Escape from the Third Reich

For my wife Aase, and our generation,
lest we forget . . .

For my children, Anne and Karin, and their
generation, so they should know . . .

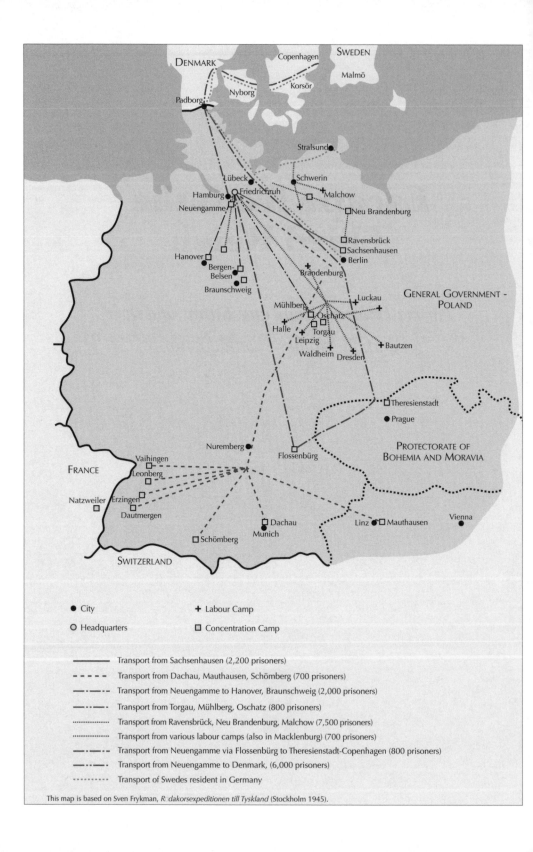

DENMARK

Copenhagen

SWEDEN

Malmö

Nyborg

Korsör

Padborg

Stralsund

Lübeck

Schwerin

Hamburg

Friedrichruh

Malchow

Neuengamme

Neu Brandenburg

Hanover

Ravensbrück

Bergen-Belsen

Sachsenhausen

Braunschweig

Berlin

Brandenburg

Luckau

Mühlberg

Oschatz

GENERAL GOVERNMENT - POLAND

Halle

Torgau

Leipzig

Bautzen

Waldheim

Dresden

Theresienstadt

Prague

Nuremberg

Flossenbürg

PROTECTORATE OF BOHEMIA AND MORAVIA

Vaihingen

FRANCE

Leonberg

Natzweiler

Erzingen

Dautmergen

Dachau

Linz

Mauthausen

Vienna

Munich

Schömberg

SWITZERLAND

● City

+ Labour Camp

○ Headquarters

□ Concentration Camp

———— Transport from Sachsenhausen (2,200 prisoners)

– – – – Transport from Dachau, Mauthausen, Schömberg (700 prisoners)

–·–·– Transport from Neuengamme to Hanover, Braunschweig (2,000 prisoners)

–··–··– Transport from Torgau, Mühlberg, Oschatz (800 prisoners)

················ Transport from Ravensbrück, Neu Brandenburg, Malchow (7,500 prisoners)

················ Transport from various labour camps (also in Macklenburg) (700 prisoners)

–··–··– Transport from Neuengamme via Flossenbürg to Theresienstadt-Copenhagen (800 prisoners)

–··–··· Transport from Neuengamme to Denmark, (6,000 prisoners)

············ Transport of Swedes resident in Germany

This map is based on Sven Frykman, Rödakorsexpeditionen till Tyskland (Stockholm 1945).

Escape from the Third Reich

The Harrowing True Story of the Largest Rescue Effort Inside Nazi Germany

Sune Persson

Translated by Graham Long

Introduction by Brian Urquhart

Skyhorse Publishing

Escape from the Third Reich

This edition published in 2009 by Frontline Books, an imprint of Pen & Sword Books Ltd,
47 Church Street, Barnsley, S. Yorkshire, S70 2AS
and
Published and distributed in the United States of America and Canada
by Skyhorse Publishing, 555 Eighth Avenue, Suite 903, New York, NY 10018
www.skyhorsepublishing.com
Skyhorse Publishing books may be purchased in bulk at special discounts for sales promotion,
corporate gifts, fund raising, or educational purposes. Special editions can also be created to specifications.
For details, contact Special Sales Department, Skyhorse Publishing, 555 Eighth Avenue, Suite 903, New York,
NY 10018 or email info@skyhorsepublishing.com.

Frontline edition: ISBN 978-1-84832-556-2
Skyhorse edition: ISBN 978-1-60239-968-6

Publishing history
'Vi åker till Sverige': De vita bussarna 1945 was originally published by Fischer & Co in 2002.
This is the first English-language edition of the text and includes a new introduction by Brian Urquhart
and new material from Sune Persson. This book includes photographs taken by Heinz Ahrens,
which have never been published before.

*The Publisher would like to thank Mr Jan Bonde Nielsen for his contribution to the production of this first English-language edition.
This book would not have been possible without his generous support.*

A CIP data record for this title is available from the British Library.

Library of Congress Cataloging-in-Publication Data

Persson, Sune, 1938–
Escape from the Third Reich : The Harrowing True Story of the Largest Rescue Effort Inside Nazi Germany /
Sune Persson.
  p. cm.
Includes bibliographical references and index.
ISBN 978-1-60239-968-6 (alk. paper)
1. Bernadotte, Folke, 1895-1948. 2. World War, 1939–1945—Jews—Germany. 3. World War, 1939–1945
—Civilian relief—Germany. 4. World War, 1939–1945—Concentration camps—Germany. 5. Svenska röda
korset—History—20th century. 6. Holocaust, Jewish (1939–1945) 7. Statesmen—Sweden—Biography.
8. Himmler, Heinrich, 1900–1945. 9. Sweden—Foreign relations—Germany. 10. Germany—Foreign relations
—Sweden. I. Title.
D804.6.P47 2009
940.53'1835--dc22

2009035365

For more information on our books, please visit
www.frontline-books.com, email info@frontline-books.com
or write to us at the above address.

Typeset by Wordsense Ltd, Edinburgh
Printed in the UK by the MPG Books Group

Contents

Abbreviations

AJDC	American Joint Distribution Committee
CICR	Comité International de la Croix Rouge
CZA	Central Zionist Archives
DRA	Rigsarkivet, the Danish Record Office
FBA	Folke Bernadotte Archives
FO	(British) Foreign Office
HIAS	Hebrew Immigrant Aid Society
HIPO	Danish Nazi Auxiliary Police Force
HL	Central Command for Norwegian Resistance Movement
ICRC	International Committee of the Red Cross
KL, KLZ, KZ	Concentration camp
NN	*Nacht und Nebel* (Night and Fog)
NSDAP	Nationalsozialistische Deutsche Arbeiterpartei
NUDA	Norwegian Foreign Office Archives
OSS	Office of Strategic Services
RSHA	Reichssicherheitshauptamt
SÄPO	Swedish Security Police
SD	Sicherheitsdienst
SRA	Riksarkivet, the Swedish Record Office
SRK	Swedish Red Cross
SRKA	Swedish Red Cross Archives
SS	Schutz-Staffel
TNA:PRO	The National Archives: Public Record Office
UD	(Swedish) Foreign Office
UDA	Swedish Foreign Office Archives
USNA	United States National Archives
WJC	World Jewish Congress

Illustrations

Introduction

The last months of the Second World War in Europe were a period of turmoil, continuous violence, confusion and, above all, appalling human suffering. From the east the Red Army was encountering desperate German resistance on its way to Berlin. From the west the Allied armies, having liberated France and Belgium, had crossed the Rhine and were approaching a link up with the Red Army. In between was a shifting territory inhabited by victims of many kinds. The homeless inhabitants of bombed-out German cities would have been pathetic enough, but as the armies advanced they came upon millions of an altogether different category, the polyglot forced labourers, desperately searching for a way home, and, most tragic of all, the barely surviving inmates of Hitler's concentration camps.[1]

Winning the war was still, inevitably, the first priority of the fighting Allies. The Swedish government, in February 1945, decided to launch a purely humanitarian effort to try to rescue at least some categories of concentration camp victims, notably those from the Scandinavian countries. The rumour that Hitler had given orders for the liquidation of the inmates of camps before the Allies reached them was among the incentives to launch this expedition, which came to be known as the 'White Buses'. Its leader was Count Folke Bernadotte.

One of the many unusual features of this unique expedition was that its leader had to negotiate its programme with the Nazis, including Heinrich Himmler, the SS and the Gestapo, only a few days before Hitler committed suicide and the whole ghastly regime collapsed for ever. In fact for Bernadotte, it was essential to effect the rescue *before* the regime collapsed because the SS had kept control of the camps until the very last, and the liquidation of all the inmates might well have been its final task.

Many of those who were associated with the White Buses have written memoirs that sometimes give conflicting accounts of this or that part of the story. Sune Persson's achievement has been to gather as much original information as survives and to create a comprehensive history of the whole Bernadotte expedition. Where necessary, he weighs disagreements and evaluates subsequent judgements. This is a major contribution to the history of the Second World War, and particularly to the involvement in it of the Scandinavian countries.

However, Persson's book fulfils another important historical purpose. Bernadotte, through no fault of his own, became a controversial figure, especially after he was assassinated, as the United Nations Mediator in Palestine, by the Stern Gang in Jerusalem on 17 September 1948.[2] The Stern Gang, trying to justify a cowardly murder, had, along with other Jewish extremists, made outrageous allegations about Bernadotte's role in the White Buses expedition. They had repeatedly alleged, for example, that Bernadotte had been a Nazi agent and was currently an agent of the Nazis' successors, presumably meaning the British. In calling for his death they proclaimed: 'Blessed be the hand that does it.'

After Bernadotte's death, the role of assassin of his reputation was assumed by an ostensibly more reputable spokesman, Felix Kersten. A masseur of Estonian origin, resident in Sweden, Kersten was indispensable to Heinrich Himmler because he could relieve the agonizing intestinal pains that the SS leader suffered from. Persson leaves no doubt that Kersten played a helpful role in getting Himmler to agree to the programme of the White Buses. Persson also points out that Bernadotte's *Last Days of the Reich. The Diary of Count Folke Bernadotte,* a 'self-absorbed and distorted account' which was published only six weeks after the end of the war, specifically mentions neither Kersten nor Jewish concentration camp victims. Kersten later wrote his own memoirs and also made available documents showing Bernadotte's contacts with Himmler and others in an extremely unfavourable light. These documents turned out to be forgeries. In the early 1950s the British historian, H.R. Trevor-Roper, who had written the first of the famous war books, *The Last Days of Hitler*, championed Kersten and his claim to sole credit for the success of the White Buses in a long article in the *Atlantic Monthly*, to the extreme detriment of the reputation and achievement of Bernadotte, already some years dead and unable to respond.

Persson analyses this tangled and extremely complicated story with great skill and understanding and, in the process, does justice both to Bernadotte and to the many others who played their roles in this fascinating episode. I believe that his conclusions, backed up as they are by years of tireless research and study, will at last lay to rest much painful controversy. His book also comes as near as we will get to a correct and fair account of a famous and unique humanitarian operation.

Brian Urquhart
July 2009

1

The Rescue

The Miracle

The year is 1945. The greatest drama in the history of the world until this point in time – the Second World War – is drawing to a close. The German Third Reich, Hitler's grand creation, by March 1945 has been reduced to a narrow strip of land between the river Oder in the east and the Rhine on the western flank. In the east the Soviet Red Army is preparing its final offensive aimed at the German capital, Berlin. To the north-west, Montgomery's army units cross the Rhine on the 24th and British forces begin to approach Bremen, Hamburg and one of the very worst of the German concentration camps, Neuengamme. On the south-western side, US and French troops have pushed into Germany, with the Americans crossing the Rhine on the 8th and setting the stage for the last big thrust into the heart of the German land mass – there to link up with their Soviet allies. The stranglehold on Nazi Germany is at hand.

The Germans, however, offered stubborn resistance and tens of thousands of German lives were sacrificed during the final months of the war. The Führer, Adolf Hitler, declared that Germany will resist defeat until the very last man. In February he issued orders for everything of value to be destroyed in the path of the enemy as it approached the central parts of Germany. Heinrich Himmler, head of the SS, was to see to the destruction of all important urban areas, industrial plants and factory premises. The only protests emerging against Hitler's instructions came from Albert Speer, minister of armaments. Hitler also gave orders for all the hundreds

1

of thousands of prisoners in German concentration camps, jails and hard labour camps to be liquidated prior to the arrival of the Allied forces. Among those condemned to imminent death in the hellish German camps were thousands of Danish and Norwegian inmates, but mainly tens of thousands of Jews.

In Stockholm, in the meantime, the Swedish government had reached a bold decision: the Scandinavian internees in German camps were to be rescued by a Swedish expedition organised on military lines – before Hitler and Himmler could bring their deadly plans into execution. This rescue operation would formally take the shape of a Red Cross expedition using the White Buses and under the command of Count Folke Bernadotte of Wisborg. During the final months of the war, from March until the beginning of May 1945, a few hundred Swedish men and women managed to rescue tens of thousands of camp prisoners from the Nazi inferno and take them to freedom and safety in Sweden. The various trips made by the Swedes penetrating an increasingly narrower corridor of land in a Germany already on fire and on the brink of collapse claimed their tribute in the shape of one fatal casualty, but only one. The other Swedes returned home alive but haunted for the rest of their days by the nightmares they had experienced.

It is with this miraculous search and rescue from the Nazi inferno that this book is concerned.

Acknowledgements

The purpose of this book has been to attempt a portrayal of the White Bus expedition of 1945. In this I have had the help of a large number of people in Sweden. At the Swedish National Record Office in Stockholm I had the indispensable help of keeper of the records Erik Norberg, of Lars Hallberg, Per-Gunnar Ottosson, Lars-Olof Welander and Lena Ånimmer. Lena's assistance at the Arninge depot led to unexpected and elucidating discoveries. The Swedish Red Cross archives were in a fairly chaotic state, but thanks to Sonja Sjöstrand's and Agneta Greayer's efforts I gained access to relevant and exciting material – including confidential documents that on my first visit were still kept in a safe under lock but no key! Daniel Backman at the Swedish Foreign Office helped me uncover some interesting documentation in their department archives. The staff at the Swedish Military Record Office (Lars Ericson), the Royal Swedish Library (Jack Zawistowski), the provincial record offices in Gothenburg (Per Clemenson) and Lund (Annika Tergius) as well as Malmö City Archives (Staffan Gudmundsson) have been invariably accommodating. At the Jewish Community premises in Stockholm I was given access to their archives in the vaults; I wish to thank the supervisor Hans Kraitsik as well as Marianne Kirsch for their generosity. Inga Gottfarb has been a marvellous help to me. On a number of points at issue I have benefited from interesting documents and/or information offered by Wilhelm Carlgren, Silvia Frykman, Svante Hansson, Uno Hedin, Barbro Jerring, Axel Molin, Karl Molin, Miriam Nathanson and Sverker Åström. I was also sent Harald Folke's memoirs in manuscript as well as his frank comments on one of my chapters only a few weeks before he passed away, in December 1999. Some of the children of key people in this book have been of invaluable assistance in gaining access to their fathers' private archives. In this respect I mostly have in mind Folke Bernadotte jr, Arno Kersten and Carin Lembre, who in 2006 sent me her grandfather Sigurd Melin's memoranda. My colleague Alf W. Johansson has read the whole of the book in manuscript and offered his comments. Parts have also been read by Bertil Bernadotte, Inga Gottfarb, Axel Molin, Marcus Storch and Krister Wahlbäck. A sincere thank you to all and every one!

I have not conducted any detailed study of original sources in Norway but instead have relied on the large quantity of research material, white books and accounts already in existence, and here mainly Kristian Ottosen's books. Ottosen has read the chapters dealing with Norwegian issues, as have Wanda Hjort-Heger, Bjarte Bruland and Anders Thunberg in Stockholm. I extend my thanks also to those who made it possible for me to see certain material in the archives at the Royal Norwegian Ministry of Foreign Affairs and the Nobelinstituttet in Oslo.

The Danish National Record Office proved to be a veritable gold mine, with more detailed source material in some respects than the Swedish. 'This inquisitive Swede' received enormously kind and obliging assistance from Birgit Lögstrup, Peter Birkelund and Hans Sode-Madsen. Finn Nielsen's son, Ole Finn Nielsen, devoted much of his time to me and granted me the use of his office, where I discovered very interesting documents about his father. *Takk til Danmark!*

I enjoyed the huge benefit of being able to meet Gilel Storch before that fantastic man left this world. He supplied me with a large number of copies of essential documents – he wanted me even then, a full thirty years ago (1979), to proceed with the work that has only now been completed. His private files are housed in Jerusalem, in the Central Zionist Archives (CZA). In the course of an intensive week's research at these archives I was provided with the greatest help conceivable by the supervisor, Rochelle Rubinstein, who went as far as allowing me to peruse still uncatalogued material from the World Jewish Congress. It was the former head of the CZA, Yoram Mayorek, however, who introduced me to the archives and who during his stay in the United States sent me copies of documents from the US National Archives in Washington, DC. *Toda raba!*

No book sees its pages printed without the purely technical work performed at a publishing house. In this final stage of production I have been lucky to have benefited from the views offered by Tomas Fischer, Leif G.W. Persson and Eva Tigerschiöld for the Swedish-language manuscript. Eva and my wife Aase have read this final Swedish draft and applied a handsome stylistic varnish to my rougher work.

Close to three years' work (1999–2002) lies behind this book, made possible by the generous financial aid provided by RJ, the Bank of Sweden Tercentenary Foundation. Grants from the Swedish–Norwegian Cooperation Fund and the Letterstedt Association have enabled me to work on this book for three intensive weeks in ideal circumstances in Norway at the Voksenåsen Centre, Norway's national gift to Sweden as a token of appreciation for the help Sweden and its people gave during the Second World War. The San Michele Foundation has also allowed me to enjoy the hospitality of Villa San Michele at Anacapri in Italy, where I was able to complete central parts of my manuscript in March 2001, immersed in unsurpassably beautiful surroundings. *Grazie!*

Jan Bonde Nielsen has very generously provided the financial assistance which made this English-language version possible and which has enabled me to research relevant documents at the UK Public Record Office in London, now part of the National Archives. Valuable pictorial material, in the shape of unique photographs taken in 1945 by the German photographer Heinz Ahrens, has been made available especially for this English-language edition by kind permission of his daughter Anita Ahrens de Mari and his grandson Marzio de Mari. The translation of this book from Swedish into English is the work of my friend Graham Long. Finally, I should like to thank my British publisher, Michael Leventhal, for his never-failing patience. To all of you: thank you so much!

The exceedingly comprehensive notes belonging to the original Swedish edition have been reduced to include only source material in English and German, although reference is made to some of the more central Swedish, Danish and Norwegian sources. Those readers wishing to gain access to the complete list of footnotes should consult the Swedish-language edition: *Vi åker till Sverige. De vita bussarna 1945* (published in Rimbo, Sweden, by Bokförlaget Fischer & Co., 2002).

Count Folke Bernadotte

The White Bus expedition in 1945 was the biggest and most important humanitarian operation performed by Sweden in the course of the past century. It was in all probability the boldest and most successful act a Swedish government had undertaken during the twentieth century. The undisputed leader of the entire operation was Count Folke Bernadotte. Who was this remarkable man?

Count Folke Bernadotte of Wisborg was born in 1895. His father, Prince Oscar Bernadotte, was the second son of Oscar II, king of Sweden between 1872 and 1907, and also king of Norway from 1872 until the two countries separated in 1905. Sweden's king from 1907 to 1950 was, then, Folke Bernadotte's uncle.

Bernadotte himself would later characterise his upbringing as strict. The home environment was fraught with gravity and piety. The children were taught early on the virtues of obedience, punctuality and honesty. Folke was not of an intellectual disposition, and suffered from difficulties in reading and writing. The term 'dyslexia' was relatively unknown at this time, and a proper understanding of this handicap was probably all but non-existent. He passed his final school-leaving examinations with difficulty. He had a gift for languages, however, and learnt fluent

English, German and French. Following his graduation he became an officer and gained a reputation as a competent horseman and organiser. Nevertheless, he was to suffer from ill-health at an early age, and in 1930 was forced to leave the army with the rank of captain. For the rest of his life he would have to put up with gastric ulcers and a regular series of treatment with vitamins.

In 1928 Bernadotte married Estelle Manville, the daughter of a wealthy American businessman. Estelle Bernadotte was a remarkable woman, of an intellectual disposition with a fine sense of judgement, and she was to mean a lot in the formation of Folke's future career. Through his wife Bernadotte gained access to leading industrial and bank circles in New York. During 1930 and 1931 he studied banking in New York and Paris and made two unsuccessful attempts in business from 1933 to 1935. He subsequently abandoned the active world of business but remained on the board of a number of Swedish companies: AGA, Facit, NK, Nordisk Resebureau and Reader's Digest, for the last of which he and his wife converted their publication into the more Swedish-sounding *Det Bästa*.

His marriage and his many travels inclined Bernadotte to take more and more interest in international issues. It was now that he received his first Swedish public commissions, all of them, significantly, in the United States. He represented the Swedish king at the Swedish exhibition in Chicago in 1933 and 1934, and was vice-chairman of the committee appointed to celebrate the Swedish colonisation of Delaware in 1638. Finally, he acted as general commissioner at the Swedish pavilion at the New York World Fair in 1939.

When the Second World War broke out in Europe Bernadotte was in the United States. According to his own account he had been appointed by a group of prominent Swedes to organise and finance a voluntary body to aid Finland in its war with the Soviet Union. This project collapsed when the two countries declared an armistice in March 1940. Following the German occupation of Norway and Denmark on 9 April 1940, Bernadotte was mobilised into the Swedish army. Promoted to major, he was in charge of the army's recreational section and internment camps for people coming from countries engaged in warfare. This latter field of activity brought him the responsibility for the exchange of prisoners – British and

American for German – carried out in Gothenburg in south-west Sweden in 1943 and 1944. His attempts at arranging similar exchanges of prisoners between Germany and the Soviet Union met with no success, however. This was because the Germans did not consider themselves bound by the Geneva Convention regulations concerning the treatment of prisoners of war since the Soviet Union had never ratified the Convention.

In addition to his dyslexia and his incurable illness, however, Bernadotte also experienced other personal tragedies. Two of his children died suddenly at a young age. His wife later related how, on the death of his elder son Gustav, Folke said: 'We weren't brought into this world to *be* happy but rather to make others happy.' He realised that his personality was more suitable for humanitarian work; this is partly why he became chairman of the Swedish Scout Association in 1937 and vice-chairman of the Swedish Red Cross organisation in 1943.

Bernadotte's other uncle, Prince Carl, was chairman of the Swedish Red Cross but was more than eighty years old. This meant that to all intents and purposes Bernadotte became the operative head of Red Cross activities. As such he played a central rôle in the humanitarian efforts being made in war-ravaged Europe. For geographical reasons Sweden and Switzerland, when it came to humanitarian work, were the only two neutral countries that had any real clout in acting between the two alliances waging war in Europe. The Republic of Ireland, Portugal and Turkey were geographically too peripheral. Since Sweden and Switzerland were both neutral nations, their formal state institutions were unable to intervene in certain issues. They therefore handed over operations to humanitarian organisations, principally the Red Cross units in each respective country. The Swiss Red Cross was in a less favourable position than its fellow organisation in Sweden.

The International Committee of the Red Cross (ICRC), which in practice was a fully fledged Swiss state body, had become discredited on the Allied side – chiefly in the Soviet Union – for its passive attitude towards the Germans during the war. The ICRC came to see the Swedish Red Cross towards the end of the war as something of a direct competitor. The Swedish Red Cross, with the support of its government, was then in a position, and had acquired such resources, that enabled it to demand the same status as that of the ICRC. Moreover, the Swedish Red Cross and Stockholm were to act as hosts for the next International Red Cross conference, and Bernadotte was therefore automatically chairman of the standing committee representing all the various national Red Cross organisations. Bernadotte had visited the ICRC in 1943, and had met the Norwegian delegate Peter Anker, who then acquainted Bernadotte with the problems involved in getting help to prisoners in Germany.

When Bernadotte was given responsibility for the Swedish rescue operation in Germany in 1945, he was fifty years old and had a wide knowledge of languages as well as a knack of organising and getting things done. He was a good negotiator, capable of wielding influence over those around him with the innate self-confidence of a member of the upper classes, and with a dash of humour and aristocratic charm. He gravitated towards a politically conservative stance, voted for what was then the Swedish Tory Party and was most of all strongly anti-Communist, entertaining few illusions regarding the Soviet Union's future intentions. He was plainly pro-American, and occupied the post of chairman of the Swedish–American Society in Stockholm. Statements to the effect that he was pro-Nazi and anti-Jewish are pure lies. On the other hand Bernadotte publicly expressed his sympathy for the enormous hardships suffered by the German people in the final phases of the war – a not particularly popular point of view in 1945's Sweden, which was trimming its sails to accommodate a new political wind. In parallel with practically all other Swedes during the war, Bernadotte was a Swedish nationalist and a convinced promoter of Nordic unity. He was deeply religious. Some of his critics believed Bernadotte had a naïve attitude – not to say a hypocritical, arrogant belief that he had been allotted a 'divine mission'; I would instead characterise this as idealism and conscientiousness, a conviction that he was here on earth to carry out good deeds.

Bernadotte had a wide-ranging network of international contacts. In the course of a visit to London in February 1944 the Norwegian king Håkon and foreign minister-in-exile Trygve Lie extended their thanks to him for the Swedish aid offered to Norway. The British foreign minister, Anthony Eden, told him that the exchange of prisoners of war in Gothenburg was 'the greatest event that had taken place during the war in the field of humanitarian activity'. Allied Red Cross representatives, nevertheless, have put forward a number of queries concerning the fate of the Danish Jews, in Denmark and at Theresienstadt. In November 1944 Bernadotte visited the Supreme Headquarters of the Allied Expeditionary Forces in recently liberated Versailles. On that occasion the Allied supreme commander, General Eisenhower, personally thanked Bernadotte for his and his colleagues' efforts in coming to the assistance of the American internees in Sweden. Bernadotte also conferred with Eisenhower on how future Swedish assistance, mainly to the other Scandinavian countries, best be organised.[1]

2

The Realm of Death: Hitler's Germany

According to the Free German Press Service in Stockholm, Hitler made the following remarks at a secret cabinet meeting on 24 February 1945:

> I shall conduct this final struggle with all my might and by all available means. In the solid spirit of National Socialism I shall see to it that none other than the German prisoners of war will be left to bewail our people's disaster.
>
> I therefore issue this order: empowered to fulfil the final extermination shall be SS national leader Himmler. Under his supervision part of the air force will have the special task of destroying all important cities, industrial plants and factories still remaining at the end of the war . . .
>
> Within the framework of this task, following the course of the war in different areas, or on special order on a pre-determined day, all prisoners in jails, hard labour camps and concentration camps will be put to death, regardless of whether they are prisoners on remand, convicts or in preventive arrest, as well as hostages from every country. In the case of prisoners of war, I reserve the right to take special measures.[1]

Hitler's Greater Germany

Following Germany's defeat in the First World War the country had acquired a democratic form of government in the form of the so-called Weimar Republic.[2] Anti-democratic forces were rife, however, and were nourished by the feelings of bitterness in the wake of the military defeat and what was commonly called the 'Stab-in-the-back Legend', the myth claiming that Germany had not really been defeated militarily but had been betrayed from within by socialists, communists, Jews and other enemies of imperial Germany. The most significant anti-democratic force, in competition with the communists, was soon to be the Nationalsozialistische Deutsche Arbeiterpartei (NSDAP; National Socialist German Workers Party), led by Adolf Hitler.

The NSDAP's predecessor had been founded in Hitler's native country, Austria, in 1918 and had already adopted the swastika as its symbol. In 1921 Hitler became the undisputed Führer (leader) of the NSDAP.* After the failed *coup d'état* in Munich in 1923 Hitler was sentenced to five years' imprisonment but was released as early as in 1924. During his not-unpleasant stay in prison Hitler wrote his book *Mein Kampf* (My Struggle) in which he set out his confused ideology combined with some brilliant analyses of political leadership and effective mass propaganda. While Germany was enjoying comparatively favourable economic conditions during the remainder of the 1920s, Hitler and the Nazis reaped no further political successes. After Hitler had acquired German citizenship in 1932, and in the wake of the deep economic crisis which reached Germany in 1930, the Nazi party gained considerably in strength. They doubled their share of the vote in the 1932 election, and with 13,745,000 voters backing them became Germany's biggest political party. On 30 January 1933 Hitler was appointed chancellor of the German Reich.

The Weimar Republic's individual rights and liberties were abolished in February 1933, the month after Hitler had assumed power. Germany's constitution was also transformed into the *Führerprinzip* (Hitler's express will), and thus the ground was prepared for Hitler's Third Reich. In no time at all the fairly independent German federal states, the other political parties and the trade unions were suppressed, and in July 1933 the Nazi party remained the sole political party. Around the same time the old German political police corps was converted into the new secret state police, Gestapo (Geheime Staatspolizei). President von Hindenburg died

---

* I shall subsequently be using the term 'Nazi party' for the NSDAP and 'Nazis' for the National Socialists (*author's note*).

on 2 August 1934 and Hitler was proclaimed Germany's Führer and chancellor of the Reich, in addition to being chief commander of the German armed forces. Hitler now occupied an omnipotent position in Germany.

Hitler's ideology was based on the myth surrounding the 'Aryans' and their supposed pre-eminent qualities and achievements. Their chief opponents were to be the Marxists and the Jews. From the time of Hitler's speeches at the beginning of the 1920s until the Holocaust during the Second World War, Hitler's aim was plain and simple: the Jews in Europe had to be obliterated. This was the main theme running from *Mein Kampf* through to the German extermination camps during the war.

In foreign policy Hitler was systematically aggressive. On 12 March 1938 German troops stormed into Austria, which was then dubbed Ostmark, a province in the new Grossdeutschland (Greater Germany). As a result of the infamous Munich conference in September 1938 Czechoslovakia was forced to cede Sudetenland to Germany. On 13 March 1939 German troops crossed the border into what remained of Czechoslovakia, which ceased to exist as a separate country and was annexed as the Bohemian–Moravian Protectorate, with Slovakia independent but under German protection. The clouds of war were now gathering over Europe. On 23 August 1939 the German foreign minister, Joachim von Ribbentrop, and the foreign minister of the Soviet Union, Molotov, signed a pact of non-aggression between their two countries. This guaranteed Germany peace with the Soviet Union, avoiding the risk of waging war on two fronts. Hitler and Stalin thus paved the way for war on a large scale in Europe.

On 1 September 1939 Germany attacked Poland. Two days later Great Britain and France declared war on Germany, and the Second World War was under way. Polish resistance was soon crushed and the country was carved up between Germans and Russians. Parts of western Poland were incorporated into Greater Germany while the remainder of western Poland was converted into a German General-Guvernement. The Soviet Union, meanwhile, occupied the eastern parts of Poland. In the course of 1940 and 1941 Hitler's triumphal march rolled on: Denmark, Norway, France, Belgium, the Netherlands, Luxemburg, Yugoslavia and Greece were all invaded and occupied. Hitler had, however, made what was to be a fateful decision: the Russians were to be defeated. In June 1941 the

Germans, allied with Finland and Rumania, launched an attack on the Soviet Union on a broad front stretching from the Arctic Ocean down to the Black Sea – the most brutal war in the history of mankind had begun. Here, too, the Germans enjoyed a number of initial successes.

In December 1941 Japan raided Pearl Harbour and so drew the United States into the war, whereupon Hitler declared war on the United States, on 11 December. Apart from its fragile alliance with Italy and Japan, Germany was now at war with practically the entire world. Hitler had completely underestimated Britain's capacity to withstand and recuperate, as well as the United States' and the Soviet Union's immense resources. The main battle scenes took place on the Eastern Front against the Russians. On 31 January 1943 the entire German sixth army corps was compelled to surrender at Stalingrad and was taken prisoner. From the summer of 1943 onwards it was the Russians who went in for massive offensive action on the Eastern Front, while Germany had to be content with putting up a fanatical defence of their positions. Along the north of Africa in October 1942 the British under Montgomery managed to break through the German lines at El Alamein. Simultaneously British and American troops went ashore in Morroco and Algeria, and German resistance in north Africa was scotched, with the entire German–Italian army corps surrendering in May 1943 and being taken prisoner. In Italy the king dismissed Mussolini in July, and in September a new Italian government entered into a truce with the Allies.

As 1944 went on it became clear that Germany was going to lose the war. On 4 June the Western Allies marched into Rome, while two days later the gigantic British–American Normandy invasion was initiated. By September all of France and Belgium was liberated, and on 11 September an American patrol crossed the German border. The war was now being waged on German territory. Although Hitler survived an attempt on his life in July 1944, this failed assassination showed that opposition to his regime now existed also within Germany. When the Soviet Red Army began a huge offensive on 12 January 1945, from the Baltic Sea in the north to the Carpathians in the south, German resistance crumbled. Greater Germany was squeezed into an ever narrower corridor, in which Soviet, British and American troops fought appalling battles ending in all resistance being crushed. Hitler's Grossdeutschland lay in ruins. The final blow came with Hitler's suicide on 30 April 1945. In his political will and testament from the day before (29 April), Hitler resigned from his position as Germany's Führer and chancellor of the Reich. He relieved the traitors Himmler and Göring of all of their duties within the Nazi party and the German state, appointing Rear-Admiral Dönitz as president, minister of war and commander-in-chief. Hitler remained consistent to the last: the final words of his will and testament spoke of urging 'merciless resistance to the poisoner of all the people of the world, international Jewry'.

Himmler's SS-State and the Concentration Camps

Starting in 1929, Heinrich Himmler built up a protective corps called the Schutz-Staffel (SS) within the Nazi party, and became its head using the title of Reichsführer-SS.[3] Initially the SS constituted Himmler's black-uniformed bodyguard, and in 1929 was made up of 250 men. The SS came to manifest itself as an elite body whose members enjoyed special privileges. In reality the SS recruited its people more and more from the ranks of the unemployed from every layer of society. The recruitees were characterised by a spirit of unconditional obedience, a tough approach and skills with firearm and truncheon alike. Within the framework of the SS, in 1931, Himmler organised his own personal security service, the Sicher-heitsdienst (SD), the head of which was the diabolical Reinhard Heydrich, assassinated in Moravia in 1942 and succeeded by Ernst Kaltenbrunner.

In 1936 Himmler became permanent secretary at the German Minis-try of the Interior, which made him for all practical purposes head of the German police. At the same time the Gestapo was ranked as 'top state authority' and directly answerable to Himmler, who then had control over the whole of the German police network. In 1939 the entire body was merged with one main administrative unit in Berlin covering all the secu-rity services: the Reichssicherheitshauptamt (RSHA), within which the SD would represent three of seven principal departments: Amt III, domestic; Amt VI, secret (foreign) intelligence service; and Amt VII, archives and research; the Gestapo became Amt IV. The RSHA built up a comprehen-sive underground organisation throughout Germany and even abroad. Head of the main department VI, SD-Ausland, was Walter Schellenberg, appointed in 1941, who was to play a key rôle in Bernadotte's rescue operation of 1945. SD-Ausland is not to be confused with the competing military intelligence service Abwehr, which from 1935 onwards was led by the legendary Admiral Canaris. Together with Schellenberg, Kaltenbrunner managed to seize control of Abwehr in 1944 while Schellenberg became head of the combined German intelligence service. Canaris was arrested following the attempt on Hitler's life in July 1944 and executed in barbaric circumstances at the Flossenbürg concentration camp on 9 April 1945. Gruppenführer Heinrich Müller was head of the Gestapo in 1945.

After the outbreak of war in 1939 Himmler also set up an armed unit inside the SS under the name of the Waffen-SS, independent of the regular army and often, indeed, in conflict with it. Himmler had obtained permission from Hitler to create his own armed units as early as 1934, after Hitler had arranged for the murder of the leaders of the then Sturmabteilungen (SA). By the end of the war the Waffen-SS comprised about one million men and women, 25,000 of them members of the SS-Totenkopfverbände (the so-called 'death's head units'). They represented Himmler's very own army for the conquest of Europe. Hot on the heels of these units and their triumphs came the SD's special liquidation groups, the Einsatzgruppen. A special organ for economy and administration, the SS-Wirtschaftsverwaltungs-Hauptamt (SS-WVHA) was created, and it was this body that was to administer the concentration camps. The SS state had now turned into an immense mammoth bureaucracy under Himmler's control. He was a very competent organiser, capable of getting his SS to infiltrate the Nazi party, then all of Germany, and finally almost the whole of Europe. It would not be too much to say that Himmler's SS body was the core of the Nazi regime.

Towards the end of the war Himmler's position was further strengthened. Hitler relied to the very end on his faithful Himmler – 'der treue Heinrich'. He was appointed minister of the Interior in 1943, and following the attempt on Hitler's life in 1944 head of the German Home Guard as well. In January 1945 he was made commander of the Weichsel army corps, which defended the Oder Front against the Soviet Red Army, but soon proved incapable of meeting this challenge and was relieved of the post on 22 March.

Following the rapid, total victory over Poland in October 1939 Himmler also took over as Reichskommissar für die Festigung deutschen Volkstums (superintendent charged with 'consolidating the German people groups'). In the lands of eastern Europe, in the spaces known as the German Lebensraum, Volksdeutsche (Germans and German-speaking people) would now colonise the entire area stretching from Weichsel to the Ural mountains. Himmler started to organise a huge German empire in eastern Europe. The newly created General-Guvernement in Poland became the model for Nazi Germany's new European order: the Jews were to be exterminated, and the inferior races, such as the Slavs, would be completely subjected to the rule of the Aryan 'master race', represented by Himmler's SS. The local populations would occupy a servile position in German-dominated industry and agriculture. From 1942 onwards Himmler began to use concentration camp prisoners as a workforce in the German war industry.

The Nazis had already had the first concentration camps – Dachau and Oranienburg – built in Germany in 1933. Initially it was communists, social democrats and other political opponents who were sent there. In 1937 the 'Bible explorers', that is, Jehovah's Witnesses, arrived, and in 1938 it was the turn of the Jews. The task inherent in the concentration camp strategy was simple but frightening: every real or supposed opponent of Nazi rule was to be done away with, and all adverse criticism was to be nipped in the bud. All types of measure would be applied: victims would be worked to death, tortured to death, shot, hanged, gassed and left to die of hunger. As a first step the SS death's-head units at the concentration camps would be trained in 'brutality'. In time the camps were to supply German industry and commerce with cost-free slave labour, and prisoners would also be used for scientific experiments.

Nazi Germany and the SS went to work systematically building up a network of concentration camps. By 1939 there were a hundred or so throughout the country, counting the so-called 'branches' and 'external units'. Following the outbreak of war the system of concentration camps spread to the occupied territories, in particular to the General-Guvernement in Poland. Here were erected the most notorious of the camps, the six extermination camps at Oswiecim/Auschwitz-Birkenau, Treblinka, Sobibor, Chelmno/Kulmhof, Belzec and Lublin-Majdanek. Camps were also

16

installed, however, at Riga in Latvia, Stutthof near Danzig and at Natz-weiler in the French Vosges. How many people passed through all these camps we shall never know, because the Nazis destroyed as many traces of the camps as they could in the final stages of the war. In 1945 Kogon esti-mated that the concentration camps contained approximately one million prisoners at one and the same time, and that overall between eight and ten million men, women and children were killed in them.

Concentration camp prisoners were in principle divided into four cate-gories: 'political opponents' (almost all foreigners belonged here); 'inferior races' (mainly Jews and gypsies); 'criminals'; and 'anti-social elements' (minor offenders, alcoholics and the like). The most vulnerable among these were the Jews and the gypsies, who were without a national govern-ment to give them support and defend their interests in the face of the barbaric German treatment. The Jews were more exposed than any oth-ers, being blamed by Hitler and Himmler for most of the misery in the world and seen thus as their principal racial adversary. In January 1942 at the Wansee conference in Berlin top Nazi officials drew up plans for *die Endlösung* (the final solution to the Jewish problem). One month later the first Jewish transport was gassed to death by Zyklon B at Auschwitz. Hilberg's classic work of 1961, on how the European Jews were extermi-nated, estimated that in accordance with the Führer's decision concern-ing their liquidation the Germans put approximately five million Jews to death during the war. The 1998 publication *Tell Ye Your Children . . .*, commissioned by the Swedish government as part of its education project Living History, after research in later years put the figure at between five and perhaps more than six million Jews, more than half a million gypsies, hundreds of thousands of handicapped and retarded persons, 'anti-social' elements, homosexuals and Jehovah's Witnesses as well as several million Soviet and Polish prisoners.[4]

What then had happened to the perhaps one million prisoners in the German camps who were still alive at the start of 1945 and who Hitler had solemnly ordered Himmler to put to death, to the last man and woman, before the end of the war?

3

The Jews and the Holocaust

According to reports in the press on the debate about estimates of 18 January, in respect of the favourable disposition shown in receiving Jewish refugees during the first two years of the war, the minister for Social Affairs said that: 'then the Swedish government was at least as generous as the Jewish Community in Stockholm'. As this statement has given rise to misinterpretation, I should like to point out on behalf of the Jewish Community in Stockholm that the Community, while expressing its deep gratitude for the far-reaching measures adopted by the government to rescue a large number of our persecuted brethren, naturally in no way wishes to influence the authorities in a spirit of restrictive practice. On the contrary, the Community has wished for natural reasons for many more members of European Jewry to have been rescued and brought to Sweden instead of meeting the horrible fate they have suffered. The Jewish Community, in its endeavours in this respect, has however quite naturally been bound by the guidelines drawn up by the Swedish authorities. There are many cases where applications for an entry permit have been sent in or recommended by the Community but where the authority in question has not considered itself competent to sanction the application.[1]

The Jews, the Western Allies and the Holocaust

How are we able to understand that Hitler's Germany during the Second World War devoted enormous resources to systematically exterminating

18

European Jewry? From a military point of view this act of genocide was utterly irrational. During the First World War the Jews had participated in their country's war efforts on the same scale as other citizens with a different background. For Hitler and Himmler, however, the Second World War was essentially a racial affair and the Jews the main enemy. How, then, did Germany's other adversaries, in other words the Allies, the neutral states and the Jews' own organisations react in the face of the Holocaust?

The first reports of the German extermination policy towards the Jews slipped through to the western Allies in 1942. By the end of 1944 it was quite general knowledge that the Germans had been systematically exterminating the Jews in those parts of Europe over which they had control, and that the mass slaughter was continuing with the Hungarian Jews. The knowledge of these circumstances did little to influence the two most important western Powers – Britain and the United States – in attaching any appreciable priority to the fate of the European Jews. Quite the opposite, in fact: Allied blockade of German-occupied areas impeded aid to the Jews. In Sweden this Allied blockade, which prevailed until the end of the war, prevented Swedish aid from reaching Norway and the camps in Germany.

In August 1944 the western Allies dismissed petitions from Jewish organisations to bomb the extermination camps at Auschwitz-Birkenau and/or the railway lines leading to the gas chambers. The full weight of the western Allies' thrust was instead applied to the job of crushing the German war machine militarily. Nor were separate negotiations with Nazi Germany contemplated – not even in an attempt to rescue concentration camp prisoners from certain death. The goal was quite simply unconditional surrender, after which the prisoners could be rescued. Moreover, the United States and Britain were fighting an equally high-priority war against Japan in the Far East, and for the Americans the war in the Pacific was the most important scene of action ever since Pearl Harbour had been attacked in 1941 and up to the Normandy landings in 1944.[2]

The European Jews, like the gypsies or Romany peoples, found themselves deprived of any protection from a state authority – the State of Israel did not yet exist. Their struggle was taken up by a number of Jewish organisations, principally by the World Jewish Congress (WJC) and the

American Joint Distribution Committee (AJDC), both based in the United States, as well as by the Jewish Agency in Palestine, still a British mandated territory at the time of the Second World War. Other Jewish organisations existed, of varying political and religious shades. These did not always collaborate with each other and could even engage in competition with each other. This element of competition characterised relations between the old AJDC and the newcomer, the WJC. This was a conflict that, as we shall soon see, spread from New York to the subsidiary organisations in Stockholm. Working together with individuals who sympathised with the predicament of the Jewish people, these organisations endeavoured to appeal to governments around the world and other influential institutions. Since the countries waging war in Europe tended to turn a deaf ear to the cause, there was no other remedy but to approach the neutral countries – Sweden and Switzerland – and the International Red Cross movement.[3]

During autumn 1944 rumours began to circulate to the effect that Hitler was planning to liquidate all prisoners at the concentration camps with the final battle at hand, a battle everybody knew the Germans would lose. Jewish leaders such as Gerhart Riegner, the WJC representative in Geneva, and the corresponding member in Stockholm, Gilel Storch, therefore feverishly began to work towards rescuing the few Jews still alive out of Hitler's Götterdämmerung.

The ICRC was reluctant, however, to intervene on behalf of the Jews in Germany. The Geneva Convention of 1929 afforded guarantees only to military prisoners of war. Attempts made prior to the outbreak of war to secure international protection for *civil* prisoners as well had met with no success. The Germans claimed that the 'civil internees' in their camps were not covered by international law and that any conditions attached were subject to domestic German legislation. The ICRC had chosen not to challenge the Nazi leaders – one reason was that the ICRC, based in Switzerland, scrupulously followed the rigidly neutral Swiss government line.

Not until 1944 did the ICRC send any parcels to civil internees and to the Jews at Theresienstadt. The single visit paid by the ICRC to the 'model ghetto' at Theresienstadt in 1944 (see Chapter 10) resulted in a positive report being written, which the ICRC had the sense not to publish as it would have justified the Germans' treatment of the Jews. In January

1945, however, a new president was appointed at the ICRC, the Swiss professor Carl Burckhardt, and he took a more active rôle during the remaining months of the war. This was motivated by Burckhardt's meeting with Nordling, the Swedish consul in Paris, and by reports from Stockholm of an impending Swedish Red Cross operation. On 12 March Burckhardt met Himmler's closest colleague, Kaltenbrunner, for negotiations. Kaltenbrunner was accommodating: more food parcels for the prisoners of war could be sent and Red Cross observers stationed at the camps – the Red Cross observers would even be allowed to enter the 'Israelite' camps. Kaltenbrunner's pledge, though, turned out to be as good as worthless. It was not until 10 April that the first ICRC convoy was able to transport 299 French women – only seven of whom were Jewish – from Ravensbrück to Switzerland. When the war reached its final two weeks, however, the ICRC managed to gain entry into several of the concentration camps and was able to rescue about five thousand prisoners before the Allies took over responsibility for the camps. Only on 2 May did the ICRC take Theresienstadt under its protection.[4]

By this time, too, the American government had begun to wake up. Following pressure over a long period from Jewish organisations, a War Refugee Board was established in 1944. In January 1945 the American secretary of state, Stettinius, instructed the War Refugee Board to propose that the ICRC and the Swiss and Swedish governments take under their protection all Jewish survivors, draw up prisoner lists and seek to gain access to the concentration camps. The bold and brave system introduced in 1944 using first 'Red Cross passports' and later Swedish 'protective passports' for the Hungarian Jews was now well known, and it had been fairly successful. At the same time the War Refugee Board was instructed to work alongside the Swedish Red Cross in hastening the dispatch of parcels to the prisoners from the ample stores in Gothenburg. The War Refugee Board's representative in Sweden was Iver Olsen, who was also the United States's secret service agent at the Office of Strategic Services (OSS) in Stockholm.[5]

In Switzerland a representative of the American Joint Distribution Committee, Saly Meyer, managed to obtain the release of 318 Hungarian Jews after negotiations with top German Nazi officials; they were brought to Switzerland in exchange for a considerable amount of ransom money. Himmler was evidently aware of this 'commercial transaction'. In Switzerland the Sternbuchs, husband and wife, were active representatives of the orthodox American–Jewish aid organisation Va'ad Ha-hatsala. The Sternbuchs found a suitable facilitator – Jean-Marie Musy, a former president of the Swiss Confederation. Musy was beginning to worry about his image: he had previously been known as leader of a number of Fascist movements in Switzerland and had already met Himmler before the war at anti-communist rallies in Germany.

The Sternbuchs financed Musy, who got in touch with Schellenberg in Germany and on 3 November 1944 obtained an audience with Himmler. By then Himmler had put a stop to the deportations to Auschwitz and had issued instructions for the 'definitive extermination' of the Jews to be halted. The two gentlemen reached a sensational agreement. The 600,000 Jews estimated by Himmler still to be under German control were to be released to Switzerland without Hitler's knowledge, and in return the Germans would receive certain commodities, mainly trucks and tractors. In January 1945 Musy concluded a firm agreement with Schellenberg – 1,200 Jews would be delivered to Switzerland every other week while the sum of five million Swiss francs would be transferred to a Swiss bank account after each transport. One of Schellenberg's closest aides, Franz Göring, was put in charge of the project. It proved to be a difficult task, however. In January Himmler had issued orders for the camps to be evacuated before the Red Army could reach them. Thousands of prisoners perished daily marching away from these camps. At the Stutthof camp thousands were shot just days before Soviet troops liberated the place. Kaltenbrunner was still loyal to Hitler, as was the head of the Gestapo, Müller, and they actively sought to thwart the plans of Himmler, Schellenberg and Musy.

In spite of everything, however, the first train with more than 1,200 ecstatically happy Jews from Theresienstadt reached freedom in Switzerland on 7 February 1945. The news was splashed all over the Swiss press, but had its sombre consequences: one newspaper claimed that two hundred German SS men would be given asylum in the United States in exchange. In Germany the news reached Hitler's ears and produced an outbreak of rage and fury. The Führer ordered an immediate stop to all further releases of Jews. On 16 March the German radio announced instead that all Jews including prisoners of war were to be killed. The Sternbuch–Musy diplomacy was a flop – there would be no more freedom rides by train from Theresienstadt to Switzerland.

Swedish Jews and Their Aid to Kinsfolk in German Concentration Camps

Most of the Jews who lived in Sweden were to be found in the three biggest cities of Stockholm, Gothenburg and Malmö. They automatically belonged to their respective Jewish Community and paid dues to it. Without doubt the most important of these was the Jewish Community in Stockholm. Its chairman in 1945 was Gunnar Josephson, a respected bookseller in the city, while the operational work was led by its secretary, David Köpniwsky. The Community's most respected member, however, was probably chief rabbi Marcus Ehrenpreis, who had occupied that position in Sweden since 1914. Ehrenpreis was an internationally acclaimed writer and had previously been one of the leading Zionists in the world. After the war both Ehrenpreis and the leaders of the Jewish Community would be exposed to harsh criticism for their submissive attitude towards the Swedish government, and for adopting a passive stance while their Jewish kinsfolk were suffering in the rest of Europe.

Activities by the Jewish Community in Stockholm in 1945 must be viewed against the background of the conditions under which it was working. Here I shall mainly be dependent on Köpniwsky's brief and largely economic report from 1951, covering the Community's aid to refugees over the period 1933–50, as well as on Inga Gottfarb's excellent and extensive book *Den livsfarliga glömskan* (The Perils of Oblivion) from 1986. Both Köpniwsky and Gottfarb were deeply involved in rescue work in 1945 and are therefore both well informed, though obviously parties in the cause. In 1945 Gottfarb was working for the AJDC, the Swedish section of which was led by her brother, Ragnar Gottfarb.

The Jews who arrived in Sweden from 1933 onwards were not classified by the Swedish authorities as political refugees – in their respective native countries 'they had, in their capacity of bread-winners, been restricted solely on the basis of race or other reasons'. The Swedish national authorities therefore assumed no economic responsibility for these Jewish refugees. In order to grant asylum the authorities therefore had to have guarantees that the immigrant Jews would not be a burden on public expenditure. The bill for such guarantees had to be met by the Jewish Communities, which had limited economic resources. Gottfarb estimated that there were about 1,500 Jewish families in Sweden. Financing was done directly via community taxes or special collections. From 1939 certain state grants were also available.

Until 1941 the burden imposed on the Communities was reasonable since the great majority of Jews reaching Sweden wished to travel on – to Palestine, the United States or to other continents. They were nicknamed 'transmigrants', and the quota for these people had been negotiated between the authorities and the Jewish Community in Stockholm, which took upon itself the scrutiny of all applications. These applications for asylum in Sweden filed by persecuted Jews now occupy a large amount of shelf space in the Community's archives. Most of them were declined, which quite certainly led to eventual death for those who were thus refused a safe haven in Sweden.

With the United States entering the war in 1941 and the port of Gothenburg blockaded, Sweden's borders were closed. The financial burden on members of the Community grew rapidly. Special efforts were made to assist the Norwegian Jews in 1942 and the Danish Jews from 1943 onwards; a subscription was started in 1943 in favour of the illegal traffic across the strait between Denmark and Sweden. The financial situation mentioned above did not affect the Stockholm Community alone – those in Gothenburg and Malmö bore the brunt of assistance to the many Jews who entered the country via Gothenburg and the southernmost province of Skåne. Contributions were made by the American–Jewish organisations AJDC and Hebrew Immigrant Aid Society (HIAS). Köpniwsky in fact described the AJDC's 'magnificent financial support' as of vital importance to the entire relief effort. In June 1945, after the war was over, a special collection was started for 'those rescued in 1945' and it raised more than 60,000 Swedish kronor. The Community's provision for the same cause was 62,000 kronor, while the remainder – 250,000 kronor –

came from the AJDC. About two-thirds of the Community's costs for Jews entering the country in 1945, therefore, were paid for by the AJDC.[6]

As far as organisation was concerned, the Jewish Community's work during the first years was carried out by volunteers and by the office staff. Later work increased rapidly, and in 1945 literally exploded. An enormous effort was steered towards 'those rescued in 1945'. Köpniwsky estimated that almost twelve thousand Jews were rescued from the German concentration camps and brought to Sweden by the end of the war in 1945. These people admittedly were mainly cared for by the Swedish national authorities, but they did require a great deal of psychological attention and social care. In addition a large amount of work was performed by various Jewish associations and private individuals alongside what was achieved through the taxes levied and the funds raised by the Communities. The size and scope of these contributions are difficult to assess. One example is the story told by Inga Gottfarb of how during the final years of the war there were as many as ten or a dozen Jewish refugees eating and even often sleeping at her home. The Jewish Women's Club offered large financial grants. One of the more active organisations was the Czechoslovak Committee for deported Jews. This committee, led by a Czech diplomat called Kucera, possessed a very energetic assistant in Kerstin Cruickshank from Gothenburg, who through her own private initiative rescued many Jews from Czechoslovakia both before and after the war. In this she collaborated with the Norwegian diplomat Ditleff, who we shall be meeting later on in this book.

What can be considered justifiable criticism of the Jewish Community in Stockholm is difficult to assess with the benefit of hindsight and in the light of historical facts. In 1951 Köpniwsky 'was not of the opinion that the Community or its members considered themselves to have achieved very much'. Gottfarb's conclusion in 1986 was that the Jewish communities and individual people in 1945 'tried in every way to come to the aid of the new arrivals. The Jews in Sweden were perhaps not much better but surely no worse than the rest of Sweden.' It should not be forgotten, moreover, that most Swedes, including the Jews, to the very last refused to believe that anything as atrocious as the Holocaust could possibly be true.

Gottfarb also went into the more controversial aspects of the criticism. She pointed out that the leading members of the communities in Stockholm and Gothenburg came from 'old' Jewish families well established in Sweden over many years. They had been completely assimilated into Swedish society, saw themselves first and foremost as Swedes, while some of them would also willingly wipe out their Jewish origin. They felt no natural affinity with the new arrivals from eastern Europe, many of whom were orthodox Jews. They were also apprehensive about a large Jewish immigration giving rise to an increase in any anti-Semitism that already existed in Sweden. The exception was the Community in Malmö, which comprised almost entirely east European Jews. There is a hint here of the feud between the leading members of the Stockholm Community and Gilel Storch, who had immigrated from Latvia in 1940. Storch in 1979 accused the Stockholm Community of 'not having wanted to have more Jews in Sweden' and of 'not having had anything to do with the rescue work'.[7]

Primary sources dealing with these internal squabbles are unfortunately rather scarce, apart from the documentation Storch left behind. According to Gottfarb, however, a few untruths were not alien to Storch's nature. The Community chairman, Gunnar Josephson, destroyed his private documents from 1945, again according to Gottfarb.[8] Chief rabbi Ehrenpreis left behind a comprehensive stack of correspondence, although it contained little of interest dating from 1945. Hardly surprising, however, since according to his daughter he was diabetic, almost blind, had undergone an operation for cancer and was senile. On top of all this he was obliged to stage a fight on two fronts: on the one hand against the Swedish authorities, and on the other with two members of the Community leadership who were opposed to further Jewish immigration in Sweden.[9]

The Stockholm Community's reports of proceedings are astonishingly meagre in mirroring their kinsfolk's desperate situation in Europe in 1945. Among the extensive records of proceedings from 1945 there exist only three paragraphs dealing with this Jewish disaster. A silver plaque was handed over to the Swedish envoy Danielson on 23 April in gratitude for the Swedish legation's rescue work in Budapest in aid of the Hungarian Jews. The Community sent a letter of thanks on 2 May to Maj von Dardel (Raoul Wallenberg's mother) for what the legation had done and in particular for Raoul Wallenberg's brave deeds, wishing him a speedy return. On 15 May the Community chairman paid tribute to the Swedish Red Cross and to Bernadotte:

> When the assembly now gathers here today, it is with a strong sense of entering a new epoch. These recent times, darker than humanity has ever known them, have reached a climax, so desperately coveted, and we stand – yearning, inquiring, hopeful – on the threshold of a new world.
>
> Our Community and we Swedish Jews have been incredibly fortunate in living our life sheltered and unhurt while all around us Jewish life is being extinguished, and our kinsfolk have been the hardest hit by the hellish forces of evil and inhumanity. These forces have finally met their match and humankind can breathe freely again after a nightmare of horror. We ourselves are brimful with gratitude towards those who resisted the evil power and gained victory. And with heart and soul we thank our dear land where we have felt secure and confident, and where the spirit of mankind has managed to bring salvation to at least some of our fellow-beings hunted down almost to death's door. To us, our respected king – both by dint of his personal intervention and through his royal standing – is an emblem of that Swedish spirit . . .
>
> We would also like to think at this moment of the admirable rescue operation undertaken by the Swedish Red Cross, bringing thousands of people – among them a considerable number of Jews – here to our country, to liberation from the horrors of the concentration camps and a terrible demise. Mention must also be made of the fact that a specially vital and active rôle has been played by members of the World Jewish Congress in Sweden, and we are extremely pleased at the wise and effective effort put in by Herr Masur.
>
> I take for granted the assembly's approval that we of the Jewish Community express our gratitude to Count Folke Bernadotte and the Swedish Red Cross for the remarkable, brave and successful rescue operation they carried out.[10]

It is worth noting – beyond the tributes paid to the king of Sweden, Bernadotte, the Swedish Red Cross and the WJC – that not a word was said about efforts deriving from the Community itself. The only person from the WJC referred to by name is Norbert Masur. The WJC man who put in most work to rescue European Jews and bring them to Sweden, Gilel Storch, was not paid a single tribute by the Community chairman.

In marked contrast to the Jewish Community's supposedly passive attitude was the feverish activity conducted by Gilel (Hillel) Storch, the Stockholm representative of both the WJC and the Jewish Agency Rescue Committee. Storch was born in Latvia in 1902 and had been a successful businessman there. He managed to reach Stockholm in 1940 after the Soviet Union had occupied Latvia. In Sweden Storch was immediately placed under the surveillance of the Counter-Intelligence Service and had his telephone tapped. He was suspected of being a Soviet spy in 1941 and characterised as 'somewhat dishonest'. During his first years he lived in constant fear of a Swedish deportation order, and it was not until 1950 that he obtained Swedish citizenship.

Storch was, however, enterprising enough to be able to wriggle out of every threat of deportation, and a few years later even managed to secure the transfer to Sweden of his wife and daughter from Latvia. In Sweden, too, Storch used his extraordinary business acumen to build up a fortune. One reason for Storch's accomplishments in Stockholm was undoubtedly his remarkable knack of establishing connections with important top Swedish people. He succeeded in avoiding his deportation in 1941 by paying a personal call on the under-secretary of state in the Ministry for Social Affairs, Tage Erlander, who was later to become prime minister of Sweden from 1946 to 1969. During the war Erlander was in reality something of a Swedish 'police minister', creating a counter-intelligence service from scratch in 1938 to attain an increasingly global surveillance by 1945. Later during the war Storch became acquainted with the, at that time, very young Olof Palme, whose mother was also from Latvia.[11]

Storch failed, however, to get the remaining members of his family out of Latvia, or those of his wife Anja either. All of them, with one exception, were murdered by the Nazis in Latvia. It was therefore not surprising that Storch worked feverishly to save the Jews languishing under threat of death in German-occupied Europe. For this task he took full advantage of his direct contacts with Swedish authorities. As early as September 1942 he was able to inform Gösta Engzell, head of the Foreign Office legal department, of the horrific state in which Jews in Latvia were living and how they were being gassed to death by the Germans. This was in all probability the first report the Foreign Office in Stockholm received of the gassing of Jews; at the end of August 1942 certain information concerning the gassing of Jews had been passed from Kurt Gerstein to Göran von Otter, but it is uncertain whether this reached Stockholm. Storch also suggested to Engzell how the Germans could be bribed. The 'head of the Gestapo' at the German legation in Stockholm, for instance, required the payment of 25,000 Swedish kronor to issue an exit permit. The transaction was to go through the Dresdner Bank, but a bank in Switzerland was also sometimes used. 'In the case of the Dutch Jews the price was higher than for the Baltic Jews.'[12]

Nevertheless, Storch's grand project to rescue Jews in Estonia, Latvia and Lithuania via the payment of generous sums of ransom money ended in failure. This task brought Storch into contact with the representative of the War Refugee Board in Stockholm, Iver Olsen, and with three Germans – Dr Bruno Peter Kleist, Fritz Hesse and Edgar Klaus. The secret talks pursued by Kleist, Hesse and Klaus in Stockholm with the Allies, including the Soviet Union, constitute an exciting story in themselves but are out of context here. These three Germans were, however, to play a certain rôle in the rescue work in 1945.[13]

Storch had greater success in his efforts to send food parcels to Jews in the concentration camps. The WJC in collaboration with the War Refugee Board set up large stores of foodstuffs in Gothenburg. During late summer or early autumn 1944 a first dispatch of 15,000 parcels, each weighing three kilos, left Gothenburg. In October a further 20,000 parcels were sent off, this time to specially listed prisoners at Bergen-Belsen, Theresienstadt, Ravensbrück and other camps with Jews in desperate need of help. In all, 72,000 parcels were sent from Gothenburg. Jewish prisoners who were later liberated were able to testify as to the importance these parcels had had for them, quite possibly saving thousands of Jewish lives. The parcels could not, however, be sent under the name of the WJC so instead were camouflaged using the Swedish Young Men's Christian Association (YMCA) and later the Swedish Red Cross as the sender's name. Finance was arranged, according to Storch, through generous credits granted by Carl Albert Andersson, chairman of the Cooperative Society and also mayor of Stockholm. A personal guarantee for the first 10,000 parcels was made out by the Stockholm WJC leaders – Storch himself, Akim Spivak and Leon Lapidus, together with Marcus Kaplan. This was necessary in order to meet the urgent need and overcome the internal bickering which persisted within the Jewish community in Stockholm. Nonetheless, conflicts spread: the WJC and Storch had obtained a Swedish licence to send the food parcels but were short of money while the AJDC had the money but were without a licence and were loath to give the honour to the WJC. It appears to have been at this point, in autumn 1944, that the AJDC sent a representative, Laura Margolis, to Stockholm. She managed to persuade chief rabbi Ehrenpreis to have the WJC licence for the parcels transferred to the AJDC. Following the successful completion of her task Margolis left Stockholm in January 1945 appointing Ragnar Gottfarb as the AJDC's new representative.[14]

Storch had already established a provisional Swedish section of the WJC in October 1944, with himself as the driving force. He had persuaded Ehrenpreis to accept the formal position of chairman. Conflicts soon arose between the young, self-willed Storch and the elderly, authoritarian Ehrenpreis. In December Storch informed the WJC management in New York that he had temporarily resigned from the WJC's Swedish executive board, complaining about scheming against him in Stockholm on the part of Ehrenpreis and other Jewish Community leaders – Josephson, Margolis and Schwartz. Storch announced that on 29 December Ehrenpreis had demanded a halt in the WJC's rescue work – it was evidently to be transferred to the AJDC. Storch continued, however, to send food parcels, now within the framework of the WJC's own central relief organisation. The Jewish Community, Ehrenpreis and Margolis (on behalf of the AJDC) refused to collaborate with Storch. On 5 February, though, Storch received unreserved support for his leadership from Stephen Wise and Nahum Goldmann, the WJC leader in New York. On 16 February Storch swiftly created his own Relief and Rehabilitation Department. The dispute between Storch and Ehrenpreis was temporarily settled by Lev Zelmanovits, the WJC London general secretary, during a lightning visit to Stockholm in March. It should be added that existing Swedish law in 1945 did not permit Storch to be a member of the Jewish Community in Stockholm. At that time Swedish citizenship was a pre-requisite for membership in all religious communities.[15]

Thus we have seen how the western Allies were uninterested during the Second World War in the Jews' survival in the Germans' concentration camps. Internal conflicts among the different Jewish organisations and their leaders were other contributory factors in complicating the sending of aid to the Jews.

4

Norway Under German Occupation

Wanda Heger's remarks on the subject of the Norwegian Jews in the German concentration camps:

> In recent years there have been several articles in Swedish and Norwegian newspapers and radio documentaries about the White Buses in which it is claimed that Bernadotte didn't wish to bring along the Jews. Kristian Ottosen has denied this, of course, and for my part I must say that these rumours really upset me. I cannot bring to mind that in our dealings with Bernadotte at the height of the action – February and March 1945 – we ever made any difference between Jews and other Norwegians and Danes. The problem was that we didn't know where the Norwegian Jews were. Auschwitz had of course been liberated by the Russians in January 1945. We knew about the three Norwegian Jews at Sachsenhausen because the Sachsenhausen prisoners managed to smuggle out full lists of Norwegian prisoners. As far as I can make out, after having spoken to many of the prisoners about this in later years, it was the prisoners themselves who fixed the index files at Sachsenhausen so that it didn't show that anyone was Jewish. Josef Berg, for instance, had a Norwegian-sounding name. Leif Wolfberg's name was really Leiba, but it was changed to 'Leif' . . . Nor was Harry Meyer a particularly Jewish-sounding name, and he wasn't arrested either during the Jewish round-up in Norway but was part of the embargo boat people who were arrested in April 1942.[1]

Norwegian Prisoners in Germany

Norway was invaded by Germany on 9 April 1940. By June 1940 the Norwegian troops in the very north of Norway had given up fighting, but the struggle continued outside the country and was conducted from London. The Norwegian king Håkon VII and Crown Prince Olav were there, undisputed symbols of unabated Norwegian resistance. Present, too, in London was the Norwegian government-in-exile headed by the old social democrat prime minister Johan Nygaardsvold, with Trygve Lie, formerly trade union lawyer, as foreign minister.

Meanwhile in Norway resistance was also taking the form of underground groups working on a small scale for the British intelligence service. The Norwegian Hjemmefronten, a cluster of resistance groups, grew stronger after the German executions which started in 1941, and in 1944 they were concentrated under a common leadership Hjemmefrontens Ledelse (HL). By then HL was so well organised that it was able to conduct a full-scale resistance movement opposing the German occupying forces, and by the end of the war the HL had enlisted more than 40,000 men and women. The views of the resistance fighters did not always coincide with those of the government-in-exile, but differences were never as great as those in other countries labouring under German occupation.

The Norwegian resistance movement in time came up against the ever more ruthless methods employed by both the German occupying forces and their Norwegian collaborators, the quislings. Their leader, Vidkun Quisling, had already tried to take power in April 1940 but had not succeeded. Instead it was the Germans who steered the country via Hitler's proxy Reichskommissar Josef Terboven. In September 1940 Terboven formed a council of state in which all except three were members of Quisling's Nasjonal Samling. He declared the Norwegian royalty dethroned and the government deposed. Political parties other than Nasjonal Samling were banned. On 1 February 1942 Quisling performed a formal act of state in which he appointed himself 'minister president' possessing all the power that king, government and parliament together had previously exercised. In reality, however, it was Terboven's state commissioner's office that still held power by virtue of their German weapons.

During 1941 a state of emergency had been declared in Norway and the first two executions occurred: trade union leaders Hansteen and Wickström were sentenced to death with immediate effect.

Meanwhile Norwegian prisoners had been deported to camps and prisons in Germany in 1940 and by June the Germans had erected their first concentration camp in Norway, Ulven outside Bergen. In summer 1941 they brought into use the biggest camp, Grini, outside Oslo. Larger waves of deportations came later: from spring 1942 to autumn 1943 more than 1,100 officers were deported, followed by 737 Jews between November 1942 and February 1943, with some 600 students and 200 policemen in December 1943. Otherwise the deportations were of an individual character and continued until autumn 1944.

There were three categories of Norwegian internee in Germany. Officers were ranked as prisoners of war and their captivity was regulated and protected by the Geneva Convention of 1929; they were treated relatively well in Germany. They were granted the right to write and send letters, and their camp could be inspected by the International Red Cross. All military prisoners also received every month a five-kilo parcel from the Norwegian Red Cross right until the end of the war. There was no special protection governed by international law for other civilian (political, that is) prisoners, and they could be treated quite arbitrarily by the Germans. Norwegian students and policemen came to be treated better than the other 'political' prisoners, while some of the civilian prisoners were sentenced to terms of hard labour and jail. These sentences in principle had a time limit, and even though conditions in German jails and hard labour camps were brutal, some of these prisoners were able to return home to Norway while the war was still on. Prisoners regarded by the Nazis as dangerous from a political point of view ended up in a concentration camp for an indefinite period of time. Most of the Norwegians were housed at the Sachsenhausen concentration camp, where they were able to receive food parcels and medicine from New Year 1943. The most dreaded concentration camps were the death camps and the *Nacht und Nebel* (NN) camps, from where no prisoner could conceive escaping alive. Prisoners would disappear into an impenetrable mist of death and destruction, and neither parcels nor letters would be delivered there.

Finally there was a special category of prominent civilian internees who had happened to find themselves in Germany against their will but who lived in relatively unfettered circumstances. Norwegians belonging to this group included the Hjort family (eight people), the Seips (university principal Seip and his wife), Welhaven (Oslo chief of police with his wife and daughter) and a few other individuals.

The Norwegian legation in Stockholm in October 1944 estimated the number of civilian internees as 8,000–9,000, added to which there were 1,125 military prisoners of war. By March 1945 the figure had dropped to 7,000 (civilian?) prisoners.

In *Norway's Response to the Holocaust*, Samuel Abrahamsen reported that 763 Norwegian Jews were deported to Germany.[2] They were transported directly to Auschwitz, where almost all of them were led to their deaths in the gas chambers. A few survived, although others perished along the way on the death marches in 1945. A total of 925 Norwegian Jews succeeded in crossing the border into freedom in Sweden, while a handful survived the war in Norway. The lists of names compiled by Kristian Ottosen and Bjarte Bruland, undoubtedly more accurate, show 766 or 767 deported Norwegian Jews, including a few who were without Norwegian citizenship. There were only twenty-eight or twenty-nine survivors.[3]

Out of these twenty-eight or twenty-nine still alive in March 1945, only three were rescued by the Bernadotte expedition: Josef Berg (a stateless citizen), Leif Wolfberg (a Soviet citizen) and Harry Meyer from the embargoed ships. Five Norwegian Jews, among them Sammy Steinmann and Julius Paltiel, were struck from the transport list for Neuengamme by the SS at Buchenwald, while one (Robert Savosnick) was knocked unconscious by an SS officer at Allach when he attempted to enlist with the Norwegian contingent. All six of these men were later rescued by the Americans. According to Ottosen it was the camp commandant at Buchenwald who decided to send the Norwegian students imprisoned at Buchenwald to Neuengamme by cattle truck, and who denied the five Norwegian Jews (as well as a Norwegian NN prisoner) passage with this transport. Heger much later has confirmed the fact that the transportation from Buchenwald was a German affair in which the Norwegian students naturally had no say in selecting who was to be transported.[4]

The five Norwegian Jews were thus separated from a German and not a Swedish transport operation, and the Swedes naturally enough were powerless in this matter. When all is said and done, however, the Bernadotte expedition's meagre results as far as the Norwegian Jews are concerned are noteworthy. An academic paper presented in 1995 by Knut-Lennart Havaas contained a detailed report which found that no later than at the end of March 1945, following the permission granted for the Swedes to establish contact with the Norwegian students at Neuengamme, the Swedish Red Cross should have known that there were five Norwegian Jews still at Buchenwald. Havaas also demonstrated that Swedish transport convoys at the beginning of April were fetching prisoners from camps quite close to Buchenwald, yet never called in there.

The problem with Havaas's version is that it depended entirely on Norwegian sources, among them Wanda Hjort-Heger, produced long after the dramatic weeks of 1945. In correspondence with me in 2002 Heger said she had had no conversation with Havaas within her memory, but stressed that those Norwegians present in 1945 did not know which Norwegians had remained at Buchenwald.[5] Furthermore, contemporary Swedish sources repeatedly referred to reports from Norwegian liaison officers that the Norwegian Jews could not be found (see Chapter 10). As late as 6 April the deputy head of the Swedish Red Cross detachment, Captain Folke, notified the Swedish Foreign Office that the Norwegian Jews had still not been located. In response von Post at the Foreign Office phoned directly the following day down to Friedrichsruh, the Swedish expedition's headquarters, stating that Steinmann was at Buchenwald and 'should be fetched from there together with the other non-Aryans'. Bernadotte reported on 8 April that a German liaison officer, Göring, would the following day be travelling to Buchenwald to check the situation regarding 'Danish and Norwegian Jews'. Lists were sent on 10 April by diplomatic bag to the Swedish legation in Berlin, to be handled by the Swedish Red Cross expedition, of 127 Norwegian Jews who had been deported to Germany, all of whom in some form had connections with Sweden. In sixty-seven cases an application for Swedish citizenship was pending. A special request for help was sent, moreover, for this very Samuel Steinmann, about whom the Jewish Community in Stockholm knew 'for certain' that on 1 February he was at Buchenwald. Steinmann's mother was

Swedish and was residing then in Sweden. The Swedes arrived too late, however – Buchenwald was liberated on 11 April by the Americans.

Norwegian Relief Work

Sweden and Switzerland became the centres for Norwegian efforts to come to the aid of their countrymen in the diabolical German prison camps. Only the neutral states – Sweden and Switzerland, that is – were in a position via their legations in Berlin and their national Red Cross units to act on behalf of the prisoners in the German camps. In Switzerland Peter Anker was active from 1942 as representative of the Norwegian Red Cross (London) at the ICRC's headquarters in Geneva. The ICRC managed after a time to secure the right to send parcels to identifiable people in the concentration camps. The ICRC, in tandem with the national Red Cross organisations, now began feverish activity sending parcels to Norwegian and other prisoners in Germany. The parcels contained not only foodstuffs but also clothing, medication, books and other items. Invoices for the parcels were sent from the ICRC to the Norwegian government-in-exile in London. Permission to conduct humanitarian relief work was also granted to the YMCA in the course of time, and in Sweden this was administered by a YMCA relief organisation called Help War Victims. In Norway, however, the Quisling government put a stop to Norway's Red Cross organisation in Oslo sending parcels to Norwegian prisoners. All the parcels had to have an acknowledgement of receipt by the prisoners. On the basis of these receipts the Red Cross units in Geneva, Stockholm and London made out long lists of prisoners in Germany, including their camp number.

The most important work, however, was carried out in Stockholm. For simple geographical and political reasons Sweden was closest for helping the Norwegians. Ever since the outbreak of war in Scandinavia in 1940 Sweden had served diplomatically in protecting Norwegian interests in Germany. The Swedish legation in Berlin tried, just as the ICRC did, to intervene on behalf of the Norwegian civilian prisoners. These efforts were repudiated by the German authorities, who claimed there were no 'political' prisoners – only common, criminal prisoners. Sweden's endeavours to help the Norwegian prisoners were further complicated after Quisling's formal assumption of power in 1942, when the Germans announced that Sweden no longer might look after Norwegian interests in Germany. From then onwards, every Swedish diplomatic bid was repudiated under the pretext that matters about Norway were of no concern to Sweden. All the same, privately the legation people continued to try to come to the aid of the Norwegian prisoners. Working in silence was a prerequisite – at the first sign of publication in the Swedish press or elsewhere the German authorities would have put an immediate stop to the Swedish activity.

A relief body, Den Norske Relief-central, had already been set up in Stockholm in summer 1940. Its head and driving force until December 1944 was the minister Niels Christian Ditleff. In his capacity as Norway's minister in Warsaw at the outbreak of war in 1939 Ditleff had already acquired some experience in humanitarian work, and was to become totally dedicated to Norwegian relief work. The Relief-central coordinated Swedish and other aid to Norway as well as to the prisoners in Germany. Ditleff came to work mainly with Sweden's Red Cross, and thus became acquainted with its chairman, Prince Carl, and its vice-chairman, Bernadotte. In addition, he acquired a large network of contacts with the Swedish financial and political elite in Stockholm, where many people in various ways were involved in the Norway relief work.

The third link in the relief work chain, after Stockholm and Geneva, was the so-called Berlin committee with its headquarters at the Gross Kreutz estate outside Berlin, where a group of Norwegian civilians were interned. The group was led by Professor Didrik Arup Seip and a lawyer, Johan B. Hjort. Hjort had been deported to Germany in 1942 after publishing an analysis of constitutional practice and the occupying administration from a legal perspective. He had earlier been one of the founders of Quisling's Nasjonal Samling, abandoning it in 1937. One of Hjort's sisters was married in Germany to a German aristocrat who also happened to be a prominent Nazi. She succeeded in getting Hjort freed, to be interned at the family's estate Gross Kreutz, forty-five kilometres west of Berlin's city centre. The condition attached by the Germans was that the entire Hjort family should travel to Germany. Thus in 1942 Hjort's wife and children – among them Wanda and Johan – arrived at Gross Kreutz. Wanda and Johan Hjort later began to improvise visits to the concentration camps in order to deliver food parcels to Norwegian prisoners. The visits gradually developed into a systematic activity devoted in the greatest secrecy and at the risk of their lives to charting the whereabouts of the Norwegian prisoners.

Professor Seip came to Gross Kreutz in 1943. Seip was a professor of Nordic comparative philology and rector of Oslo University, and had been arrested and sent to Germany in 1941. During the first of her many trips to the German camps, Wanda Hjort had found Seip, an almost broken man, at the Reichssicherheitshauptamt at Lichterfelde Ost. Because he was interested in Nordic ancient history, Himmler reasoned that Seip was more useful alive than dead. He had Seip released for research work on old Nordic writings – first at libraries in Munich and later in Berlin, which enabled him to settle at Gross Kreutz. It was here that the young medical student Bjørn Heger arrived at the New Year in 1944. Thus the Hjort–Seip–Heger trio began to operate; its restless and dangerous activity was devoted to collecting the names of Norwegians imprisoned in Germany. They built up an efficient Norwegian intelligence centre at Gross Kreutz, right in the heart of Nazi Germany.

The other Norwegian relief centre consisted of the two Norwegian seamen's chaplains, Arne Berge and Conrad Vogt-Svendsen, in Hamburg. They were blessed with relatively large freedom of movement around Germany, and owned the right to supply food parcels, clothing and medication to Norwegian prisoners. They also engaged in smuggling goods to the prisoners and in intelligence matters, making up lists of Norwegian prisoners and receiving information about escape routes. Captain Sigurd Melin was later to write the following about Svendsen:

> Svendsen . . . was a remarkable man of the Church. He had evidently managed to visit practically every jail and knew the prisoners by name, appearance and family circumstances. Time after time and week after week he would drive all around Germany, with no change of clothes – for the simple reason that he had nothing to change into. He seldom grabbed any sleep, negotiated with the supervisors of hard labour camps like a practised diplomat, he'd reconnoitre aircraft activity stretched out on the mudguard, and he preached a sermon at the stretcher of our dead colleague Ringman

which brought tears to the eyes of the entire congregation in the little Danish country church filled to capacity.[6]

Larger and longer lists of Norwegians imprisoned in Germany were all the time being compiled, and were forwarded from Hamburg and Gross Kreutz to the Swedish legation in Berlin. Amazingly, Seip obtained permission to use the Swedish diplomatic bag when it was sent to Stockholm – a totally illegal procedure. Via the courier's bag the lists reached Stockholm and the Norwegian legation there, and from there on to London and to the Red Cross in Geneva. In spring 1945 two parallel card indexes were available, one in Stockholm and another in London. This was what enabled Ditleff to hand over to Bernadotte in February 1945 on the eve of his first journey to Germany a complete two-volume list and a survey of concentration camps, jails and hard labour camps in Germany together with the number of Norwegian prisoners in each and every one of them. These Norwegian lists were to be of invaluable help to the future Swedish expedition in planning and charting transportation within Germany.

In January 1944 Ditleff established contact with the Berlin Hjort–Seip–Heger circle of people. In the course of 1944 Ditleff also met the Danish admiral Carl Hammerich on several occasions, and in this way was informed of his secret plans to form the Jyllandskorps, a body of Danish men and women dedicated to the rescue of Danes and Norwegians from German camps. Norwegian, Danish and Swedish projects aimed at retrieving Scandinavian prisoners from Germany thus began to be interwoven in Stockholm. Ditleff was undeniably the driving force in all of this, although many others belonging to the Norwegian colony were also involved. A committee was formed on 26 April 1944, abbreviated as the Prisoners Board, with Ditleff as chairman. Working alongside the Berlin trio, the Prisoners Board started to draw up plans for the rescue of the Norwegian prisoners in conjunction with the chaos expected to arise in Germany when the country collapsed, but before an Allied occupation. The committee knew full well that all such projects had to be agreed by London, but insisted that Norway itself had to build up a relief network of its own to bring back its people. Relief organisations should therefore be mounted in Switzerland (under Anker), in Denmark (by the Jyllandskorps) and in Sweden. Ditleff felt the pulse of his secret contacts at the Swedish Foreign Office and his excellent relations with leading members of the Swedish Red Cross. There were benevolent reactions from the Swedish side.

Ditleff's planning operations in Stockholm were given a kind of silent blessing by London. In summer 1944, however, the government-in-exile in London considered that Ditleff had exceeded limits, which led to them formally dissolving the Prisoners Board and leaving Ditleff out in the cold.

For a long time Ditleff had been of the opinion that the London government was too passive concerning the prisoner issue. The reason might have been that the department in London was far too bureaucratic in order fully to understand the seriousness of the matter. The reason might also have been that the London government possessed an all-embracing responsibility for the entire Norwegian war effort, and that the prisoners' situation had to be seen in this much wider perspective. Above all, the Norwegian London government had to ensure that the prisoner issue be integrated in the total inter-Allied war planning, which was led by the Supreme Headquarters of the Allied Expeditionary Forces (SHAEF).

A subsidiary organisation to SHAEF, the newly created United Nations Relief and Rehabilitation Authority (UNRRA), was designed to administer the sending home of Allied prisoners of war *after* the end of the war. The Norwegian London government's social department created a special so-called 'R Office', sanctioned in July 1944, which dealt with planning the Norwegian prisoners' return home after the Allies had secured military control over Germany. Its head of department, Juel, subsequently travelled to Stockholm to dissolve the over-active Prisoners Board. The London government took the view that as they needed full control of the prisoner issue they could not allow an organ to operate from Stockholm with such a free hand.

For the Allies the question of what was to be done with displaced people after the end of the war began to be an increasingly urgent issue. A planning department at SHAEF dealt with this problem while its Norwegian liaison officer, Major Johan Christie, in a memo from 23 September 1944 drew up guidelines from SHAEF and UNRRA. The point of departure was that SHAEF should exercise full control over the occupied territory both during the war and after a German collapse. All relief action would be subjected to the strict control of SHAEF and 'it was presupposed that no civilian or foreign relief organisations would be involved'. The prisoners in Germany were issued a strict order to 'stay put': remain at their respective camps until such time as Allied relief arrived. UNRRA alone was to supervise the sending home of prisoners. In this respect prisoners of war would be given priority while for the first two or three months civilian prisoners would not be able to reckon on any repatriation at all.

Christie's memo found its way to the Gross Kreutz trio in October 1944 and according to Heger they were 'exasperated and terrified'. It was evident to Seip that such a piece of information could not be passed on to the Norwegian prisoners. It would be impossible to retain the prisoners in the concentration camps in the chaotic circumstances that might arise, since this could risk their lives. In a report sent to Stockholm Hjort pointed to the imminent risk of the prisoners being liquidated as the Allies approached. The only way to save them was to get them out of Germany *before* the country was occupied:

> An urgent request is therefore made for the Norwegian government to consider whether the Swedish government cannot be persuaded to intervene on behalf of at least the Norwegian and Danish civilian prisoners in Germany, including those in jails and at hard labour camps, with a view to transferring the prisoners to Sweden possibly to remain there until the end of the war.

This was, in the words of Jakob Apalset, probably the first time a proposal for a purely *Swedish* action on behalf of the imprisoned Norwegians and Danes was put forward to the Norwegian authorities. The reaction in London was not long in coming, and as late as in December 1944 Norwegian foreign minister Lie appears to have been opposed to requesting aid from Sweden. Johan Christie commented:

> There existed, not least in all of our London offices, a very strong notion that this was 'our pitch' which 'we' – the Norwegian authorities in London – were to make a good job of. We were also somewhat reluctant to start something that might give the Swedes credit or praise in connection with this special issue, which had considerable prestige attached to it.

In Stockholm the Norwegian legation's Evacuation Office now eschewed Ditleff's efforts. He was still, however, head of the Norwegian Relief Centre. Subsequent official and semi-official Norwegian findings underestimate the antagonism that existed during these months between Ditleff and the London government. Ditleff himself in 1955 didn't mince his words: he called Christie's memo 'depressing' and 'appalling'. He made reference to a report later received from Seip in which the information came from a commandant at one of the larger German camps: 'liquidation of the contents of the camps, as soon as the risk appears that the Allies will take them over, has been decided upon and planned to the very last detail'.

After waiting two months for some action, or at least reaction, from London, Ditleff's patience was tried to the limits and towards the end of October 1944 his personal, unofficial, private dealings in Stockholm were now resumed. He renewed his what were now 'illegal' contacts with the Foreign Office, principally with the head of the political department, who was Eric von Post, and his deputy, Sven Grafström. Ditleff's project now focused on a purely Swedish operation, which would even embrace the Danish prisoners. It was to be undertaken *before* chaos arose in Germany. Ditleff secretly got in touch with Bernadotte, who immediately accepted Ditleff's propositions. Consequently Ditleff on 30 November 1944 presented the Swedish Foreign Office with his *Momenter til svensk aksjon for fangehjelp* (Proposals for Swedish Aid for Prisoner Relief), which would be the prelude to Bernadotte's Red Cross expedition to Germany in 1945. Ditleff's proposition was a trial balloon sent up by a private individual which did not coincide with the London government's standpoint at that moment.

Not until 29 December 1944 did the Norwegian Foreign Office in London give the signal to its legation in Stockholm to explore the possibility of a Swedish intervention on behalf of the prisoners in Germany. Ditleff was now reinstated and given the job of canvassing the Swedish Foreign Office in accordance with the Norwegian social department's general principles. These guidelines could now be interpreted in Stockholm to mean that a Swedish relief expedition would be sent off *before* the Allies had occupied Germany!

5

The Danish People Under German Occupation

Postcard sent 20 April 1944 from R. to R.S., Hauptstrasse 22, Theresienstadt:

Dearest,

I'm writing to you but don't know whether you'll be replying. I've already written so many times without a reply. I wonder what the reasons can be. Something's happened to you? We're sent news every day, though. Maybe you've lost interest in me . . . you don't really know me and you don't understand me either. So, where are we? . . .

I've got so much to tell you, but there's not enough paper to get it all down. So I pray to God that we shall see each other in the future and tell each other about everything. Please write to me, meanwhile, something about yourself and I'll answer you. Everything's as usual with us. I work from early morning to five. I'm alone, abandoned and live in my dreams.

All my love and kisses,

R.[1]

Danish Prisoners in Germany

Denmark's situation at the time of the German invasion there on 9 April 1940 was different from that of Norway's. Denmark had signed a pact of non-aggression with Germany in May 1939. When the German army invaded, Denmark was practically defenceless and was occupied in a single day. When, under protest, it yielded to the German forces, the Germans promised that Denmark could retain its internal self-government. The Danish government made no change until it was reshuffled in July and a national coalition was formed. The king, Christian X, remained in the country and the Rigsdag (Danish parliament) continued functioning. The new government began a period of collaboration with the Germans, and in July 1940 it declared that it foresaw a new Europe under German hegemony, and that Denmark was prepared to play an active rôle in cooperating with this Greater Germany.

The Danes delivered agricultural products and other items to the Germans in the entire course of the war. In return the Germans desisted from putting the Danish Nazis into power throughout the country. After the German attack on the Soviet Union in 1941, however, Danish authorities were compelled to imprison approximately two hundred communists, who were interned at the Horserød camp, and Denmark's Communist Party was banned. The Danish foreign minister, Scavenius, signed an anti-Comintern pact in Berlin in November 1941, though with strong reservations. From the German point of view, Denmark was to be a model example of benevolent German occupation. Seen from the Allies' standpoint, Denmark was regarded as a state associated with Germany.

Nevertheless, the signing of the anti-Comintern pact led to large demonstrations of protest in Copenhagen, and the first illegal resistance publications began to appear. The elderly prime minister, Stauning, died in 1942 and was succeeded by another social democrat, Vilhelm Buhl. Relations during 1942 and 1943 deteriorated between the German occupying power and the Danish people. Parliamentary elections in March 1943 were seen as a national manifestation in favour of popular Danish government, while at the same time illegal activities were on the increase. In summer 1943 there was an increase in large-scale stoppages in provincial towns and cities in protest at German excesses.

The conflicts came to a head on 28 August 1943. The German plenipotentiary, Bevollmächtiger des Deutschen Reiches in Dänemark, Dr Werner Best, demanded that the Danish government declare a state of emergency and introduce martial law, the death penalty for acts of sabotage and German press censorship. This ultimatum was rejected by the government which ceased to function from the following day. The Germans now formally took over power in Denmark: parliament no longer functioned, although it was not formally dissolved, and the king was put under surveillance. The Danish army and navy were disbanded, and Danish defence establishments were manned by the Germans. The Germans then proclaimed a state of emergency and on 8 September 1943 they performed the first execution. Simultaneously the Danes began to assemble an illegal army, including a Danish brigade trained in Sweden.

After the Danish government ceased to function on 29 August 1943 a legal and political vacuum was left behind in the country. During the period 1943 to 1945 power in Denmark was confined to four major centres. Formally, Denmark was now governed by a German 'State Commissioner'. The Germans also had the military might on their side and were to a certain extent able to force their policies through. They were, however, without the support of the native population. In place of the non-functioning Danish government it was the heads of departments who became a sort of non-political governing body in charge of the administrative work – it came to be dubbed the 'Departmental heads government'. Politicians, who previously had been active in their governing capacity, remained in a 'non-official' rôle, and Buhl acted as a kind of *de facto* prime minister. Gradually the resistance movement's illegal units, united under an umbrella called Danmarks Frihetsråd, constituted a fourth power centre. The course of Denmark's history from 1943 to 1945 turned into an intricate web of interplay and resistance between these four power centres.

Danish Jews began to be arrested on 1 October 1943 and sent to Germany, an action that aroused widespread protests throughout the country. Thanks to Denmark's favoured position, however, the Jews were not bundled off to the extermination camps but transported instead to what was made out to be the model ghetto of Theresienstadt. Swedish radio made a public announcement on 2 October in which the Swedish government invited Germany to allow all Danish Jews into Sweden, an announcement that made world press headlines. Leni Yahil regarded the Swedish decision of 2 October as signifying Sweden's first public stand *vis-à-vis* Nazi Germany – a Swedish demonstration that the country firmly stood in the free, democratic world.

The vast majority of Danish Jews were assured protection by their countrymen, and close to 8,000 Jews were helped to reach Sweden. Swedish citizenship had already been granted to nearly two hundred Danish Jews. A number of these, as well as Danish Jews married to Gentiles, had been allowed by the Germans to travel from Denmark to Sweden. Danish resistance people, ministers, civil servants, officers, sick people and many others were also transferred to Sweden, illegally, and by the end of the war there were about 18,000 Danish refugees in Sweden. Exactly how many of these were actually Jewish is hard to say: the Danish refugee administrative unit in Stockholm refused to use the label 'Jewish' in registering Danish refugees.

Danmarks Frihetsråd's first proclamation, made in October 1943, managed to unite the whole of the illegal Danish resistance movement under its leadership. That same autumn the Germans began deporting non-Jewish Danes as well, to the concentration camps. The day before New Year's Eve 1943 a new phase opened in German terror tactics, with attacks on prominent Danish public figures. A well-known clergyman and poet, Kaj Munk, was murdered on 5 January 1944. The Danish heads of department then made concerted efforts to avoid further deportations. On a Danish initiative, the concentration camp at Frøslev in southern Jutland close to the German border was brought into use in August 1944, and prisoners from the Horserød camp were transferred there. The Danes opened the Frøslev camp partly on condition that those Danes who had previously been deported to Germany would now be allowed back in the country, and partly on the understanding that deportations would no longer be carried out. Best confirmed this agreement, but the German's pledges were soon to be broken.

During 1944 Danish acts of sabotage increased and the Germans responded using terror. Danish executions of those they considered traitors, so-called *stikkere*, were met by what were known as 'clearing assassinations' on the part of the Germans or the Danish Nazis. Danish resistance people arrested by the Germans were subjected to torture and executed. During the big 'people's strike' that took place in Copenhagen in June and July 1944 eighty-eight Danes were murdered. On 19 September 1944 the Germans put the entire police force under arrest and sent all two thousand of them to Germany – exceptions were those who managed to remain in hiding. Law and order in Denmark would in future be the task of civilian 'home guards' and the Hilfspolizei (HIPO; the Danish Nazis's auxiliary police force). Until the German surrender on 4 May 1945 Danish acts of sabotage became more and more frequent, mostly by blowing up rail transport on the main island of Själland, to which the Germans responded with their own terror tactics .

Danish Relief Work and the Jyllandskorps

Responsibility for the extensive humanitarian work in aid of the Danish prisoners in Germany lay with the Ministry of Social Affairs.[2] Since at least part of this work would involve illegal actions few people were initiated into its details. Head of department Hans Henrik Koch took the main burden of the work, together with office manager Mogens Kirstein and the secretary Finn Nielsen. They were faced with a growing mountain of routine business concerning the Danish internees first at Horserød, later at Frøslev and lastly also in Germany. They had to seek information as to where the prisoners were and what their living conditions were like, and they had to maintain contact with them and send them relief parcels. They began planning relief action, and all this required money. Liaison with the Germans was maintained at the foreign ministry by section head Frants Hvass.

Some 472 Jews and 150 communists were deported on 2 October 1943, and in November the first food parcels were dispatched to the communists at the so-called 'labour camp' of Stutthof. There later followed parcels containing clothing, medication, cigarettes and other items. To begin with the Germans allowed one parcel a month, but from 1944 onwards this was increased to two, plus an extra special parcel per month, containing for example chocolate and sweets, marmelade and honey. Deportee relief was often formally coordinated by 'Ladies' Committees' in conjunction with the Ministry of Social Affairs. The practical work was carried out by the Danish Red Cross, although Rosting, its head official, harboured certain misgivings about this.

Parcels would also be sent to the Danish prisoners at Sachsenhausen and Ravensbrück, and the Jews at Theresienstadt were also permitted to receive parcels. They had to be of a personal nature, however, and equipped with name of sender and receiver. Once again, it was the Danish Red Cross which handled the dispatch of parcels. It was trickier to get the parcels through to Danes in German jails, but sometimes the Danish and Norwegian seamen's chaplains in Hamburg succeeded in smuggling in vitamins and other items, although food parcels hardly ever arrived. As far as the prisoners in the external labour camps were concerned, the Danes never obtained permission to supply them with parcels.

German deportations of Danish men and women continued, Best's pledges notwithstanding. Deportations in groups were carried out between November 1943 and January 1944, the men being transferred to Sachsenhausen and the women to Ravensbrück. The mass deportation of policemen to Buchenwald in September 1944 presented the Danish relief network with a fresh series of serious problems. The Danish policemen were soon classified, however, as 'prisoners of war', and most of them sent on to the Mühlberg prisoner of war camp, where conditions were better. The Danish Red Cross was even able to install a medical post at Torgau in March 1945 with Dr Troels Thune Andersen offering his services to the Danes at the prisoner of war camp. A further shipment of Danes was deported between September 1944 and February 1945, this time principally to the Neuengamme camp outside Hamburg.

The Danish foreign ministry's carefully compiled statistics show that the total number of Danish men and women deported to Germany amounted to 6,083. Of these, 1,981 were policemen, 472 Jews were transported to Theresienstadt and 150 communists to Stutthof. Some 531 of these Danes died in Germany, ten under transportation home and another forty-four later as a result of their ordeals in Germany. Privations suffered at the concentration camps accounted for 585 Danish fatalities in all, close to ten per cent of the number deported.

The Danes were swift in starting plans to bring their prisoners home, Admiral Carl Hammerich being the driving force in this enterprise. He and his Norwegian-born wife Borghild had canvassed for Danish aid to Norway from the very start of the war. They had established a broad network of contacts with Norway and with Norwegians in Stockholm (mainly

Ditleff) as well as in Germany (the seamen's chaplains in Hamburg and Heger and Seip at Gross Kreutz).

In 1944 Hammerich initiated plans for a body of volunteers formed on military lines, and which came to be known as the Jyllandskorps. It was to be more of a paramilitary operation, the majority of the 425 people recruited being military personnel. Hammerich counted on both rail transport and shipping being out of operation in a Germany on the brink of total collapse. Transportation home of Danish and Norwegian prisoners would have to be by road using buses and fish vans. Danish vehicles had supplied fish, an important export commodity, directly to Germany throughout the war, and the Germans should, it was reasoned, be anxious for these transports to continue for as long as possible. Geographically, Denmark's position favoured such an operation. Hammerich paid visits to Stockholm in February, April and July 1944 and enlarged on his plans for Ditleff. In July the newly created Norwegian Evacuation Office was also present at the talks, as well as Koch, who confirmed the Danish administration's support for Hammerich's project. Its name had by now been officially changed to Det danske Hjaelpekorps (The Danish Relief Corps), but it was of course as yet merely a theoretical exercise.

Hammerich, however, had the backing of the Ministry of Social Affairs, with all its administrative and financial resources. The ministry began to prepare seriously for a Danish relief operation in the unknown future, and while doing this it drew up lists of Danish deportees with their prison camp clearly marked.

The assumption in the planning procedure at the talks in Stockholm was that Scandinavian prisoners were being rescued, even if other nationalities would not be excluded. In reply to a query put by the Norwegians the Danes made it clear that the project should rather be seen as a 'camouflaged state enterprise'. Hammerich was arrested by the Germans in December 1944 and was killed when the British bombed Shell House, the Gestapo headquarters in Copenhagen, on 21 March 1945. With the Danish ministry now directly involved in planning operations, preparations were intensified following a new pledge from Best, on 1 December 1944, that all Danish prisoners on German soil would be gathered at Frøslev, with the exception of:

1   those active in sabotage and partisan groups;
2   murderers;
3   communist officials;
4   spies.

The Danish–Norwegian talks concluded with an agreement in Stockholm on 23 February 1945 in which the Danish Ministry of Social Affairs approved a proposal made by the Norwegian government concerning 'repatriation of Danish and Norwegian prisoners interned in Germany'. It was hardly by chance that this happened one day after Bernadotte's return from his first successful trip to Germany (see Chapter 7). It must then have been plain in Stockholm that a Swedish relief operation in aid of these Danish and Norwegian prisoners would soon be launched. Nowhere in the Danish–Norwegian agreement, however, was anything mentioned of an active Swedish unit. Arrangements were for the Danish and Norwegian prisoners to be conveyed to Ramlösa (in southern Sweden, oddly enough) where they would be taken care of by Norwegian repatriation units.

Danish records showed that Danish preparations were largely ready to be launched, and that all that was needed was a formal go-ahead:

• 120 vehicles with room for twenty-five people in each (i.e., a transport capacity of some three thousand people) could be requisitioned in a matter of days;
• preparations had been made for recruiting essential personnel such as group leaders, doctors, nurses, drivers and mechanics;
• a command office was planned in southern Denmark;
• depots had been set up supplying foodstuffs, medication, vehicle equipment, etc.

This Danish–Norwegian project, however, never saw the light of day. It was not intended to be implemented until *after* the end of the war and was no longer relevant when the Swedish rescue mission in Germany came into operation. The Danish–Norwegian plans and their practical preparations would be of invaluable help, nevertheless, when the Swedes started work in March 1945. On a smaller scale the Danes, too, had begun to bring home a number of their prisoners by December 1944. The practical work for this was the responsibility of the National Serum Institute in Copenhagen, and it involved obtaining a supply of food, medication, fuel, instruments, road maps, tobacco, beer and not least of all Danish vodka: 'Schnapps – and food parcels, of course – were extraordinarily useful means in Germany in certain situations to get unpopular or unattainable requests met.' Every conceivable measure had been taken at the Danish–German border to be able to welcome thousands of prisoners from Germany, and the quarantine units at Padborg and Kruså had been reinforced. Inside Germany, at the Danish senior citizens' centre Stift Rosenborg near Neuengamme, the Danes had prepared large stores of food parcels for the prisoners. Stift Rosenborg was to be the Danes' gathering point in Germany.

The first convoys of 198 Danish policemen were brought home from the Buchenwald concentration camp between 5 and 11 December 1944 for internment at Frøslev. They were fetched by four buses – painted red – pulling trailers with producer-gas units, four ambulances (one of the policemen died after an operation performed under transport), a truck and a passenger car. Subsequently only individual Danes could be brought back while political negotiations were becoming deadlocked – there were eight sick people moved home on 12 December and two internees from Neuengamme on 20 January 1945, an occasion that afforded the Danes an opportunity to gain an insight into the abominable conditions prevailing at this concentration camp. Fresh convoys on 2 February fetched thirty border guards and twelve 'anti-social elements' from Neuengamme as well as seventeen policemen from the Mühlberg and Buchenwald camps. Mühlberg proved to be operating under far better conditions than the other concentration camps. Later on that February more Danish convoys collected forty-two policemen from Mühlberg and thirty-one 'anti-social elements' plus one labelled as a 'political prisoner' from Neuengamme. Regulations required that the policemen and the 'political prisoners' be interned at Frøslev while the 'anti-social elements' were set free. All of these minor transport operations, which by the end of February had succeeded in bringing home 341 Danes, were carried out entirely on Danish initiative and using solely Danish vehicles. Most of those collected and brought home were ill.

6

Sweden's Balance Between Neutrality and Activism

Swedish cabinet ministers in March 1945 on the subject of military aid to Denmark:

> Bramstorp: recommend rejection; if the Allies find out, they'll do nothing.
> Rubbestad: recommend rejection, there's no mood for it, might even be a revolt, from the farmers at least, clear reluctance.
> Günther: perhaps the petition is not to be taken too seriously. It's unrealistic that such a situation should arise as to call for Swedish intervention.
> Domö: recommend rejection.
> Sköld: we shouldn't get ourselves involved in these matters, out of the question, in any case without a request from the Allies.
> Wigforss: just an abstract possibility, but difficult to dismiss the notion, say that for the moment we don't want to commit ourselves.[1]

Sweden Changes Course in Favour of Scandinavia

Following the change in fortune in hostilities around the turn of the year 1942/3, the Swedish government slowly but surely altered course in a more pro-Western direction. In conjunction with this change of attitude, it also became necessary to improve the icy relations with the sister nations Norway and Denmark. An increase in aid to the Norwegians and Danes was also something that an ever stronger public opinion in Sweden, chiefly the so-called Norway Movement, had been urging for some time.

The Social Democratic party, too, contained many leading politicians and moulders of public opinion – finance minister Ernst Wigforss and the Myrdals, for instance – who were firm believers in Nordic solidarity. The latter had even suggested, in 1941, uniting the Nordic countries in a new 'Nordic Union'. Foreign minister Günther was also a keen supporter of the Nordic idea, although at this time it might be more appropriate to talk of Scandinavian rather than Nordic unity – Finland was of course for the time being an ally of Hitler's Germany, and it was difficult to claim that what mattered for Finland now also mattered for Sweden. After Finland had entered into a truce with the Soviet Union in September 1944 (assisted by Sweden) and turned its weapons on its former German warring part-ners, Finland's future standing within the Nordic Union was to become a permanent headache for the decision-makers in Stockholm.

Judging by the source material, and not least by his own private archives, the Swedish prime minister, Per Albin Hansson, was deeply involved in training the Norwegian and Danish police forces (in other words, military units) on Swedish soil. It was Hansson, too, who received the direct propos-als for military aid. His Danish party counterpart and Denmark's former prime minister, Vilhelm Buhl, in November 1943 informed Hansson that if circumstances made it absolutely necessary *'we shall request the assistance of military forces'*, while in March 1945 Buhl expressly mentioned the possibil-ity of a Danish petition for Swedish military aid (3–5 divisions) in order to forestall disintegration and anarchy in Denmark. Hansson's response was elusive and in no way binding: his objective continued to be that of keeping Sweden out of the war, to the bitter end. Following Buhl's cautious proposal, Hansson summed up the dismissive views of other members of his cabinet (see p.53) as well as his own balance sheet:

A *no* best meets Sweden's interests in the short run, but will:
- depress the Danes;
- complicate cooperation in the future;
- cause us damage in others' eyes should the matter be made public.

A *yes* would not correspond to 'the mood of the people' at this moment:
- would inspire the Danes to perhaps premature action;
- would, if it were necessary, tend to subdue the Germans.

Similarly the prime minister coolly refuted Norwegian expectations of Swedish armed intervention in Norway. It was instead within the humanitarian field that the Swedish government would concentrate its efforts on behalf of the sister nations in the final stages of the war. Hansson had no hand in this work, it would appear from source material available. These matters came instead to be handled by the head of the Foreign Office political department, Eric von Post, and by the head of its legal department, Gösta Engzell, under the ever-watchful eye of the Honourable Christian Günther, the foreign minister.

Swedish Humanitarian Aid to Norwegian and Danish Prisoners in Germany

A turning point in Swedish policy came with the Germans' deportation of six hundred students at Oslo University at the end of 1943. The Swedish government presented a petition to the German government on 1 December to cancel the measures taken against teaching staff and students at the university. There was a very strong response from the Germans. Their foreign minister, von Ribbentrop, declared to Sweden's chargé d'affaires in Berlin (still Eric von Post) that the German government was surprised at Sweden's petition and particularly at the fact that it had been served to the Swedish press. Ribbentrop made it clear that 'Germany recognised in no way the Swedish government's right to make overtures in Norwegian affairs and that the Reich government in principle must reject any discussion of such issues.' According to German sources Sweden's petition was supposed to have aroused ill will in Hitler who had experienced the Swedish *démarche* as a personal 'rap on the knuckles'.

Following this sharp German reproof no more Swedish diplomatic overtures were made for some time. In all secrecy, however, the Swedish legation in Berlin, under minister Arvid Richert, from spring 1944 started to mediate between the Norwegian minister Ditleff in Stockholm and the Norwegian intelligence centre at Gross Kreutz with the Hjort–Seip–Heger trio. At the same time the Swedish Berlin legation attempted to provide relief to Norwegian internees in Germany with food parcels, medication and money. In Stockholm exchanges between the Foreign Office and the Norwegian legation became more and more frequent. Sven Grafström, deputy head at the Foreign Office political department, on 6 September sent instructions to Richert in Berlin to present Günther's appeal to the Germans for Norwegian internees in Germany to be released and sent home to Norway, with priority given to the Norwegian students. As an alternative Richert was to request the Norwegians' release in order to travel to and remain in Sweden. The Swedish appeal was admittedly not complied with, but as distinct from the treatment received in December 1943 it was not abruptly rebuked. Subsequently a number of Swedish appeals were made in Berlin and Stockholm, for the most part on behalf of the Norwegian students. When Sweden in September 1944 gave the Germans permission to transport seriously wounded Germans from northern Finland to Germany over Swedish territory, it was expected that Germany in return would grant sick Norwegian students the right to be transferred from Germany to Sweden. At the same time Richert also began to stress the risk of a further deterioration in Swedish–German relations through the German deportation of thousands of Danish prisoners.

In private conversations Richert threatened, although probably without express permission from Stockholm, a possible rupture in Swedish–German diplomatic relations. At the same time Swedish trade with Germany during autumn 1944 had been reduced to a minimum and all Swedish shipping movements to Germany as well as German movements to Swedish Baltic ports had been axed. Both Himmler and Hitler appear to have begun to fear that Sweden would be entering the war on the Allies' side. Hitler's reasons for refusing to evacuate by sea the German troops cornered in Courland in Latvia were that it was only by these troops remaining there that Sweden could be prevented from entering the war.

Parallel with the contacts existing between the Swedish and German foreign offices intensive discussions were also under way between the Norwegian legation in Stockholm, the Swedish Foreign Office, the Swedish legation in Berlin and the Norwegian 'intelligence' group at the Gross Kreutz estate. Several Norwegian documents dealing with the way in which the Norwegian prisoners could be rescued would be produced in the months to come by Ditleff and Seip. A proposal for an operation under Norwegian leadership but supported by Swedish means following a

German collapse was soon shelved in favour of a purely Swedish operation with fairly immediate effect.

Ditleff enjoyed excellent relations with the Swedish Red Cross and with the Swedish Norway Aid organisation. Bertil Kugelberg, deputy managing director of the Swedish Employers' Confederation, also formed part of the board of directors of Norway Aid. Kugelberg in his memoirs described how on 22 September 1944 he brought together at a dinner party representatives of the British and American embassies, the Norwegian legation (including Ditleff) and the deputy chairman of the Swedish Red Cross, Bernadotte. Ditleff suggested to Bernadotte that he (Bernadotte) put in a word with King Gustaf concerning a Swedish operation in aid of the Norwegian internees. In Kugelberg's words Bernadotte's response was: 'I'll go out to Drottningholm Palace first thing tomorrow and have a chat with the king about the matter.'

Subsequently, by virtue of 'extremely cautious private contacts' within the Swedish Foreign Office, Ditleff succeeded in winning over to his cause Eric von Post and Sven Grafström, head and deputy head respectively of the political department. Ditleff and Grafström had known each other ever since they had both been diplomats in Warsaw in 1939. Their backing assured, Ditleff on 30 November 1944 submitted his proposal to the Foreign Office. Since this is generally regarded as the origin of the entire 'White Bus operation' and the first time Bernadotte was brought into the picture, we are reproducing here the introductory section in full:

1   Delegation to Berlin: Swedish Red Cross delegation with Folke Bernadotte as leader, one general, one of Göring's or Himmler's several friends, head of dept. Grafström; royal letter addressed to Hitler(?); support from CICR (Dr Marti).

2   Delegation's task: on the basis of Scandinavian sister nationhood and in a spirit of human charity, request that:

(a) either certain groups of Norwegian prisoners be released, possibly reprieved, to be interned in Sweden until the end of the war;

(b) or these groups be transferred for internment in German-occupied Scandinavian country (Denmark or Norway) with access to material aid from the Swedish Red Cross; or

(c) the Swedish Red Cross, in conjunction with respective German authority in charge, immediately prepare an exclusively Swedish relief expedition capable of visiting German ports in order to collect and repatriate Scandinavian prisoners in Germany and within German domain in the event of a truce, declaration of peace or whenever the German government, either earlier or later, can permit the passage of a Swedish humanitarian expedition acting in collaboration with German authorities.

Ditleff's presentation was not an official Norwegian one but instead a private proposal. Simultaneously the Swedish Foreign Office was in the process of changing its strategy towards Germany. Auswärtiges Amt and its pompous chief von Ribbentrop were beginning to be seen as fairly powerless. In his place the Swedes started to focus their attention on the head of the SS, Heinrich Himmler, and one of his closest colleagues, SS-Brigadeführer Walter Schellenberg. In the final stages of the war Himmler stood out as a progressively more powerful man in the Third Reich. Secret reports dispatched in November to the Foreign Office spoke of Hitler having been wounded in the attempt on his life on 20 July 1944. Consequently he would no longer be capable of functioning as head of government. Rumours then pointed to Himmler as Germany's future minister–president or as the Führer's formal deputy. The Swedish legation in Berlin on 26 November reported that its 'outspoken friend', undoubtedly Schellenberg, had communicated the fact that by virtue of illness and Himmler's intervention Hitler had now been 'neutralised'. Himmler was now seeking via Stockholm to gain contact with the western Powers for peace overtures. In the event of the western Powers not immediately rejecting these moves, Hitler would definitely be removed from the leadership.

Sweden Seeks Direct Contact with Himmler: Schellenberg and Kersten Enter the Scene

At the start of 1945 Heinrich Himmler as Reichsführer-SS was formally head of the enormous complex of German concentration camps. German jails and hard labour camps admittedly came under the formal supervision of the Ministry of Justice, but as Himmler was also Germany's minister of the interior it was quite probable he had the last say in matters concerning these institutions too.

It was common knowledge that Himmler had a bit of a soft spot for Sweden. One likely reason was his infatuation with the ancient Germanic races and for Scandinavians as the purest of 'Aryans'. He was also afraid of Sweden entering the war in 1945. His main interest as far as Sweden was concerned, however, was in getting the country to act as intermediary in his endeavour to establish contact with the western Allies in order to conclude separate peace terms with them. A German research team has revealed such efforts on Himmler's part from as early as 1941. In 1943 and 1944, moreover, Himmler had in vain tried to use the services of bank executive Jacob Wallenberg in Stockholm to probe the possibilities of contacting the western Powers.[2]

Walter Schellenberg had succeeded Admiral Canaris in 1944 as head of the Abwehr (German military intelligence service). He had been Himmler's closest confidant and possibly also the driving force behind his plans for a *coup d'état* to remove Hitler and achieve a separate peace with the West. Whatever the matter, this is how he wished to present his case after the war at the Nuremburg trials:

> Himmler had already realised during 1942 that Germany was not going to win the war, and that only a peace compromise could save Germany from defeat. From then on Himmler was pondering over plans to stage a coup and remove Hitler and subsequently initiate peace talks with the western Powers. As Himmler's representative Schellenberg got in touch with western Power representatives, joining them for talks both in Switzerland and Sweden.
>
> The coup that was being planned came under discussion in detail between Himmler and Schellenberg during 1943. Himmler, though, always unable to make firm decisions, postponed the plans time and time again, but through Schellenberg maintained steady contact with British and American circles via connections in Switzerland and Sweden. Schellenberg travelled to Stockholm some ten times for talks, a few times using his own name but often under the pseudonym of Schellenkampf . . .

On one occasion in the course of 1943 Himmler consulted Kaltenbrunner about the contacts and plans established via Schellenberg. Kaltenbrunner warned Himmler (who then began to fret and hesitate) that Schellenberg's activities could put his position at risk and even cost him his life since this was tantamount to high treason. Notwithstanding this, Himmler continued to entertain hopes of further contact with the western Powers.

Questioned as to whether after Himmler's change of heart and following Kaltenbrunner's knowledge of the plans he didn't fear for his own safety, Schellenberg replied that he did indeed feel a certain anxiety but that through the 'masseur' he had managed to keep his hold on Himmler and exert influence on him, more than anything else by repeatedly revealing to him 'Hitler's horoscope of death'. Both Himmler and Hitler believed in the study of astrology, and Schellenberg exploited this superstition to his own ends.

After Sweden had cut off trade relations with Germany by closing its ports in autumn 1944, Himmler feared that Sweden would declare war on Germany, and he was therefore anxious for Schellenberg to maintain connections with Sweden. This was why Schellenberg continued to visit Sweden even after Kaltenbrunner's warnings.[3]

On 25 May 1944 Richert reported to the Foreign Office that Schellenberg had been appointed head of the Abwehr. He had evidently enjoyed his pleasant conversation on 15 November with Schellenberg who, in Richert's words, 'left a sober, intelligent, easy-going and not unagreeable impression'! Schellenberg showed that he understood the Swedish view of the Norwegian–Danish–Swedish conundrum, reaffirmed Himmler's positive attitude towards Sweden and added that he was 'positively in favour of satisfying our requirements concerning Norway (Schellenberg expressed himself more vaguely on the subject of Denmark), but that he often came up against difficulties from other quarters – Ribbentrop and Terboven – and was often unable to have his way with Hitler since it appeared that Hitler was still swayed by Swedish press notices to our detriment.'

The 'masseur', Himmler's private doctor Felix Kersten, then became involved. Kersten was born in 1898 in Estonian Dorpat but became a

Finnish citizen in 1920, and had the title of 'medical counsellor' bestowed on him for his services to Finland during the Second World War. He had trained to be a masseur and nature-healer in the period between the wars, and had acquired a fashionable circle of clients including the Dutch royal family. Following the German occupation of the Netherlands in 1940 Kersten was obliged, according to the account he gave *after the war*, to remain in Germany as Himmler's Privatartz. All sources agree that this assured him a large measure of influence over Himmler, who suffered from chronic stomach pains and became totally dependent on Kersten's skilful treatment. It is quite plain that Kersten exploited Himmler's dependence on him to extract a whole series of concessions in matters of a humanitarian nature. How many and how large those concessions were has, however, remained controversial.[4]

Schellenberg informed the Allies after the war that he too from 1942 onwards had begun to rely on Kersten's excellent massage. He received treatment from Kersten both in Germany and on his visits to Stockholm. Schellenberg and Kersten shared uneasiness about Germany's imminent defeat. For Kersten, this meant the loss of his country estate and other assets in Germany. According to Schellenberg Kersten in 1940 had declined an offer from the United States and stayed instead in Germany, accepting a lump sum of 100,000 Reichsmark plus a large wooded area close to the Harzwalde estate. When it came to property, Schellenberg claimed, Kersten was 'like a small child, primitive, at times utterly unscrupulous'. When Kersten moved to Sweden in 1943, promising Himmler to return to Germany every fourth month for treatment, he was granted a further 50,000 Swedish kronor in order to start a practice in Sweden. All work at his Harzwalde estate was carried out by the so-called Bible students, the Jehovah's Witnesses, all of them former camp prisoners. Kersten on the other hand emphatically declared that he 'refused to accept fees' and had not got a single penny from Himmler.[5]

From 1943 the Swedish Foreign Office made use of Kersten's services for its humanitarian work. He was given a residence permit in Sweden in autumn 1943, acquiring living quarters in Stockholm. His first real success, thanks to his mediation in December 1944, was Himmler allowing fifty Norwegian students and fifty Danish policemen to return home, as well as releasing the last three of the so-called Warsaw Swedes. These were seven Swedish businessmen working for STAB (the Swedish Match Company) as well as L.M. Ericsson, who had been arrested by the Germans in Poland in 1942 for unlawful activity that was deemed to be of benefit to the Polish London government. In 1943 four of them had been sentenced to death and one to a hard labour camp, while two were acquitted. Hitler had commuted the death sentences to life imprisonment at a hard labour camp after a personal appeal from King Gustaf V.

In 1944 a further two Swedes had been released. In addition, Richert reported back that, according to Kersten, Himmler was subsequently prepared to satisfy further Swedish requests concerning Norway and Denmark. A prerequisite was that Swedish parliamentary opinion or the like should not bring pressure to bear on the matter, in which case the very opposite would be the result: 'In such circumstances a concession would appear to be a sign of weakness.' By the end of the year 143 Norwegian students had been able to return home. The fact that this had been possible because of Swedish intervention was something that had to be kept quiet in order not to hurt German prestige.

Himmler's 1944 Christmas present to Kersten demonstrated that the new Swedish strategy was working: with the aid of Schellenberg and Kersten Sweden succeeded in wresting from Germany's top executioner, Himmler, permission to open up the gates of freedom for a tiny number of Scandinavian prisoners. The Foreign Office then saw fresh hope for further German concessions, not least because the war situation was worsening for the Germans. At the same time death and destruction loomed ever larger for the remaining prisoners, especially those confined to concentration camps. This applied particularly to Jewish prisoners.

Swedish Humanitarian Aid to Jews During the Second World War

The policies pursued by the Swedish Foreign Office in the so-called 'Jewish question' have been described in detail by Paul A. Levine in his excellent dissertation *From Indifference to Activism. Swedish Diplomacy and the Holocaust; 1938–44*. Unfortunately Levine's analysis finished with the initial stages of Raoul Wallenberg's 1944 activities in Budapest. Two other reports – Monty Penkower, *The Jews Were Expendable. Free World Diplomacy and the Holocaust*, and Steven Koblik, *The Stones Cry Out. Sweden's Response to the Persecution of the Jews 1933–1945*, covering the last year of the war, that is 1944 to 1945 – were more superficial. It is interesting, and significant to Swedish research scholars, that all three authors were American Jews.[6]

The general picture is clear. In Sweden's struggle for national survival during the Second World War the Jewish question for a long time had a low priority for Swedish decision-makers. Up to 1942, the official Sweden, with few exceptions, was uninterested in the fate of the European Jews. In some cases restrictive Swedish practice created a direct hindrance to Jews being rescued through the refusal of entry into Sweden. From 1942, however, and quite definitely from 1943, Sweden changed the direction of its policies, towards an increasingly more resolute attempt to rescue Jews, *in their very capacity of being Jews*, from the Nazi inferno in German-occupied Europe. The man behind this remarkable volte-face appears to have been Gösta Engzell, head of the Foreign Office legal department. Together with his closest colleague, Svante Hellstedt, Engzell was directly responsible for handling refugee matters. It is reasonable to assume that the change of policy was influenced by the fact that fortunes had now turned in the Allies' favour. The Germans had lost the battles of El Alamein and Stalingrad, in 1942 and 1943 respectively, and as from autumn 1942 the indescribable cruelties inflicted on the Jews by the Germans were well known by all those acquainted with the real state of affairs, not least within the Foreign Office.

Another reason for a more active stand on the part of the Foreign Office in favour of the Jewish cause was undoubtedly the work done by Jewish organisations in Stockholm and their attempts to pressure Swedish authorities. The driving force in these attempts was Gilel Storch (see Chapter 3).

The first stage in the new Jewish policy adopted by Sweden was the demand from 1942 that *all Norwegian Jews* be allowed to cross into Sweden. Close to half of the total number of Jews in Norway had succeeded in illegally making their way over the border into Sweden. Of high priority for the Foreign Office in 1944–5 was the bid to extract the very few Jews still remaining in Norway for a safe passage to Sweden – a steady flow of correspondence concerning this issue went between Oslo and Stockholm.

The next step in Sweden's new policy was the decision that Sweden was prepared to welcome all *Danish Jews* when German deportation of Jews from Denmark started in October 1943. In this way the majority of Danish Jews were able to escape to Sweden. On 2 October the Swedish public radio announced the government's decision. Sweden was now set on a collision course with Germany on the Jewish question. The year 1944 saw the start of the celebrated Swedish action aimed at rescuing *Hungarian Jews* by equipping them, among other things, with protective Swedish passports. These events have been linked chiefly to Raoul Wallenberg, although in reality the action was initiated by the Swedish Red Cross delegate Valdemar Langlet and the Swedish legation in Budapest under minister Danielsson prior to Wallenberg's arrival there. The Swedish action in Hungary was to save the lives of tens of thousands of Jews up until liberation by the Soviet army. The number of Jewish refugees in Sweden in November 1944 was estimated at 13,115, of whom 500 were Norwegian, 5,000 Danish plus 2,000 'half-Jewish' Danes, while 4,500 were German and Austrian Jews.[7]

With the war almost over it was now a question of trying to rescue the Jews from the 'heart of darkness', the German concentration camps. The Allied fronts penetrated ever more deeply into Germany proper and, with Hitler's threat of total extermination hanging over their heads, at the start of 1945 for the Jews it was now a race against time and a matter of life or death. The Foreign Office was bombarded with pleas for Swedish aid for the Jews during the early months of 1945. The American minister in Stockholm on 27 January proposed measures that Sweden could adopt to protect Jews in German concentration camps.[8] From 6 February the Foreign Office at frequent intervals received lists from the American legation in Stockholm naming hundreds of Jews trapped in enemy-occupied territory, people with close relations in the United States who had applied for visa entry there and had it approved. The lists were forwarded to Richert in Berlin – fifteen such lists arrived by 20 April 1945 (which happened to be Hitler's birthday). Jewish organisations in Sweden and Argentina approached the Foreign Office with similar petitions.

The WJC, too, brought pressure to bear on the Foreign Office. Von Post informed Richert on 25 January that Boström, the Swedish minister in Washington, had been asked by the WJC whether the Swedish government could not approach the German government, urging it to abandon its policy of extermination of European Jews. The WJC had also wondered whether the Swedish protective passport system as used in Hungary could not be extended to other Nazi-dominated areas. Richert's response, with quiet resignation, was total rejection. The WJC refused to give up: on 3 February Storch delivered directly to the Foreign Office a desperate appeal from the WJC reporting alarming news about Theresienstadt, now feared to be about to be converted by the Germans into another Oswiecim/Auschwitz. There was a quick reaction from the Foreign Office, which sent a sharply worded telegram to Richert urging him – together with the Swiss minister and the pope's emissary to the German Foreign Office – to express 'Sweden's strong concern for the fate that is befalling the Jews at Theresienstadt, Bergen-Belsen and elsewhere in Germany and *dem deutschen Machtbereich.*' Richert's immediate response was just as negatively formulated as before. The Swiss minister, the pope's emissary and Richert himself were all of the opinion that a protest would be directly damaging and, as Richert put it, 'at best, a shot in the dark'.[9]

In Stockholm, however, there was no stopping. The Foreign Office discovered via Berne that in addition to the 1,500 Jewish internees already transferred to Switzerland, a further 1,200 were on their way from Theresienstadt. Engzell noted on 12 February that Ehrenpreis had sent word that 2,000 Jews could be released from Bergen-Belsen on condition that Sweden was prepared to take them in; that he had obtained the foreign minister's and the social minister's agreement, and that the American attaché Olsen had guaranteed the necessary finance. An urgent telegram in support was sent the same day to Richert, who called on the German Foreign Office:

> At my *démarche* today with Steengracht I delivered the Swedish government's note declaring its willingness to receive Jews interned in Germany, making special mention of Theresienstadt and Bergen-Belsen and expressing particular interest in every individual case

which in recent years has been registered with the Auswärtiges Amt. Besides which I handed over Hellstedt's lists of Jews who have obtained entry into the United States, explaining our readiness to care for them in the meantime. The general offer I presented applied to Jews without restriction. The pope's emissary and the Swiss minister have already left Berlin.[10]

The Swedish government had now officially informed the Germans that Sweden was prepared to take in *all Jews*, without restriction.

7

Folke Bernadotte and the Swedish Relief Expedition

Confucius he say: 'It is better to light one small candle than to curse the darkness.'[1]

Folke Bernadotte Commissioned to Negotiate with Himmler

In November 1944 the Swedish Foreign Office shelved Ditleff's proposal to send a Swedish negotiating team to Germany, led by Bernadotte. In February 1945, however, Ditleff returned to the Foreign Office with a new memo, dated 5 February, in which he set out a series of proposals to prepare for a Swedish rescue operation in Germany – with or without German or Allied consent – and the dispatch of a Swedish Red Cross delegation to Berlin for talks. Once Ditleff had received telegraphic consent from the Norwegian government-in-exile in London, his plan became official. Things then happened swiftly: Ditleff's formal petition on 10 February to the Swedish foreign minister Günther immediately met with a positive response. Günther reported that the Swedish government had agreed to Bernadotte engaging in talks in Berlin in order to 'attempt to obtain the release of Norwegian and Danish internees in Germany and their transportation to Sweden or Denmark, etc.' That same evening, instructions were sent to Richert to explore the possibility – via Schellenberg – of Himmler being willing to receive Bernadotte for discussions on Swedish–German relations.

Why had the Foreign Office reconsidered the matter, and why the hurry? Why had the Foreign Office surrendered its desire to exercise

67

control over Swedish–German relations? Why had they even abandoned Ditleff's former idea to send a delegation to Berlin together with a representative from the Foreign Office? And why was it quite alright now to entrust these important negotiations to a single man, and to an outsider, into the bargain?

We shall probably never have any clear perception of what kind of considerations in Stockholm lay behind the 10 February decision. The rescue operation in Germany seemed never to have been dealt with on a formal level at government meetings between February and May 1945: no records are to be found covering the issue either in the protocol for cabinet meetings at the Foreign Office or at the Ministry of Defence. Nor is there anything mentioned either in prime minister Per Albin Hansson's private files or in Günther's. The Foreign Office, too, was forced to admit in its *White Book 1956*: '. . . there is no information from documents available as to the discussions that must have preceded the government's consent to Bernadotte's journey. . .'[2] This same *White Book*, it should be added, reported that from the Swedish side: 'Serious misgivings existed as to the wisdom of dispatching a large Swedish rescue operation to Germany in the midst of a war still being waged . . . an operation that could not be guaranteed safe from violent incidents and which might quite possibly involve Sweden in conflicts and complicated relations with either or both of the warring parties.'[3]

We can only speculate – as with the *Swedish Foreign Office White Book 1956* – on what deliberations actually took place. Plainly, those messages that arrived in December 1944 concerning Himmler's readiness to comply with further Swedish requests must have been both tempting and challenging. Kersten's own contribution should not be overlooked: according to later testimony it was Kersten who, at Günther's request, introduced Bernadotte to Himmler by telephone.[4]

Time was running out for the Swedes. A total German collapse was clearly not far off. Reports had come in that Hitler had given orders for all traces of the German concentration camps to be wiped out before such a collapse took place. The Swedish consul general in Oslo had warned the Foreign Office as early as November 1944 of German plans, in the event of defeat, to liquidate all the concentration camps and 'annihilate the internees'. The Norwegian legation in Stockholm – and mainly Ditleff – were unremitting in their efforts to call upon the Foreign Office for aid for the Norwegians in Germany. The Foreign Office was also subjected to considerable pressure from Jewish and American quarters to succour the Jewish concentration camp prisoners. This was not an impossible task, either; on 9 February 1945, in fact, it was reported that the Swiss ex-president Musy had managed to rescue 1,200 Jews from Theresienstadt (see Chapter 3).

Another important consideration must have been the increasingly desperate reports emanating from Richert at the Swedish legation in Berlin. The beginning of February saw a major Soviet offensive reach the shores of the Oder, a mere eighty kilometres from Berlin, and the city was being punished by air raid after air raid. Communications were steadily getting worse, and working conditions at the legation were deteriorating. The Swiss minister and the pope's diplomatic representative had already left Berlin. Business at the Swedish embassy had to all intents and purposes been transferred to a rallying point, Alt Döbern, a country residence outside Berlin. The embassy's main task now consisted of assisting Swedish nationals wishing to leave the country, in an endeavour to escape the terrible destruction that threatened Berlin. Richert regarded as fairly hopeless any attempts to high-pressure the Auswärtiges Amt into releasing any further Norwegian and Danish internees. For one thing, this German department had been losing more and more of its influence over developments, and for another foreign minister Ribbentrop was not in much of a mood for concessions to Sweden without something in return from the Swedes. In addition, the legation no longer had any contact with either Schellenberg or Himmler. In a gesture of resignation Richert had sent a telegram on 4 February to the effect that Kersten 'was now the only path along which, in my opinion, we can proceed in order to deal with actual Norwegian cases'. Kersten, though, was now back in Stockholm.

The Swedish government had evidently reached a decision at the start of February 1945 that Sweden would play an active rôle in attempts to rescue prisoners from Nazi concentration camps and prisons. My conclusion is that the Foreign Office by then had given up any hope of the legation in Berlin – with an undeniably exhausted Richert (both physically and mentally) at the helm – ever being able to do anything of benefit for the people interned in the German camps. What was needed was an additional effort, from someone who was thoroughly rested, bold, optimistic and energetic, full of drive and initiative. This is where Bernadotte was an ideal choice; he had long had a favourable network of contacts with the old German upper classes; he spoke perfect German; his long experience of negotiating difficult issues stood him in good stead; his reputation was excellent after his efforts in the exchange of German prisoners of war; he was in charge of the Red Cross which would bear formal responsibility for the operation; he would be in a position to exploit his royal descent, if need be (which usually impressed the Nazi bigwigs, most of whom were simple upstarts); he was, in fact, a fearless man always ready to perform good deeds.

A cynical view of the circumstances would suggest that the Swedish government and its Foreign Office regarded as fairly small any chance of the Germans changing their tune, and that it would therefore be better to heap the blame for any failure on the outsider Bernadotte. Perhaps the silence surrounding what deliberations lay behind the decision points in that direction. The unreserved memoranda written by the deputy head of the political department, Sven Grafström, showed a similar tendency. Grafström never mentioned the fact that in November 1944 Ditleff had proposed him – Grafström – as negotiator, despite almost certainly being aware of the proposal coming from an old friend of his. Grafström linked the February decision to the government's refusal to intervene militarily in Norway and Denmark, in the wake of which some 'bright boy' concocted the idea instead of sending Bernadotte to Himmler to bring home the imprisoned Norwegians and Danes. In the political department Grafström categorically advised against adopting the Bernadotte operation, 'which would certainly not lead to any positive result'. The same opinion was expressed by the chief of the defence staff, Ehrensvärd, who depicted the following scenario:

And now this finely polished convoy of vehicles will wind its way through Germany, with corpulent and well-nourished Swedish 'Red Cross partisans', unarmed to the teeth. They come up against one or two companies of famished and poorly clad Germans in a desperate mood, retreating from the east or from the west. The Germans' leading officer requests information as to where such a pretty caravan is headed, and in reply learns that it consists of Swedes on their way to gather together Norwegians and Danes, and on board they happen to have food and clothes for these poor blighters. It may so happen that discipline holds, the German stands to attention and then moves off with his troop. But it may so also happen, quite differently, that he fails to see what is so great with this humanitarian errand in which the Swedes find ourselves, yet both he and his fellows fully recognize the value of the vehicles and the advantages attached to possessing their contents. This is the sort of situation which can lead to trouble . . .[5]

What, then, does Bernadotte himself have to say about the preliminaries to 1945's rescue operation?

For a long time the most important source for Bernadotte's actions was his book *Last Days of the Reich. The Diary of Count Folke Bernadotte*, in English translation and republished in London in 2009. The Swedish version was published as early as 16 June 1945, approximately six weeks after the end of the war. This remarkable achievement on the part of the author is explained by the fact that the book – as Bernadotte made clear in his Preface – was based on his notes and reports completed during his travels between the middle of February and the end of April. The book was completed, with Bernadotte dictating, by his ghostwriter Ragnar Svanström at the Norstedt publishing house. Svanström advised Bernadotte to restrict the story solely to Bernadotte's own experiences, which is why, for instance, Kersten was not even mentioned. Bernadotte's wife later confirmed that the publisher was very eager for the book to come out as soon as possible, and that Bernadotte was sure that all the other personalities involved would be publishing their own books in time, too. A number of what were obviously defects in *Last Days* . . .(as I shall be referring to it) can be explained away by the haste in which it was prepared – by the fact that it was a kind of personal log, with no pretence to being a scientific and objective account of historical events. This is not to exculpate entirely

Bernadotte's failure to mention Kersten's and Storch's significant rôles; or his belittling of Ditleff's and the Danes' significant contributions; or the almost total absence of any mention of the Jews and their extermination. Bernadotte certainly possessed fundamental knowledge of all of these elements during the 1945 rescue operation. Bernadotte's self-absorbed and distorted account led to a state of full hostility between him and Kersten as well as bitter relations between him and both Ditleff and Günther. A further consequence was that after 1948 an anti-Bernadotte campaign blossomed from the Jewish side as well as from the pen of the British historian Trevor-Roper and that of the Danish physician Holm. Storch, on the other hand, a man who had fought his battles with Masur and other Jews in Stockholm, defended Bernadotte until his dying day.

In *Last Days . . .* Bernadotte claimed that the seeds of the Red Cross operation in Germany were sown during a conversation he had on 3 November 1944 in Paris with the Swedish consul general Raoul Nordling, who had made major contributions as a mediator between the two warring parties after the liberation of Paris, saving thousands of French men and women from deportation to German concentration camps. Couldn't Bernadotte possibly 'do something' for those languishing in the German concentration camps?[6] Back in Stockholm Bernadotte came into contact with one person who was to play a decisive rôle: the Norwegian diplomat Ditleff. He it was who suggested the idea of trying to gain permission to have the Norwegian civilian prisoners transferred to Sweden. Attracted by the notion, Bernadotte joined Ditleff in their mutual conclusion that the only possibility lay in seeking contact with Himmler. The next step for Bernadotte was to consult with both the chairman of the Red Cross and members of its board, as well as with the Swedish government. Following this, Bernadotte presented the government with a proposal that he and Ditleff together had worked out. In the course of discussions at the end of January and the beginning of February 1945: 'We agreed that it was much more difficult for the head of a legation (i.e. Richert) than for a private individual (i.e. Bernadotte himself) to get into contact with those authorities in charge of the concentration camps'.[7]

Bernadotte's account in *Last Days . . .* does not tally well with what primary sources have to tell us. The notes he made indicated that in November 1944 Nordling's original ideas concerning Swedish aid were confined to sending foodstuffs and clothing to one camp – Ravensbrück – 'where about 20,000 (French) women are interned'. The fact that Bernadotte made no mention of Nordling's reference to Ravensbrück in *Last Days* . . . is puzzling since the biggest rescue operation undertaken by the White Buses would in fact involve Ravensbrück.

Just as mystifying is the fact that Bernadotte's meetings in London on 8 November 1944 with 'a representative of the Jewish rabbi and a representative of the Jewish organisation Aguda Israel' was passed over in silence in his book. The representative Bernadotte met in London was in fact L. Zelmanovits, general secretary of the British section of the WJC. Zelmanovits noted the problems discussed at the meeting in a letter posted the following day:

1 Could the Swedish Red Cross help out by sending food parcels to Jewish camps in Germany?
2 Could the Swedish Red Cross send a mission to camps for Jewish children in Slovakia?
3 Could the Swedish system of so-called protective passports, which had proved to be of 'enormous value' in Hungary, be extended to Jewish internees in Germany, particularly at Theresienstadt?

In January 1945 Zelmanovits complained that he had not received any reply. Bernadotte then sent a brief note, in a letter dated 9 February, saying that immediately on arrival home in November he had contacted Rabbi Ehrenpreis regarding possible solutions to the problems, after which he had had a further series of meetings with Ehrenpreis. Ehrenpreis was of course a member of the WJC executive committee in Stockholm, and entries in Bernadotte's diary reveal the fact that he had indeed met Ehrenpreis on 28 November 1944.[8]

What Bernadotte did, then, was to leave Ehrenpreis with the responsibility for keeping the silence. What Ehrenpreis did as far as the WJC's wishes were concerned is unknown to me. Nor have I found any traces in either Ehrenpreis's or the Jewish Community's archives in Stockholm. Storch reported, however, in another context, that Ehrenpreis had been sceptical and repudiated Storch in Bernadotte's presence on the subject of talks that could lead to the release of Jews from Bergen-Belsen. There was a general spirit among Jews in Stockholm of resistance to the work done by the WJC, which they considered to be too heavily politicised. Storch, on the other hand, was also a good friend of Bernadotte. Bernadotte's diary for this period showed three meetings with Storch: 25 November 1944, 4 March 1945 and 11 April 1945. According to Storch, Bernadotte had already given him and the WJC permission to use the Swedish Red Cross as a cover to send food parcels to Jews at Nazi concentration camps. The Red Cross placed an entire truckful of Red Cross material such as writing paper, forms and labels at the WJC's disposal. 'Bernadotte was very favourably disposed to the Jewish issue', Storch has assured me in my conversation with him.[9]

Nor does Bernadotte have anything to say, strangely enough, about the earlier, far-reaching plans from both Norwegian and Danish quarters for aid to the camp prisoners. In his capacity as vice-chairman of the Swedish Red Cross Bernadotte clearly kept in contact with the sister organisations in Norway and Denmark. These contacts were, however, maintained at a very low level as it was suspected in Sweden in both cases that each of the chairmen in those countries was something of a yes-man towards the Germans. In the case of the Danes, all planning had to be carried out in the utmost secrecy. Bernadotte was, however, deeply involved in relief work for Norway. He had, of course, already in February 1944 discussed this matter with top representatives of the government-in-exile in London, and had later corresponded with them at length, as well as with Ditleff. A Norwegian *White Book* reveals the fact that Bernadotte repeatedly promised Ditleff that the Swedish Red Cross would lend its assistance in every shape and form should the Norwegian government request help in repatriating Norwegian prisoners. This, however, only concerned aid to Norwegians in Norway, or following the end of the war. Nevertheless, there remains not a single trace in either Bernadotte's own archives or those of the Swedish Red Cross or the Foreign Office of Bernadotte's supposedly close cooperation with Ditleff between November 1944 and February 1945. All the documentation that exists concerning would-be rescue operations in Germany is unmistakably Norwegian, and in the majority of cases has a 'Ditleff-ish' slant. The Foreign Office documentation showed unequivocally that it was Ditleff and not Bernadotte who was responsible for the decisive proposal. Bernadotte's own diary showed quite clearly that he met Ditleff just once – 23 October 1944 – in the course of these months. Obviously there may have been other occasions, but he did not bother to note them. The conclusion drawn by the Swedish Foreign Office in its *White Book 1956* is overwhelming: 'no further information has been found' concerning Bernadotte's participation in and significance for discussions prior to his journey to Germany – the prime mover behind these discussions was 'in all certainty Ditleff' and 'Bernadotte's presentation of events in his book *Last Days* . . . undoubtedly does little justice to Ditleff's efforts to get the rescue operation off the ground.'[10]

Folke Bernadotte and His Talks in Germany: Round One

Foreign minister Günther paved the way for Bernadotte's mission by sending a couple of unusual messages to Richert, his minister in Berlin. On 10 February he instructed the head of the political department, Erik von Post, to send this telegram:

> Purpose is to send Folke Bernadotte to Berlin to inspect Red Cross operations but in reality mainly try bring about in Germany Norwegian and Danish internees' transport to Sweden or Denmark (etc.) *(handwritten and added – author's comment)*. For this purpose contact probably required with Auswärtiges Amt but mainly with Himmler. Ascertain through Schellenberg whether Himmler willing receive Bernadotte discuss issues concerning relations Sweden–Germany.
>
> Departure should be soonest possible. Telegraph whether you consider necessary resort to Kersten, whose services we prefer not to use *(all of the last sentence was deleted in pencil – author's comment)*.
>
> For information. Swiss Musy's successful negotiation Jewish question appears give us certain prospects our requests being heeded.[11]

On this telegram the foreign minister had scrawled in ink 'By order of His Excellency', which seemed particularly sharp wording. Richert was given a further hint that a Swiss had successfully negotiated the Jewish issue –

so why not Sweden? Finally, the Foreign Office had first of all wanted to make it clear it preferred not to have to resort to Kersten (as opposed to Richert's attitude on 4 February), but then changed its mind. Or was von Post repudiated by Günther or Boheman? Whatever the case, instead of closing the door on Kersten, with Bernadotte now prepared, so to speak, to step through it, they have left it open. Kersten may remain as an alternative or as a complement to Bernadotte, a move that turned out to be a wise one.

Three days later Günther wrote a personal letter to Richert explaining how aware he was of Richert's and the legation's distressing situation. He asked Richert, however, to retain the legation in Berlin:

> Don't forget the terribly important task we have in front of us is coming to the aid of Norwegian and Danish prisoners in Germany, as far as and for as long as possible. It would be extremely helpful if we could make a worthwhile contribution in this respect, and for such a purpose alone it seems to me there is every reason to hold on to the legation.[12]

The legation had also been reinforced in the shape of a Red Cross unit, led by Captain Hultgren, together with six other people, two buses and a passenger car. These were to transport back home those Swedish-born women who had married in Germany and who wished to return to Sweden. It was to inspect this small Red Cross unit that Red Cross vice-chairman Bernadotte was now – officially – to travel down to Berlin.

Richert was admittedly anxious to remain as long as possible in Berlin, but when it came to Bernadotte's mission he proved to be as defeatist as before:

> Firstly . . . It is doubtful whether a meeting can be arranged in all haste with Himmler, who has command of the front and is very likely at headquarters.
>
> Secondly . . . I see no reason to assume that the Germans would agree to such far-reaching measures, nor that with the present situation, completely changed as it is, any reference to more or less favourable impressions in Sweden has any importance provided there is no threat of war. Considering, moreover, the current catastrophic

situation regarding transport facilities the action proposed would seem to be quite difficult to carry out . . .

. . .

Fourthly . . . The successful Jewish operation carried out by Switzerland should be seen against a background in which this country does not have Norwegians and Danes to work for, as Sweden does, and in other respects has initially been in a better position than we have with regard to political and trade policy.[13]

Fortunately, Richert was being assisted by two able young colleagues, legation counsellor Lennart Nylander and secretary Torsten Brandel, both of whom in future would be Bernadotte's closest assistants at the Berlin legation. On 14 February Brandel was able to phone through a message to the effect that Kaltenbrunner would endeavour to arrange for Bernadotte actually to meet Himmler. A couple of days later Count Bernadotte was on his way to Berlin:

. . . There they stood, these Berliners, queuing up for food, or else they were working away on their barricades, waiting for the enemy to enter their city. All around them lay destruction and desolation. Wandering through the streets in the central part of the city, you got the impression that of every five buildings four lay in ruins following the Allies' mighty bombing raids. In spite of everything people continued living in the cellars – many had of course already been evacuated – and life went on, if not in its usual way quite, in any case as normally as the situation permitted. The Underground system was working with a number of power cuts after each air raid, and the same applied to gas, electricity and the telephone services. What went through the minds of these people in situations such as these, what lay behind their rather apathetic facial expressions? Not so easy to pinpoint. What was evident was that their trust in Nazism had suffered a severe blow. Just as evident (notwithstanding Dr Goebbel's each and every propaganda speech) was the fact that they clearly saw that Germany was heading straight for defeat. What was odd but also quite characteristic was that, among some of them at least, they couldn't understand – or wouldn't understand

– that Hitler was mainly responsible for all the misery. With all that sentimentality, surely so distinguishing a mark for the German people, large sections of the population hung on to their faith in the Führer during these last months of the Reich.[14]

No written instructions had emanated from the Foreign Office for Bernadotte to take with him to Berlin. He did, however, have a memorandum signed by his immediate supervisor, Prince Carl:

> The chairman of the Swedish Red Cross has therefore deemed it convenient on behalf of the Scandinavian neighbouring people to propose to the German authorities, who possess the right of determination over the civilian internees in Germany, that they accept that those Norwegians and Danes who form part of these civilian prisoners be transferred to Sweden and there be taken in charge and interned until such time as the final outcome of the war decide the question of their further treatment.[15]

During the following five hectic days, 17–21 February, Bernadotte had meetings with the head of the German security service, Ernst Kaltenbrunner, foreign minister Joachim von Ribbentrop, head of intelligence, Walter Schellenberg, and lastly with Hitler's closest colleague, Reichsführer-SS Heinrich Himmler. With the exception of Hitler, Bernadotte was able to meet pretty well all of the leading men in Nazi Germany. Hitler, however, had to be kept unaware of the far-reaching Swedish plans as he would otherwise undoubtedly have put a stop to them. The news of Musy's successful liberation of 1,200 Jews had leaked to the foreign press and come to Hitler's knowledge. His fit of rage was directed against Himmler, and he had straightaway given orders to forbid any further transport of Jews which did not involve compensation for Germany. An unequivocal prerequisite for the success of the Bernadotte mission was therefore absolute silence in the Swedish mass media.

Kaltenbrunner and Ribbentrop were essential go-betweens for reaching the target – Himmler. Bernadotte left detailed descriptions of his talks. These indicate that he actually implied to Kaltenbrunner the possibility of Sweden entering the war. 'I called attention to the fact that relations between Sweden and Germany were particularly bad, that the mood of the people – especially due to events in Norway and Denmark – is very bitter towards Germany, and that *this popular mood can end up in Sweden no longer being able to remain neutral.*[16] Schellenberg then declared that it would be very harmful for Germany if Sweden abandoned its neutrality. Kaltenbrunner and Bernadotte agreed on one point: Germany losing the war would involve a great risk of Europe being Bolshevised. As far as Ribbentrop was concerned, Bernadotte had learnt beforehand that relations between him and Himmler 'were not of the heartiest nature'. Ribbentrop started by thanking Bernadotte for helping with the exchange of prisoners of war. Then followed a monologue from Ribbentrop which lasted exactly one hour, seven minutes and seven point three seconds. Bernadotte, who had been warned by Richert and was a habitual athletics team leader, measured the time on his stopwatch. Ribbentrop, too, gave warning of the eventual Bolshevisation of Europe. Ribbentrop, though – and we will remember that he was the brain behind the German–Soviet Pact of 1939 – came to another conclusion: Germany would rather see the Russians swamp Europe than the western Allies, and should Germany prove incapable of holding the Oder line it would be preferable to 'throw itself into the hands of the Russians by moving divisions from the eastern to the western front'. He gave assurances, however, of Hitler's friendly feelings for Sweden, adding that 'there was no other person that Hitler looked up to as much as to Sweden's king.'[17]

On 19 February Bernadotte was granted his first meeting with Himmler. The impression he left on Bernadotte was one of:

> . . . a rather insignificant civil servant – if you'd passed him in the street, you wouldn't have noticed him. He had tiny, delicate, sensitive hands – I observed how well manicured they were, despite the fact that manicuring was forbidden within the SS. He proved to be remarkably and surprisingly engaging, showing every sign of humour, with a slight tendency towards a grim humour, and was quick to crack a joke to create a pleasant mood. Least of all was there anything diabolical about his appearance. I found nothing of the cold hardness in his look that has been so much talked about.[18]

Bernadotte presented Himmler with a seventeenth-century work relating to Swedish runic inscriptions. It was a good start to a more than two-hour meeting – Bermadotte had no doubt been tipped off by the Norwegian professor Seip. Soon, however, Himmler launched out on a severe attack on the Swedish press, which he accused of being unilaterally hostile to Germany. Bernadotte countered by referring to the German destruction of the north of Norway and the Germans' executions and taking of hostages. Gradually Bernadotte broached the real purpose of his trip to Berlin: he asked whether it would be possible for Norwegian and Danish prisoners in Germany to be shipped over to Sweden for internment. Himmler's response was totally negative. 'Are you implying that these people should be trained in Sweden for police duty? The others have been given a similar training. Do you really consider that a neutral country should take such steps?' Bernadotte was forced to rely on his second-best proposition: couldn't at least all the Norwegian and Danish prisoners be placed together in a camp of their own in Germany so that the Swedish Red Cross could thus more easily serve their needs materially and spiritually? Himmler adopted a positive attitude to this proposal and had no objections to Swedish Red Cross staff being allowed in the camps to help take care of the prisoners. Bernadotte's estimate of the number of Norwegian and Danish prisoners in Germany came to some 13,000 whereas in Himmler's opinion there were only 2,000 or 3,000 people. Himmler also thought it would be feasible for the elderly, the sick and mothers to be able to return to Norway and Denmark after they had been gathered together in the camps.

Bernadotte now brought up the question of exit visas for Swedish women in Germany married to Germans while at the same time being German citizens. When Himmler got to see the lists compiled by the Swedish legation, his face darkened. There were a number of children on the lists. The fathers of these children, he suggested, would undoubtedly 'rather see their children grow up in a German log cabin than have to seek refuge in a palace situated in a country hostile to Germany'. The lists were, however, handed over to Schellenberg, who later informed Bernadotte that the matter would probably be resolved satisfactorily. Finally, Himmler too made reference to the dangers threatening Europe with the advance of

Bolshevism. He pointed to the Allies' bombing and shelling of the civilian population of Dresden where at least 40,000 civilians were killed in the course of some thirty-six hours. What propaganda this sort of thing would be for Bolshevism, that 'only the western Allies and not the Russians carry out bombing raids on cities which are without real war industries, terrorising the civilian population!' Parenthetically Bernadotte confirmed these reports about Dresden.[19]

At a fresh meeting on 21 February Ribbentrop pointed out that the transport of prisoners could not be undertaken by the Germans. In consenting, Bernadotte replied that the Swedish Red Cross would stand responsible for a transport operation providing its own fuel. Bernadotte had lunch the same day with Schellenberg, who confirmed that Himmler had definitely given his approval to the proposals discussed. The Scandinavian prisoners would be gathered together at one and the same camp, Neuengamme, near Hamburg. As to the number of Norwegians and Danes imprisoned, Schellenberg's and Bernadotte's figures did not tally. Bernadotte was unable to verify whether the figures covered all the prisoners of war, including the Norwegian officers and those confined in hard labour camps. Schellenberg also undertook to facilitate a number of practical details, such as supplying visas for passports and the like, in anticipation of the arrival of the Red Cross convoy. Schellenberg in general made a good impression on Bernadotte, who right from the start gained 'a measure of confidence' in this man.[20] In turn, Bernadotte promised Schellenberg he would try to have the convoy in Warnemünde in ten days' time at the latest, by 3 March.

Bernadotte's report to the Foreign Office ended as follows: 'It would appear most convenient first of all to evacuate those camps which at present lie in the danger zone. Undoubtedly <u>greatest possible</u> speed is essential' (*underlined in the original – author's note*). These were indeed words of wisdom which it would not be so very easy to carry into practice!

During his stay in Berlin, apart from the staff of the Swedish legation, Bernadotte met the Danish minister and legation counsellor, and among the Norwegians professor Seip (on two occasions, 19 and 20 February), the chaplain Vogt-Svendsen, Miss Wanda Hjort and Dr Heger. Bernadotte had been given a survey of the prevailing scene by Richert, and had had talks concerning tactics and arguments to be used in the coming negotiations with the Germans. The same concerned Bernadotte's later rounds of talks in Germany. Bernadotte and Richert had long been the best of friends, and it was Richert who presented Bernadotte with what was to become his second proposal to Himmler: bringing Norwegian and Danish prisoners to a special camp. The suggestion had come, in point of fact, from a 'young Norwegian' – a medical student, Bjørn Heger. On the whole, Bernadotte was fairly ungenerous in his reporting of the contributions made by the Norwegians. Seip had by now moved his card index listing the Norwegian prisoners over to the Swedish legation, and this proved to be of invaluable help for the coming rescue work. We also know that Bernadotte met Professor Seip on at least two occasions, and that Seip provided him with much valuable background information. According to Seip's own account, at these meetings Bernadotte received all the information possessed by the Gross Kreutz trio, as well as a memo relating to Ditleff's 'memorandum' of 30 November 1944.

In a letter to Günther, minister Richert praised Bernadotte's achievements which he regarded as particularly satisfactory. This outcome could hardly have been achieved without the direct contact established between Bernadotte and Himmler – the Swedish legation had years of sad experience of the sabotage technique employed by the Auswärtiges Amt. Bernadotte was praised for his considerable negotiating skills, and was judged to have achieved a large measure of goodwill, which in time to come would definitely be of good use to Norwegian and Danish prisoners alike. His results must of course be seen in the light of the ongoing war situation, and – Richert assumed – in view of the fact that Himmler also perhaps 'had been influenced by a desire to create goodwill in Sweden as well as opportunities to mediate in the event of establishing peace-making contacts'.

Evidently another contributory factor was what Richert called 'the sudden change in the balance of power between Sweden and Germany'. One man who realised this was Schellenberg. Bernadotte's *Last Days* . . . included an account by Schellenberg, which described how Hitler completely repudiated a meeting between Himmler and Bernadotte. 'A clown like him won't get us anywhere in this war' was Hitler's comment.[21] Schellenberg did, however, manage to persuade Himmler to see Bernadotte behind Hitler's back: Bernadotte's visit represented the last opportunity to manoeuvre Germany out of the war.

Back in Sweden Bernadotte now balanced King Gustaf V on the Swedish scales, too. In a letter to Schellenberg dated 26 February he reported from a visit to his uncle, His Majesty the king of Sweden, that the latter had expressed his gratitude to Himmler and Kaltenbrunner, with the wish that 'our' action might lead to happy results. The same royal gratitude was forwarded to Ribbentrop via the German legation in Stockholm.

Organising the Swedish Red Cross Expedition – with the Exclusion of the Danes

Back in Stockholm on 22 February, Bernadotte had a busy time before setting off once more for Berlin on 6 March. His diary showed that during this bare fortnight he was able to meet, apart from the royal couple, ministers from the Soviet Union (Mme Kollontay twice), Germany (Thomsen) and the United States (Johnson). The first name of all on his list, however, was that of Ditleff on 23 February. On the last day but one, 4 March, he again met both Ditleff and Storch.

Storch continued his feverish campaign to rescue his kinsfolk. He had thanked Engzell, the head of Foreign Office political affairs, for the government having granted an entry permit to the Jews from Bergen-Belsen, had forwarded a desperate appeal from the Jewish Agency which told of how the retreating Germans were probably murdering the Jews, and had asked the Foreign Office to contact Bernadotte in Berlin to intervene with Dr Kleist to help the Jews in the concentration camps. Bernadotte's report showed no sign of this having taken place, however. On the other hand Nylander, the legation counsellor, on 23 February reported that he had visited Dr Kleist and discussed the issue of the Jews at Bergen-Belsen and Theresienstadt. He had also supplied a list, which Engzell had given Bernadotte, of Jews who the legation had intervened on behalf of in recent years. This was probably the so-called 'short list' of fifteen names, five of whom were Swedish, eight Norwegian and two Danish citizens. Nylander then asked Kleist to clarify 'the technical details pertaining to the exit passage of those concerned'. Writing to Storch on 26 February, Bernadotte explained that he saw a slight change for the better in the Swiss – Musy's, that is – transfer of Jews from German concentration camps to Switzerland. As for the Swedish permit allowing a number of Jews to come to Sweden, this matter 'looked very hopeful', was Bernadotte's message from Berlin. A day or two earlier Storch had thanked Bernadotte for 'the valuable assistance you have offered us in these times of utter desperation'.

According to *Last Days . . .*, Bernadotte on arrival home had his plans sanctioned after an audience with the government and commander-in-chief Jung, whereupon the Swedish military authorities set about the task of equipping the expedition. This is probably correct even though I have not been able to discover any sources confirming this. In light of Bernadotte's pledge to Schellenberg to have the convoy in place in Germany by 3 March, nine days after Bernadotte's arrival back home in Stockholm and including an approximately three-day journey for the expedition between Sweden and Germany, this planning would appear to be quite unrealistic. The practical preparations must have started, as Ditleff pointed out, in all probability straight after the 10 February decision. That this was the case was borne out by a letter sent by Ditleff to the Swedish Red Cross on 15 February thanking them for mediating the day before in the loan of military vehicles. The Norwegian Evacuation Office had been unsuccessful in its bid to acquire civilian buses. Instead the Norwegians were to hand over to Bernadotte their card index material containing the names of 7,500 Norwegians interned in German camps.

Ditleff was in a state of frantic activity. On 26 February he sent Bernadotte a sixteen-page memo on the subject of the coming rescue operation together with an enclosure written by the Norwegian chaplain in Hamburg, Vogt-Svendsen, listing the Norwegians believed to be imprisoned in German camps and jails and based on the latest information. This was followed by another letter from Ditleff, dated 2 March, with a new memo. In addition, the Swedish Red Cross records contained a comprehensive ten-page Norwegian memo compiled by Hjort and Vogt-Svendsen which dealt with how the Scandinavian prisoners were to be gathered together at the Neuengamme camp. The authors of this memo were joined in its composition by the Danish legation chaplain Jeppesen and the Swedish attaché Giron. According to Seip, Bernadotte now received a note about the Jyllandskorps, the body of volunteers organised to fetch home Danish and

Norwegian prisoners. No such equivalent planning was documented on the Swedish side, either among the Foreign Office and Red Cross records or Bernadotte's private archives. The chief impression that emerges is that the Swedes took over, in portions that were suitable for the moment, Norwegian and Danish planning operations already in existence.

The Swedish Red Cross approached the Swedish army, which very quickly provided a transport convoy that was placed at the Red Cross's disposal. In the words of the *Swedish Foreign Office White Book 1956*, this was in reality 'an action undertaken by the Swedish state – the personnel to a very high degree consisted of volunteers from the armed forces, equipment was transferred from defence supplies, and the costs were defrayed by the national exchequer'. A formal decision regarding the Red Cross detachment was made by order-in-council, Royal Defence department, on 2 March 1945. Wages paid to the conscripts were said to be the same as those payable for normal military service in Sweden. Most of those serving in the detachment were ordinary soldiers who received two-and-a-half Swedish kronor a day, the equivalent in those days of a normal restaurant meal.

From the start the Swedish Red Cross detachment was planned to comprise 340 men and women and fifteen Red Cross delegates, as well as 75–100 vehicles of various types. The Germans insisted on the force being reduced to a maximum of 250 people. The Swedish press were informed by Bernadotte on 5 May that the final figures had been 250 people and seventy-five vehicles. The specification offered by what came to be known as the 'Bernadotte Society Germany detachment 1945' put the figures at 308 people in all and close to a hundred vehicles (thirty-six buses for the conveyance of sick people, nineteen trucks, seven passenger cars, seven motor cycles, a breakdown truck as well as a number of supply vans with meals-on-wheels). Every supply item, such as food, fuel (a petrol-alcohol mix) and repair equipment had to proceed from the Swedish side. None of this was available in Germany. A vessel called the *Lillie Matthiessen* was also chartered to ship 350,000 litres of fuel to the port of Lübeck, plus other stores and 6,000 gift parcels for prisoners at the German camps.

The romantic but tragic background to the story of the *Lillie Matthiessen* was not revealed until 2008 in a Swedish magazine. It appears that Bernadotte in 1921 had become the illegitimate father of a baby girl, born to a revue artist called Lillie Ericsson. The two of them were deeply in love and engaged, but Bernadotte's strict and extremely conventional parents refused to allow their son to marry Lillie. She later married shipowner Carl Matthiessen. When Bernadotte in 1945 came to charter the *Lillie Matthiessen* it was something of a silent gesture and, why not, a plea to the love of his youth for forgiveness.

Among the personnel there were a score of people – doctors, nurses, auxiliaries, almoners – drawn from the Swedish Red Cross organisation. Professor Gerhard Rundberg was in charge of these people, while the team of nurses included Bernadotte's sister, Maria Bernadotte. The remainder were military people. The commander of the army, General Lieutenant Archibald Douglas, gave orders for three army service corps – Svea in Linköping, Norrland in Sollefteå and Skånska in Hässleholm – to organise the major part of the troop. Colonel Gottfrid Björck was appointed head of the detachment in his capacity of inspector-general of army service corps units. Officers were hand-picked from a large number of volunteers at the three service corps. According to Åke Svenson, orders to this effect were sent out on 25 February. Recruiting other ranks proved to be a tougher task. First-year recruits could not be considered, and questionnaires were sent out from respective mobilisation units to possible applicants. All this was done amidst a total mass media black-out. Special requests were dispatched from the National Board of Information on 22 and 28 February to editorial desks to refrain from mentioning anything about the Swedish Red Cross expedition. Recruitment therefore went more slowly than expected, and led to the first delay experienced by the expedition. All the equipment was selected from stock, brand-new. All military badges of rank and emblems were exchanged for Red Cross badges on caps and tunics. One advantage the delay brought was that more time was available to trim the vehicles for the job. The engines were all driven by a petrol–alcohol mixture the better to resist the strains and hardships expected, and like many other vehicles had often been standing idle in a garage unused for some period of time.

The core of the detachment was divided into three platoons, each consisting of twelve buses, a truck platoon of twelve vehicles, and a quartermaster platoon. Added to these was the very important supply van. Transport capacity was about 1,000 people at a time, which could be stretched for shorter distances, and making use of the trucks, to 1,200 persons. On 7 and 8 March the detachment gathered at Hässleholm, and the serious nature of the expedition was made clear to the crew: there was a risk of heavy casualties, perhaps as many as fifty per cent.

The Swedish action was received with immense gratitude by the Norwegian government-in-exile and by the Danish legation in Stockholm. All the same, as we have already seen, plans had existed in Denmark for a Danish expedition to Germany for a long time, and Danish prisoners had in fact already been brought home from the German camps. On 13 February the Danish minister in Stockholm had reported to Prince Carl the huge Danish interest in the planned Red Cross operation and offered Danish assistance. While in Berlin in February Bernadotte conferred with the Danish minister there, Otto Carl Mohr. No records from this meeting are available, however, from the Swedish side. Mohr's own records, though, showed that Bernadotte originally imagined a common effort on the part of the Swedish and Danish Red Cross organisations, with each responsible for half of the personnel and material necessary to accomplish the task. Bernadotte's proposal was phoned through to the Danish Red Cross on 22 February. The following day the Danish foreign ministry offered the Swedish legation in Copenhagen no less than forty Danish buses, fourteen of which were equipped with a trailer and had room for 1,400 people, as well as thirty trucks, eighteen ambulances, a dozen passenger cars, not to mention personnel, doctors, nurses, fuel, foodstuffs and medication. The only condition attached was that the action involved evacuating Danes to Denmark, Sweden or any other safe place. The following day, however, Bernadotte gratefully acknowledged the offer but rejected it 'since the expedition should be entirely Swedish for organisational and other reasons'. Later Bernadotte explained his rejection of the offer by referring to the necessity of 'reducing the total force'. This motivation has also been accepted by Mohr: 'since this (common effort – *author's note*) would have come up against difficulties from the German side, it was decided that transport should be carried out by the Swedish Red Cross alone'.

The rescue expedition to Germany, then, became a fully Swedish operation in its initial stages. Criticism later on was levelled at this decision
and more specifically at Bernadotte. It was suggested, not least from the
Danish side, that the Swedes were anxious to keep the credit for the action
for themselves for reasons of prestige, and Bernadotte personally for himself. As far as Sweden was concerned it would also be a means of improving its somewhat tarnished image in the eyes of the other Scandinavian
countries. There appears to be no support for these accusations in my
source material. On the contrary, Bernadotte quite plainly wanted a joint
Swedish–Danish effort from the start. It was the German demands that
put a spoke in the wheel and compelled the expedition to limit its strength.
This was also accepted by the Danes. In some Swedish quarters, however
– people within the Foreign Office, that is – irritation was felt over the
Danish enthusiasm. Richert, for instance, complained from Berlin on 28
February that the Danes were intending to send up to 115 vehicles for the
rescue operation: 'As German authorities doubtful let in our personnel
hardly room Danes apart from reserve stationed in Denmark.'

What really lay behind Bernadotte's 'other reasons' for the expedition
to remain wholly Swedish? It is worth noting that the rejection attributed
to Bernadotte was communicated to the Danes by von Post at the Foreign
Office, undoubtedly after discussions with Günther. As the *Swedish Foreign
Office White Book 1956* put it: Bernadotte admittedly had a free hand in the
conduct of his negotiations, but he always had to proceed in line with the
foreign minister's guiding principles. Interestingly enough, this *White Book*
made no mention of the fact that Bernadotte had intended the expedition
to be a joint Swedish–Danish operation. In a 'strictly confidential' letter of
1 March, moreover, von Post announced that it was the government that
had decided to reject the Danish offer. It may be assumed that this decision was linked in some way with the notion coming from some 'bright
boy' – in Grafström's words – that Bernadotte's operation would serve as
compensation for the Swedish government's reluctance to intervene militarily in Norway and Denmark – in which case the operation would have
to be entirely Swedish.

8

The White Buses: Neuengamme

Let us be as patient as we can, just as long as we know that Swedish influence and Swedish supervision are prevailing and being extended as much as possible in a situation of crucial importance for thousands of Danish and Norwegian prisoners. Similar experiences in other countries and in other war-like conditions indicate that very much can be done with a resolute and bold mind and personal authority.[1]

I don't mind who you tell, articles such as DN's leading article in Monday's edition may very well make a mess of everything.[2]

The White Buses

The Swedish Red Cross detachment left Hässleholm in the far south of Sweden on 8 and 10 March and travelled via the Malmö ferry to Copenhagen. The route to Germany had earlier in March been reconnoitred by Captain Sigurd Melin. A problem cropped up at the very last minute. The vehicles had been camouflaged in accordance with Swedish army practice, with Swedish flags and Red Cross designs painted on roof and sides. The evening before departure, however, it was announced from the Swedish Foreign Office that the British had insisted that all vehicles were to be painted white in order to be identified by Allied aircraft. All hands were put to the task of painting the buses white, and the last of the vehicles was painted on the ferry by a specially recruited crew of painters from Malmö.

The White Buses, as the entire expedition gradually came to be known as, had been created in a flash.[3]

The journey that the Swedish contingent took through Denmark was a triumphal one. To be on the safe side, von Post had informed a representative of the Danish resistance movement in Stockholm – the legendary journalist Ebbe Munch – of the Swedish plans. He in turn had passed on the information to the Danish underground movement so as to hinder any acts of sabotage that might be plotted and directed at the Swedish convoy. Odense was the centre of resistance to the occupying forces. There the Swedish contingent was given accommodation in a school which a large mass of people guarded, as they did the hotel where Colonel Björck spent twenty-four hours. It turned out that a report had come in to the effect that the Danish Quisling police, the HIPO, had drafted plans to assassinate Björck in an effort to stop the Swedish expedition. Almost the entire population of Odense was on the alert to protect the Swedes.

Colonel Björck was already in Copenhagen on 8 March. He had conferred there with representatives of the Danish ministries for foreign affairs, social affairs and traffic as well as with the Danish Red Cross. The meetings were devoted to a mutual presentation and planning of the passage through Denmark. Björck also obtained thorough-going information from the Danish side: lists of the Danish and Norwegian internees and where they probably could be located, in addition to reports from previous Danish Red Cross expeditions. He also managed to get hold of road maps for Germany, a lucky strike as it turned out that none would be available at all in Germany. Bernadotte had earlier reminded Schellenberg of his promise to produce German maps, but evidently in vain.

On 12 March the White Buses reached what would be their headquarters, Friedrichsruh, twenty-two kilometres east of Hamburg city centre, not too far, that is, from the border with Denmark. The detachment was welcomed by Bernadotte. The Friedrichsruh castle belonged to the Bismarck family, and it was here in 1890 that the old Iron Chancellor, Otto von Bismarck, had retired and written his *Gedanken und Erinnerungen*. In 1945 Friedrichsruh was the property of the grandson, Prince Otto von Bismarck. He was married to Swedish-born Ann Mari Tengbom, who also had happened to be a schoolmate of Bernadotte's. Colonel Björck and the oldest officers were accommodated at the castle and the staff at a local inn, while the troops and troop officers were ordered to pitch camp in the surrounding forest. Only twenty kilometres away was situated one of the most notorious of the concentration camps, now intended to be a gathering point for the Scandinavian prisoners.

The White Buses had been joined in Germany by the German liaison officers, the most important of whom was Himmler's own, SS-Obersturmbannführer Dr Karl Rennau. Rennau has been characterised in a positive light by Swedish, Danish and Norwegian sources – he appeared to be eager for the Swedish expedition to be a success. Another key player on the German side was the link between the Swedish legation and the Gestapo, detective superintendent Franz Göring, according to Brandel 'a very energetic and reliable man'. As we saw in Chapter 3, Göring had been involved in Schellenberg's project to exchange Jewish camp prisoners for Swiss francs. Rennau's and Göring's efforts to facilitate the success of the expedition would later prove to have paid off.

Forty German liaison officers, SS officers and Gestapo were assigned to the detachment, all of them in civilian clothes. It was stipulated that at least every other Swedish bus should have a German Begleitungsoffizier. In the beginning the evidently somewhat naïve Swedes wondered what sort of task these Germans were supposed to have, but soon they realised that their real commitment was to watch the Swedish personnel, not the passengers. Swedish records described the initial atmosphere between Swedes and Germans as cool but correct. As the Swedish personnel gradually got to see the horrendous conditions in the concentration camps tensions increased, and the Swedish officers had to deal with problems involving frequent conflicts between the Swedes and the Gestapo. Serious encounters of this nature might well have led to a total interruption of the expedition's work on the part of the Germans. The Swedes were, of course, all the time dependent on different permits in the German bureaucracy – visa controls at the border, identity documents, *Ausweis* (permits to be in Germany), *Bescheinigungen* (special travel permits) and permits for access to the various camps. In the last resort it was always the Germans who made the decision as to where and how the buses went. A more positive way of expressing this is the conclusion drawn by Sergeant Åke Lööw in a statement he made thirty-five years later. 'The Germans' help was invaluable – thanks to their Gestapo passes, the Swedes were able to get around practically everywhere!'

Concerning the real-life conditions that the prisoners and the Swedish personnel had to contend with, one of the bus drivers, Helge Andersson, left the following description from a later date:

> We had no weapons ourselves, but on most of the buses there was a Gestapo officer. They were dressed in civilian clothes, in suits of various shapes and sizes. The only uniform article of clothing was their black, wide-brimmed hat. They carried pistols under their left arm, in holsters underneath the jacket. We used to mount guard together with a Gestapo man. Mine was called Gideon Walter, about forty years of age, a thick-set man with a coarse, scarred face, probably the result of pimply skin during his youth. He was a serious type, quite friendly, but very correct. You could imagine what it would be like to be his 'victim'! I mounted guard together with him at Friedrichsruh. My only 'weapon' was a road spade used when the convoy was on the road, like the type of spade you see on police wagons. I had a torch, too. We used to walk around in the dark, without a word. We didn't understand one another's language, although there was always a suspicion that they could understand a Scandinavian mix, so we were to be careful in general with what we said whenever they were within hearing distance . . .
>
> Our buses were not exactly comfortable long-distance coaches. As I mentioned before, they were really army hospital vehicles. Quite small in size, which was well suited to the type of tricky roads we had to manoeuvre at times. There were, if I remember rightly, eight stretchers, which could be folded and dismantled. In the course of our transports we rarely had to use more than one or two of them. On each side of the bus there was a fitted bench, upholstered, and another wooden bench in the middle, this time loose-fitted. The driver sat to the right, and he was the only one who had a seat with a back to it, and it was also the only place where it was comfortable to sit. Right at the front on the left-hand side was a metre and a half-long

solid bench, where the companion driver and the Gestapo officer would sit. When this driver needed to sleep and gather strength for his next turn at the wheel the Gestapo officer had to move over to the bonnet of the engine or somewhere else . . .

There was fairly acceptable room for about thirty people to sit, but we often had more passengers. These were of course no luxury trips, but the concentration camps were not exactly known for comfortable living either. Faced with the prospect of being able to escape alive the prisoners were capable of enduring a great deal, while on the other hand they had of course no choice in the matter. On the occasions when the capacity of the buses was insufficient a number of people even had to travel on covered truck platforms. The buses were equipped with black-out material made of masonite to cover the windows, and the Germans wanted this to be fitted to the passenger section of the buses to prevent the prisoners looking out and outsiders looking in. The Swedes managed to get their way, insisting it was not necessary except in special cases. Many of the prisoners were lice-ridden, which was not considered unusual. Lice can transmit serious diseases, however, and to forestall these our hair and underclothes were thoroughly dusted with DDT powder, among other things. Using special dusting sprays we helped each other disinfect vests and underpants.[4]

One Problem After Another

The White Buses were fated to encounter many obstacles on their way, such as the delay the expedition suffered at the start. Contrary to the commitment Bernadotte made to Schellenberg the detachment arrived nine days later than planned. It was much smaller than originally planned, which meant that its transport capacity was severely reduced. If it had been possible to include what the Danes had wanted to offer, the transport capacity would have more than doubled and the rescue work could, in principle, have been carried out in less than half the time. In the light of Danish experiences from previous transports from the German camps, the expedition's degree of efficiency would probably have more than doubled.

One major reason for the delay was the hectic work involved in Stockholm securing some form of safe conduct for the expedition on the part of the Allied powers. The latter now had complete control of air space over Germany, and the low-flying attacks particularly from British fighter aircraft on traffic on the German highways became more and more common and more and more ruthless. The Swedish expedition's regional base came to lie within the British war operational zone. According to the *Swedish Foreign Office White Book 1956* the American, British and Russian legations were all informed of the expedition. No objections were raised, but no guarantees were offered either. The Swedish Foreign Office promised as far as possible to supply the Allies with information concerning the various routes the vehicles would be plying and timetables for the transportation through Germany. The Soviet Union legation appears never to have responded formally. It was not until April that the American legation announced that the State Department had no objection to the expedition itself, but that no commodities from Sweden were to be sent to it. Abundant correspondence does exist, however, between the Swedish Foreign Office (in the person of the young third secretary, Sverker Åström) and the British legation on the subject of safe conduct.

On 5 March the British promised that their air force authorities would issue instructions to avoid attacks on Swedish Red Cross convoys, but concrete guarantees were not forthcoming. A definite reply came on 8 March (the same day that the detachment received its orders for embarkation) to the effect that the British government in principle was in agreement with the Red Cross action but was *unable to give a safe-conduct* and was compelled to announce that those Swedes who entered Germany and territory occupied by Germany did so 'at their own risk'.

Connections by land were not the only unsafe ones. Plans to have a Red Cross plane fly between Malmö and Hamburg were shelved after the US and British legations failed to promise an Allied safe-conduct. Similarly, Prince Carl of Sweden reported that the Red Cross had chartered a large vessel to transport the detachment directly from Malmö to Lübeck in northern Germany. In the absence of a safe-conduct, however, the Gothenburg shipping line refused to assume the risk . A further source of trouble was the voyage undertaken by the *Lillie Matthiessen* to Lübeck.

Its cargo of 350,000 litres of fuel was of course a prerequisite for the Swedish vehicles being able to continue driving throughout Germany. The ship's departure was delayed day after day, in part as a result of the Allies refusing to grant a safe-conduct and in part because of Swedish red tape. According to Frykman safe-conduct was finally given by the warring parties while the resistance put up by the Swedish Chamber of Commerce to grant a permit for an extra ten men to watch over the cargo was overcome through a government decree.

I have not found any confirmation of these reports. There do exist, on the other hand, a number of petitions, ever more furiously worded, from Bernadotte demanding the departure of the ship. Finally a memo dated 12 March mentioned von Post informing the British and American legations that the *Lillie Matthiessen* had been given the all-clear to depart even though 'notice had not been accepted'. My impression, therefore, is that the Swedes allowed the vessel to leave without receiving guarantees from the Allies. The objections forwarded by the Chamber of Commerce are also easy to understand. The 350,000 litres of an inflammable petrol–alcohol mixture was an extremely risky cargo. Towards the end of the war ruthless attacks were performed on shipping in the Baltic by the Allies. The *Lillie Matthiessen* reached Lübeck, however, on 17 March. Instead of serving as a depot vessel, as was first intended, the ship was unloaded in a hurry by the Swedes – and at the start even with the help of prisoners of war! The stores were then transported in the Swedish vehicles to Friedrichsruh, but by then the expedition was already running late by three days and nights.

The news from Denmark was worrying. On 1 March the Swedish minister von Dardel had sent a telegram indicating that, according to the chairman of the Danish medical association, the mortality rate at the Neuengamme camp was desperately high. As a result of poor hygiene, every month 2,000 people were dying out of the 80,000 interned there. Could the Swedish Red Cross send barracks for the sick?

Nevertheless, the worst of the problems were to be found, not unexpectedly, on the German side. On the same day (1 March) a message reached Bernadotte from the legation in Berlin stating that 'all' (as it was put in the original) of the Norwegian and Danish prisoners were on their way by train from Buchenwald to Neuengamme, something that as a consequence rendered the entire Swedish Red Cross expedition unnecessary. Torsten Brandel, undoubtedly dismayed, retorted that the Swedes considered that the action by no means was unnecessary and demanded to be allowed to speak to Schellenberg. Bernadotte declared that it was impossible to discontinue the action, and that he would be going to Berlin to settle the matter. The following day, in a doubtless unpleasant conversation with Brandel, Schellenberg admitted that he had run into greater difficulties than he had imagined and the reasons for these were beyond his control. What exactly happened during the next few days up until Bernadotte's trip to Berlin on 5 March is not clear from the primary sources. According to the account in Bernadotte's *Last Days* . . . (and the relevant chapters here are somewhat confusing), 'a phone call came from Berlin' in which somebody (presumably Brandel) reported from a very reliable source that Kaltenbrunner had tried to quash Bernadotte's agreement with Himmler.

The 'very reliable source' had been Schellenberg, who revealed after the war that Kaltenbrunner had been furious when he was kept out of Himmler's meeting with Bernadotte on 19 February, and that from that moment Kaltenbrunner had sought to thwart both Bernadotte's plans and Schellenberg's. Kaltenbrunner had told the Danish representative in Berlin that Bernadotte was a particularly naïve man. How could he believe that Danish and Norwegian prisoners would be permitted to be transported to Sweden, or that Swedish Red Cross delegates would be allowed into German concentration camps? Bernadotte did all the same understand this line of reasoning – if the Swedes gained insight into the German camps 'the Third Reich's gruesome secrets, maintained until the very last, would be revealed . . . and what remained of Nazi-Germany's prestige would disappear'. Bernadotte's sharp response was that he could not accept his agreement with Himmler being broken by an outsider, and that it could only be revoked by a new agreement between him and Himmler. In his book Bernadotte went on to state that it was Schellenberg who rescued the entire undertaking 'during these critical days'.[5]

On 1 March, the same day that the alarm had gone off at the Foreign Office in Stockholm, von Post was sending Richert a personal letter in which he reported that the following day Kersten would be travelling to Berlin to resume treatment on Himmler:

> Kersten will then (together with Himmler – *author's note*) as far as it is possible put in a word for the transfer of the Danish and Norwegian internees to Sweden, or in any case for the successful completion of the Bernadotte expedition, and intends to draw attention to a number of special cases, mainly concerning exits to Sweden.
>
> The foreign secretary told me yesterday that he was going to write to you and ask you to afford Kersten all support, naturally not least should he unexpectedly come up against difficulties.[6]

Günther had once again produced an ace from his sleeve – Himmler's masseur Kersten. The letter showed quite clearly that Kersten had now been commissioned by the Foreign Office – at least indirectly – to pressure Himmler into releasing the Danish and Norwegian prisoners for transfer to Sweden, on a parallel with Bernadotte's own negotiations, as well as a number of other Swedish requests.

Folke Bernadotte and His Talks in Germany: Round Two

The results of Bernadotte's first negotiation round, it must be admitted, were very good. For Himmler to have conceded 'from the very first meeting' that all interned Norwegians and Danes were to be transferred to Sweden was probably, as von Post had written on 1 March, almost beyond the realm of possibility. Von Post's report is interesting inasmuch as it hints at what was very likely the Swedish government's (and Bernadotte's) negotiation strategy – gradually to move forward the Swedish positions 'stage by stage' and present the Germans with increasingly tougher demands. It was known of course in Stockholm that in step with the imminent collapse of the Third Reich the balance of power between Germany and Sweden (to use Richert's phrase) was quickly to change in Sweden's favour.

When Bernadotte landed again in Berlin on 6 March, however, the situation was precarious. In top German circles his expedition was considered 'unnecessary'. In Sweden the Red Cross detachment had not yet even been assembled, much less arrived on German soil by 3 March as Bernadotte had promised.

He undoubtedly took along with him a detailed memo resulting from a telephone conversation with Berlin on 3 March. Here was laid out, 'as a result of a meeting today in Berlin', the organisation of the Swedish expedition's future activity via a series of ten items. Since the agreement involved both Swedish and German obligations it was very likely the result of the Swedish legation's negotiations with the German side. Ten camps were enumerated, for example, with more than seven thousand Norwegian and Danish prisoners to be evacuated. It may be noted that Theresienstadt was missing from the list, and also that 'Count Bernadotte . . . might well be able to arrange for further evacuation'. Attached to this memo is another list of 'documents relating to talks with Germany regarding Danish and Norwegian internees'. From this we can deduce the fact that Bernadotte took along not only his own letter to Schellenberg but also nine different Norwegian memos and two Danish ones. Once again it may be noted that in one of these – the Reverend Vogt-Svendsen's list of Scandinavian prisoners in Germany – Theresienstadt was conspicuous by its absence.

Finally there was also an unpleasant report that an 'SS general is governing north-western Germany'. Names and dates were missing from the report, but presumably it derived from the Swedish National Security Service's 'own correspondent'. Thus it was that Bernadotte found out that the Waffen-SS general, Count Bassewitz, had been appointed by Himmler with extraordinary powers in north-western Germany. During the attempt at a *coup d'état* against Hitler in July 1944, Captain Mayendorf in Hamburg, acting under the orders of the coup architects in Berlin and with the tacit consent of the military in Hamburg, had held the SS headquarters under occupation for forty-eight hours. After the failure of the coup attempt Bassewitz had been given a free hand by Himmler, and in a mopping-up operation had executed Mayendorf and eighty civilians 'after prolonged torture'. This was the man who now ruled as a dictator over Lübeck, Hamburg, Friedrichsruh and Neuengamme – the very same area that served as the Swedish detachment's base.

Bernadotte, moreover, had received a new letter from the tireless Storch the day before his departure. Storch was able to inform Bernadotte that, according to 'unverified information', the Germans were possibly prepared to release all the remaining Jews and transport a small number of them over to Sweden. Storch begged him to apply his 'extraordinary authority' to this matter and also try to establish the fate of the Norwegian and Danish Jews. He further drew attention to the fact that provisions at the concentration camps were at a catastrophic level, and that the Allied authorities who were exercising a blockade were not granting larger permits for deliveries of parcels. Big amounts of foodstuffs could be sent from the WJC and from the American Red Cross stores in Gothenburg, but only on condition that the Swedish Red Cross be allowed to check distribution of the parcels at the camps. Was Bernadotte able to initiate talks to this effect? Bernadotte pencilled the following remarks on the original copy of Storch's letter (positive as such, but only concerning Storch's last request): '1. A Swedish Red Cross centre at Lübeck. 2. Delegates able to check distribution through visits to camps & confirm parcels reach addressees.'

Bernadotte arrived in Berlin on 6 March and left the city again on 19 March. His stay was one of almost two weeks. In the light of this, and in view of the critical situation prevailing on his arrival, the slender account given of his negotiations during the month of March is rather striking. The *Swedish Foreign Office White Book 1956* pointed out the fact, quite briefly, that Bernadotte 'stubbornly and successfully refused to go back on his agreement in principle with Himmler'. This is correct. At the same time it should be added that this 'agreement in principle' was never put on paper. It is, furthermore, noteworthy that this time Bernadotte never got to meet Himmler, notwithstanding his long stay in Germany. The *White Book* further established the fact that Bernadotte's conversation with especially Kaltenbrunner and Schellenberg between 6 and 8 March 'removed the last difficulties'. This, however, as will transpire later, was totally incorrect. Finally the *White Book* quoted a telephone message home from Bernadotte on 7 March stating that 'the German authorities concerned did everything to ensure the successful outcome of the action', and that a subsequent second action – the transfer to Sweden of those who had been transported to Neuengamme – did not appear to be out of the question.

I have not been able to trace this telegram, and Bernadotte's overall report from 15 March neither reproduces nor reflects such an assessment. He painted here a far more dismal picture. 'Himmler's subordinate officers, chiefly Obergruppenführer Kaltenbrunner, head of the security police, is dead against the project and has tried to get Himmler to retract his promise to me of a couple of weeks ago. Himmler has however declared that he is willing to stand by his promise.' It is worth noting here that Bernadotte is not talking about any 'agreement' with Himmler but only a 'promise'. Himmler's 'promise' to Bernadotte of 19 February evidently had the character of a 'gentlemen's agreement'. Bernadotte himself was a gentleman to his fingertips while Himmler, Kaltenbrunner and their subordinates were quite the opposite. It should, then, have been an easy matter for them to sabotage Himmler's verbal 'promise'. This was also confirmed in a report from Brandel on the same day: the Swedish Red Cross delegation was still not being allowed into the Neuengamme camp as long as the Norwegians and Danes were not separated from the other prisoners. Bernadotte, who considered the delegation's work inside Neuengamme to be a 'cardinal point', now threatened to return home with the entire expedition. 'The Germans are particularly sensitive about our getting an inside view of the camp and conditions in general.'

Bernadotte's account of his March visit in *Last Days* . . .was also striking.[7] The only reference to any of his many talks with the Germans was this brief exchange of words with Kaltenbrunner:

> Kaltenbrunner: I don't intend contributing to a positive solution of the issues you have taken up . . .
> Bernadotte: And I cannot submit to having one of Himmler's subordinates try and sabotage an agreement concluded between him and myself.

Otherwise *Last Days* . . . did not include anything of interest from this trip, save a few descriptions of Friedrichsruh, Schönhausen (another of Bismarck's estates, two hundred kilometres west of Berlin, where the Swedish legation was now accommodated), how people were coping in the midst of Germany's state of collapse, as well as his journey home through Denmark and an audience with the Danish king Christian. Nor did he mention, in his report home of 15 March, the result of his lunchtime conversation with Kaltenbrunner on 7 March, or his two meetings (at least) later on with Schellenberg, or those with other high-ranking German officers. He did include the fact that he would be requesting an audience with the

German Minister of Justice Thierack, whose department dealt with matters concerning internees detained on charges of discipline. Whether he was successful or not is unclear. What is noteworthy, in the light of the Foreign Office's considerable interest in the Jewish question and Storch's proposals, is the fact that we have no account of what happened when Bernadotte (according to his diary) met Dr Kleist on 8 March or Kersten at his estate Harzwalde on 17 March. The latter, who had been treating Himmler since 3 March, should of course have had a lot to say about the state of mind of the Reichsführer-SS. Evidently, following the initial political negotiations of 6–8 March, Bernadotte largely occupied himself with matters of a practical and organisational nature concerning the Red Cross expedition and its rescue work.

Fortunately there are a large number of detailed notes dealing with most of the political meetings – partly those produced by legation secretary Brandel and Nylander's replacement the attaché Marc Giron, and partly one left by the Danes. Bernadotte's own report of 15 March also mentioned this first meeting with Schellenberg as well as meetings with the Danish minister on 6 and 8 March and with the Norwegian representatives on the 7th.

Bernadotte had previously given advanced notice that the success of the expedition might be a matter of weeks, perhaps days. He now discovered in Germany that the prisoners at Auschwitz – where all the Norwegian Jews had been interned – and at Stutthof (the Norwegian military and Danish communists) had already been evacuated, and that these prisoners were now *auf Trek*, which meant for many that they were out on a forced march towards a certain death. The Germans suggested that the Stutthof prisoners might be evacuated by sea under Red Cross supervision, but only if the ship also took German refugees. Bernadotte allowed this project to lapse. 'In the case of the Stutthof camp we've got here too late', Bernadotte concluded – and the same concerned the Jews at Auschwitz.

A different version of the Stutthof fiasco appeared in the Stockholm newspaper *Stockholms-Tidningen* on 11 April 1956. Without disclosing its source (although probably it was Hultgren) the newspaper reported that negotiations had taken place at the Danish legation in Berlin at the beginning of March involving Bernadotte, the Red Cross representative Captain

Hultgren, head of the first modest Swedish detachment in Berlin, Hvass from the Danish side and the Norwegian professor Seip. This man claimed to have discovered that Hitler intended blowing up Stutthof with all the prisoners inside. Stutthof contained political prisoners, a particular source of hatred for Hitler. The Norwegians and the Danes then tried to get Bernadotte to rescue the Scandinavian prisoners at Stutthof, by fermenting a coup if necessary. Captain Hultgren offered to travel to Stutthof, by air or torpedo boat, in order to attempt to prevent the destruction of the camp, if only by the presence of his Red Cross uniform. But Bernadotte refused: he would not risk the life of a Swedish Red Cross member for such a hazardous enterprise. Those present at the meeting guessed at another reason for Bernadotte's refusal – he feared that such a bold action would reach Hitler's ears and upset his entire rescue undertaking. Bernadotte's refusal in this case may have been another source of the rumours later on which hinted at his reluctance to rescue Norwegians, Danes *and Jews as well*.

Folke Bernadotte and the Jews

On arrival in Germany on 6 March Bernadotte was informed by Schellenberg that, all in all, there were approximately five thousand Norwegian and Danish prisoners to be transported to Neuengamme. Bernadotte noted that the tally was far too small, and that the Danish policemen and the Norwegian and Danish Jews were not included.

A memo resulting from a conversation on 8 March led to the broadcast on Swedish radio in April 1998 of a notorious programme entitled 'Take the Jews last':

> Memo concerning conversation with Göring 8 March.
> Present among others Count Bernadotte, Brandel and Giron.
> 1   Concerning *the Jews*: majority evacuated from Auschwitz.
> Jews should be collected last.[8]

Drawing the conclusion, on the strength of this one phrase, and in a single document, that Bernadotte and the Swedish expedition in future would put the Jews last on their agenda would seem rash. Item 1 in the above was followed in the original document by a further eight items which as a whole clearly showed that the memo referred to the German view (Göring's, that is) of the situation – together with Swedish comments – prior to the arrival of the White Buses. The last item, for example, read: '9 Border officials today received orders from Göring.' The idea of a German detective inspector taking part in decision-making together with Count Bernadotte and two representatives from the Swedish legation is extremely far-fetched. This interpretation is confirmed by another document dated the same day, but clearly later in the day. Under the letterhead Der Chef der SicherheitsPolizei und des SD Göring issued direct instructions for the Swedish action. No reference is made here to the Jews. All other documents point, in fact, in the opposite direction, namely that Bernadotte was actively working for the Jewish cause. The matter was taken up with the Danes directly on 6 March:

> Theresienstadt. As the war scenario is now approaching Prague, these people should be moved northwards to Neuengamme, even though they are particularly comfortable where they are. After some discussion the Danes, in reply to a direct query, declared themselves to be of the opinion that this was advisable, despite the fact that it could temporarily lead to some displeasure. The matter should be raised with Kaltenbrunner.[9]

The same thing happened the following day with the Norwegians, who reported that there ought to be 371 Jews at Theresienstadt moved there from Auschwitz:

> In reply to Bernadotte's direct enquiry the Norwegians expressed a request that the Jews be moved to Neuengamme. Conditions at Theresienstadt were no longer as satisfactory as before, and for the Norwegians worse even than for the Danes.[10]

In his report Bernadotte expressed his surprise that the Danish policemen were reluctant to leave their camp where they were being treated very well in their capacity as prisoners of war. It was the same with the Jewish question:

> Concerning the Jews, both the Norwegians and the Danes considered that they likewise would be particularly disinclined to be moved to Neuengamme since they, too, are now enjoying very good treatment,

a circumstance which came as a great surprise to me as well. In consultation with the Norwegians and the Danes it was decided, however, to try to obtain permission for the Jews as well to move to Neuengamme, and in this respect I have also achieved a positive result. It must be assumed, though, that especially to begin with the Jews are going to accept the arrangements with very little enthusiasm.[11]

It was Bernadotte, then, according to the Swedish sources, who was pressing the Jewish question in relation to Norwegians and Danes. He it was, too, who during a lunchtime conversation got Kaltenbrunner to consent to the transfer of *all the Scandinavian Jews* as well as *the Danish policemen* to Neuengamme. When Bernadotte gave his final orders to the Red Cross detachment at Friedrichsruh on 20 March prior to his journey home, of the five categories the Jews occupied second place in priorities, after the Danish policemen: '2. Approximately 800 Scandinavian Jews are to be transferred to Neuengamme from sites as yet unknown.'

What, then, do the Danish sources have to say about these conversations? Unfortunately I have not been able to find any Danish record of the meeting of 6 March, but I have for the conversation that took place two days later. The Danish record stated that Bernadotte gave information of his meeting the day before with Kaltenbrunner – as well as with under-secretary of state Baron von Steengracht – and of the agreement by which *all* Danes and Norwegians would be moved to the main camp at Neuengamme. Nothing specific was said about the Danish Jews. On the other hand Bernadotte reported that von Steengracht had favoured the Danish policemen being returned as soon as possible to Denmark while Kaltenbrunner opposed such a move on account of the situation in Denmark. Similar circumstances are recorded in minister Mohr's private archives. Very little material is to be found here on the Danish Jews or Theresienstadt, but a lot, however, on Bernadotte and the Danish policemen, including a twelve-page report. There was, though, an interesting article in the Danish newspaper *Berlingske Tidende* in 1946 in which Mohr made the following statement:

Conditions at Theresienstadt in the view of Hvass and Dr Juel Henningsen did not seem to be as bad as the persistent rumours had one believe. Among other things it appeared that the food parcels and medical items sent through the Danish Red Cross did indeed reach the prisoners. There had been some doubts in this respect. It further appeared that the prisoners enjoyed a certain degree of self-determination with institutions of their own . . . Theresienstadt was no concentration camp as such, but a separate community within which the Jews had certain freedom of movement.[12]

In the view of Holm, the Danish medical officer, Mohr showed 'very little' concern for the Danish prisoners in Germany. Mohr's statement from 1946 mirrors quite well, I think, the picture portrayed by Swedish sources of Mohr's lack of interest in 1945, particularly as regards the fate of the Danish Jews at Theresienstadt.

The Danes Negotiate in Parallel

For a long time the Danes had of course been insisting that Danish prisoners be transported home, and indeed they had already been successful in sending home from the camps several hundred of their own people, mainly elderly people and the sick. The Swedish Red Cross expedition was welcomed by Denmark, which still however continued to press independently for the release of its prisoners. On 28 February Nils Svenningsen, head of the Danish foreign ministry and thus to all intents and purposes Danish foreign minister, made a reference in a letter to Werner Best, the German 'High Chancellor' in Denmark, to Bernadotte's negotiations and plans for reuniting all Danish prisoners in one camp. Svenningsen reminded Best of his undertaking of 1 December 1944, to allow all Danish prisoners on German soil, with few exceptions, to be transferred to the Danish camp at Frøslev. The exceptions were Danish saboteurs and partisans, murderers, communists and spies. Svenningsen asked Best to arrange for all other Danish prisoners, chiefly policemen, border guards and those under arrest who were sick, now to be able to return to Denmark, either to be released or to be interned at Frøslev. Those 'saddled with serious charges', however, would be moved to an assembly camp chosen by Himmler and Bernadotte.

At more or less the same time Mohr, the minister in Berlin, called on the under-secretary of state at Auswärtiges Amt, Baron von Steengracht, and read him Svenningsen's letter. Von Steengracht had asked not to be given 'anything in writing', adding that this sharply worded Danish request could lead to the halt of the Swedish plans for gathering all the Danish prisoners together under Swedish Red Cross care. Mohr's response was that 'the Swedish issue' would not be affected by the Danish proposal since Himmler's undertaking had already been forwarded to the Swedish government.

As we have said, the Danish negotiations focused on the issue of the Danish policemen. The reason lay in the increasing unrest and crime in Denmark following the wholesale deportation of the Danish police force to Germany in 1944. A state of affairs in Denmark soon reaching anarchic levels was also a source of worry to the Germans, who were forced to raise the level of their own patrol numbers. The Germans quite logically wished to release these for duty at the front. The unrest and the acts of sabotage, moreover, threatened production in Denmark and export to Germany, mainly of essential foodstuffs. It was, then, clearly of interest to the Germans for a Danish police force to be reinstated. Those responsible for these talks were Kaltenbrunner for the Germans while the minister in Berlin, Otto Carl Mohr, was chief Danish negotiator.

During March and April 1945 the Danes and the Swedes were negotiating in parallel with the Germans. Their objectives were not exactly identical – the Swedes wanted to bring together all the Danish prisoners at Neuengamme as a first step, while the Danes wanted them moved straight home for release or for internment at Frøslev. The Danes' negotiating partner was Kaltenbrunner and the Swedes' was Himmler or Schellenberg. Kaltenbrunner on the one hand and Himmler and Schellenberg on the other were bitter enemies and sought to thwart each other. Clearly the two negotiation processes threatened to counteract each other, as von Steengracht had warned, unless some sort of careful coordination could be arranged.

Mohr managed to arrange two meetings with Kaltenbrunner for 6 and 8 March, the same days on which he also met Bernadotte. Mohr was quite frank with Kaltenbrunner and criticised German excesses during the occupation. He also mentioned all the breaches of promise on the part of the Germans, and gave a reminder of Best's commitment of 1 December 1944, to send to Denmark all the deportees, with the exception of those answering to Best's four categories. Kaltenbrunner promised now to send home and release seventy-four gendarmes from Neuengamme, eighty sick policemen from Buchenwald, and to permit the transfer of sick policemen from Mühlberg to Frøslev. Kaltenbrunner further held out the prospect of half the remaining policemen (approximately one thousand men) 'soon' being moved to Frøslev, with the rest within another month. The first half could then be released and the remainder shortly afterwards. The prerequisite for this generous concession was – said the Germans – that 'the Danish side show itself favourably disposed to the idea of the reinstatement of a Danish police force.' In response to a Danish query as to the tasks such a police force would be required to perform, it was said that they should also be prepared to deal with sabotage. Department chief of staff Hvass replied that it would not be possible to establish such a police organisation.

The Danish and German negotiators now turned to the matter of the Swedish expedition. The Danes took up the abominable conditions prevailing at Neuengamme where some two hundred Danes had died in the course of a few months. The Danes were loath to risk their policemen suffering worse treatment at Neuengamme than that they had already been receiving as prisoners of war. Kaltenbrunner promised new regulations, or new management, for the Neuengamme camp, and saw no difficulty in the Danes being offered a 'separate section'. As regards the Swedish proposal for Swedish *Betreuung* (responsibility) for the Danish–Norwegian section at Neuengamme, he had certainly not promised anything of the kind. Schellenberg may have put forward a suggestion which arrived at his work desk, but he was strongly opposed to it: it might well lead to espionage. One or two Danish doctors, on the other hand, could be allowed into Neuengamme, on the understanding that they subjected themselves to camp rules and regulations for internees.[13]

The following day the Danes informed Bernadotte of Kaltenbrunner's declarations, but this did not bother Bernadotte – the agreement about Swedish *Betreuung* at Neuengamme had been entered into with Himmler himself. Mohr, too, confirmed the agreement that the Swedish contingent should transport the Danish policemen to Neuengamme – after that the Danes themselves could move them home to Frøslev.

And so it was. First, though, between 12 and 21 March the Danes were able to shuttle to Frøslev for internment 140 policemen, seventy border guards and fifty-two so-called 'socially maladjusted individuals', all of whom were released on arrival in Denmark. Then the Danish convoys ceased for a time and were replaced by the Swedish White Buses transporting the Danes to Neuengamme.

The Danes had achieved considerable success in their negotiations for their policemen. As far as the Danish Jews were concerned, however, the news was less promising. Svenningsen had on 16 March put the question direct to Dr Best as to whether the Jews at Theresienstadt too were to be moved to Neuengamme. Best assumed that the permission did not cover these Jews as they were hardly to be classed as 'prisoners', strictly speaking, in the same way as the prisoners in the concentration camps.

Kersten and Himmler

Kersten arrived in Germany on 3 March 1945 and stayed until the 23rd. We can mostly discern the results of his treatment of and discussions with Himmler only from Kersten's own reports. Some insight derives, however, from the Swedish Foreign Office reports. The Foreign Office wrote to its legation in Berlin on 14 March that: 'If Bernadotte unsuccessful release Swedish Jews per enclosed list question whether request Kersten try.' Bernadotte's silence over this matter implies that he had been unsuccessful in the Jewish question. This is confirmed by Kersten's diary entry to the effect that Bernadotte had 'got stuck'.[14] Eight days later Richert communicated that Kersten had received the legation's 'Jewish list' together with a couple of additional names plus a list of all the Swedish nationals under arrest in Germany. Bernadotte had also added a number of special cases. In Richert's letter to von Post of 22 March we learn that when Bernadotte and Brandel visited him on 17 March Kersten informed them that:

> . . . 'the Jewish list' was ready, and that the Swedish prisoners would be released, with the exception of those sentenced to death, for whom Himmler was not in a position to make a definite decision but had committed himself to further discussion in the best possible spirit, and that most of the special cases had also been settled. It is

now sincerely to be hoped that we shall be able to see the promises given Kersten honoured while there is still time.

Concerning the Danish and Norwegian internees, Kersten has been pressing for their transport from Neuengamme to Sweden. According to his own statements it would appear that Himmler has been won over to this idea, but materialising it obviously requires collaboration from other quarters . . .

Kersten seems to have worked for other Jews than those on our list, with, as he believes, good results.

Kersten's deliberations regarding Jews occupy pride of place in Richert's letter. According to Kersten's own petition to the Foreign Office a few months later, at the end of February he became acquainted with Gilel Storch, the WJC delegate in Stockholm, through Ottakar von Knierem, who was the Dresdner Bank representative in Scandinavia. Both he and Storch were Latvians, and von Knierem happened also to be uncle on his mother's side to Olof Palme, who was to become the prime minister of Sweden 1969–76 and 1982–6. Kersten claimed later that the target for his and Storch's work had been the release of every Jew in Germany and their transport 'abroad'. The WJC, however, regarded it as unrealistic immediately to get all Jews out of Germany, and the concrete proposals sent from the Congress to Kersten were confined to attempting to obtain:

1   permits for the Swedish Red Cross to distribute food parcels and clothes direct to the concentration camp prisoners;
2   release from Bergen-Belsen of some 3,000 Jews with South American passports;
3   release to Sweden of other groups of Jews;
4   information as to where in Germany various groups of Jews were to be located and their numbers in different camps;
5   release to Sweden of four individuals (Rabbi Samuel, from Oslo; Dr Stricker, Theresienstadt; Elieser Grünbaum; Dr Idelsohn, from Riga);
6   release of large groups of Jews, possibly by means of internment under Swedish government custody until the end of the war.[15]

As was the case with Bernadotte's 'agreements' with Himmler, however, the latter's so-called 'promises' to Kersten could indeed be called into question. In his petition to the Foreign Office in June Kersten claimed that as Bernadotte was going to discuss the same matter with Himmler: 'it would be superfluous for me to request written confirmation of the course of my negotiations. I did, however, acquire on 21 March a confirmation from Dr Brandt (Himmler's adjutant) of the release of those people the foreign minister had particularly requested to have handed over, and all of whom have arrived in Sweden' (12 June, that is – *author's note*). This is not true, or at any rate only part of the truth. Brandt's letters of 20 and 21 March merely promised a 'positive treatment' of three particular cases and 'benevolent consideration'. As regards the Swedish Foreign Ministry's list of individuals for release, evidently amounting to some seventy-two names all told, Brandt only mentioned on 21 March that the SS-Reichsführer 'intended' to meet Kersten's request for *five* of these (the Norwegian Aulie, Princess Sapieha, Countess Fleurieu and the two Swedish Bondy children). These children were discovered much later in Hamburg, at the beginning of July, when they had been liberated by the Russians. It was not until 4 July that Bernadotte could cable the good news to their parents, the Löblowitz family in Gothenburg, that the children were alive and well.[16]

Kersten's report from June is also very sparse in relation to the release of the Norwegians and the Danes. On 3 March Himmler was totally averse to releasing them, in view of Hitler's negative attitude. Gradually Kersten managed to get Himmler to come around at least to discussing with Bernadotte the release of the women and children interned. The matter was therefore passed on to Bernadotte, and Kersten's further proposals were dismissed by Himmler with a 'please don't bother me, I'm not a free man'.

The important progress Kersten was able to report concerned the Jews. His report included a truly sensational document: a *Vereinbarung* (contract) between Kersten and Himmler:

AGREEMENT

I do hereby certify that, together with Medical Counsellor Kersten, of Stockholm, I have entered into the following agreement:

1   I shall not pass on the Führer's order to blow up the concentration camps together with their internees at the Allies' approach, and forbid every attempt at causing an explosion. The same applies to the killing of prisoners;

2   at the Allies' approach a concentration camp shall be surrendered in due order and displaying white flags;

3   further killing of Jews is to be discontinued and forbidden, and Jews are to be put on a par with other prisoners in the concentration camps;

4   the concentration camps are not to be evacuated, and prisoners are to remain where they are for the moment; all prisoners may receive food parcels from Sweden.

Hohenlychen, 12 March, 2 p.m.

In the name of humanity.

Felix Kersten	Heinrich Himmler
Finnish Medical Counsellor	Reichsführer SS
Stockholm	

Should this document be genuine, it would imply a sensational break-through in the work to rescue the Jews in the concentration camps. The problem is that the copies I have been able to find are copies of other copies and are unsigned. The authenticity of the original and its car-bon copy, however, have been certified by Elisabeth Lüben and by the Dutch experts van Nagell and Jacobus Nieuwenhuis. The Dutch certifi-cates appeared more than seven years later, when Kersten was embroiled in his bitter struggle to gain Swedish citizenship.[17] Elisabeth Lüben had been Kersten's private secretary for many years and he regarded her as his 'half-sister' and as a member of the Kersten family. Arno Kersten, his son, recalled that Lüben typed out all of Kersten's notes as he dictated them.[18] Strangely enough I have not been able to find this important docu-ment in the National Record Office at the Swedish Foreign Office, or any original copy in the Kersten family's private archives. Still stranger is the fact that Kersten, writing his book *Conversations with Himmler* in 1947, did not substantiate with a picture this sensational agreement, or that Dutch professor Posthumus, proposing Kersten to the Norwegian Nobel Prize

Committee on 31 August 1951 as a candidate for the Nobel Peace Prize that year, made no mention of this agreement. My own belief is that the Kersten–Himmler agreement of 12 March 1945 is false and had probably been written out much later by Lüben, the same lady who plausibly typed out the Bernadotte–Himmler letter, proven false, two days previously.

Kersten wished to get the commitments made by Himmler, as described above, confirmed before he flew back to Sweden. In the only letter (dated 21 March) addressed to Kersten and personally signed by Himmler that I have been able to detect from this trip, Himmler did not speak of these commitments at all. Himmler boasted instead of already having saved the lives of 2,700 Jews by sending them to Switzerland, and in the letter further spread the rumour of a serious epidemic of typhus having broken out at Bergen-Belsen. It was thought to be under control, declared Himmler, thanks to modern and the best possible medical counter-measures. Writing to Brandt earlier, however, Kersten spoke of 'stormy discussions' with Himmler resulting in the Reichsführer's undertaking to release 800 French women from Ravensbrück for transfer to Sweden in the White Buses, plus the further release of 1,000 Dutch, 400 Belgian and 500 Polish women. This should be carried out swiftly enough to prevent Kaltenbrunner from intervening.[19] I have been unable to find any reply from Brandt to this letter.

Most of the promises given Kersten by Himmler regarding the Jews are confirmed, however, in Kersten's petition to the Swedish Foreign Office of 12 June, and mainly in a letter he sent to Storch as early as 24 March, straight after his return to Stockholm. These promises included:

- the distribution of food parcels and perhaps also medication for the concentration camp prisoners;
- possible regrouping of the Jews in special camps to be placed under Red Cross supervision;
- a reconsideration of the release of certain Jews to Sweden or Switzerland as well as a stop to cruel treatment and killing of Jews.

All such releases and measures to relax the harshness of the situation would be rescinded, however, if they were leaked to the world press and thus might be construed as signs of weakness on the part of Germany. Everything must be performed with the utmost discretion, Kersten stressed. Finally Kersten delivered Himmler's personal invitation to Storch to have direct talks with Himmler on these matters. The issue of the release of the Jews, however, was evidently shifted over to Bernadotte: Himmler promised to 'discuss this matter with Count Bernadotte'.

The Scandinavians are Assembled at Neuengamme

The Swedish Red Cross detachment was split into two operational groups at Friedrichsruh. The first platoon was responsible for the transport of Scandinavians from the Sachsenhausen concentration camp, situated just north of Berlin (see map, p.iv). The journey covered about 540 kilometres. Transportation began on 15 March and there were seven trips in all, during which some 2,200 Norwegians and Danes were transferred to Neuengamme (Greaver/Sjöstrand put the tally at 2,161). The journeys soon acquired a routine schedule with one trip about every other day, starting from Friedrichsruh at 5 p.m., arriving at Sachsenhausen around midnight and back again under cover of darkness, returning to Neuengamme close to 11 a.m. the following morning. Sven Frykman, in charge of one of these convoys, gave an account:

> The bus platoon set off at five in the afternoon from Friedrichsruh on the 540 kilometre journey in brilliant spring weather. The radio, which was switched on all the time, played merry tunes from light operas, announcing every half hour that no enemy planes had been sighted over northern Germany. Everything was plain sailing and we kept a good speed – an average of sixty kilometres an hour. From time to time we had to reduce speed whenever we ran into long convoys of 'Trecks', which never seemed to stop coming in this war-ravaged Germany. The sides of the road were full of horses and cows dead from exhaustion, and it was an eerie sight, their swollen corpses spreading a disgusting stink . . .
>
> The northern suburbs of Berlin were relatively free of damage. Entire districts still stood, fully fit to live in. In between there were huge empty spaces made up of piles of gravel. Berlin itself however presented a dreadful scene. A full moon shone from a cloudless

sky so you could see the awful extent of the damage. A ghost town of cave-dwellers was all that was left of this world metropolis. We drove along the largest and most famous streets. The imperial palace, all the splendid castles, the prince's palace, the Royal Library, Tempelhof, the buildings along the Unter den Linden – hardly anything was left of all of these. Because of the moonlight which shone through all these empty windows and doorways, the city gave an even more grotesque impression than by daylight. Here and there a flame was still burning after the most recent bombing raids, and the fire brigades were at work. Burst pipes on some of the streets made you think of Venice and its canals.

We had done all we had to do apart from one last job. The Gestapo officer was about to go up to his service post to fetch the courier's bag when the sirens began to wail. Suddenly the scene changed dramatically. People streamed out of their cellars and basements clinging to their odds and ends and rushed towards the air-raid shelters. Cars hurtled along, their horns blasting away like ambulances. Police and air-raid wardens shouting and making a lot of noise, with the civilian population in a state of apathy. Most of them went around like sleep-walkers, some cursed the 'murderous angels' from above, others weeped softly. The minutes that lasted before the Gestapo officer had returned at the gallop with a healthy colleague to replace the sick one seemed an eternity. He told us we had ten minutes before all hell broke loose in the sky over Berlin, and asked what we intended doing. 'Drive as fast as the wheels will let us,' we replied. He seemed satisfied with this answer and was obviously very much in favour of getting out of Berlin as quickly as possible. The radio broadcast an ominous warning: 'A large enemy bombing unit is approaching Berlin from the west and is estimated to be over the centre of the city within five minutes.' We put on even more speed. Repeatedly we were halted by police who yelled at us to stop and seek shelter. But we had to keep going. We were compelled to make a detour of the main thoroughfares which were badly damaged and had to switch off our headlights. I've rarely heard so much abuse as that which was heaped upon us by uniformed

Right: Friedrichsruh castle, which was the headquarters of the Swedish Red Cross expedition in Germany, March–April 1945. It was bombed by the RAF on 20–21 April and again on the 29th.

Below: Swedish Red Cross tented accommodation at Friedrichsruh castle.

Above: Swedish, Danish and Gestapo officials at Friedrichsruh castle. The Danish doctor Johannes Holm is second from left, Count Bernadotte is fourth from left and expedition military leader Colonel Björck is second from right. The Gestapo officials are wearing civilian hats.

Below: Swedish Red Cross officers, including Captain Harald Folke (second from left), in discussion with their Gestapo liaison officers at Friedrichsruh castle. As usual they are wearing civilian hats.

Above: Swedish Red Cross despatch rider Sven Nilsson on his motorcycle. In the background is a Danish White Bus.

Left: Swedish White Buses in convoy, 5–29 April 1945.

*Lübeck, northern Germany, 5–20 April 1945: White Buses outside the Swedish legation ready for the onward repatriation to Sweden. Near the front (**above**) is the Swedish legation official Lüning, whose married name was Countess von Eickstedt. The Gestapo officials are in their usual civilian hats. The lady nearest the Danish White Bus (**below**), with the Danish driver at the door, is legation official Countess von Eickstedt. At the front in the centre is Ingrid Ahrens (who was married to German photographer Heinz Ahrens); their daughter Anita is waving.*

Above: Swedish women who had arrived at Lübeck and were then waiting for repatriation on the Swedish White Buses, April 1945.

Below: The German Nazi film producer Veit Harlan and his Swedish film star Kristina Söderbaum waiting at Lübeck for repatriation. On the far right is the Swedish legation official Countess von Eickstedt.

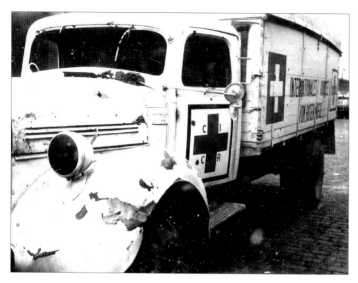

Left: An International Red Cross truck that had been attacked at Schwerin by the RAF on 25 April 1945. The Swedish driver, Eric Ringman, was killed as was a Canadian auxiliary driver and several women rescued from the Ravensbrück concentration camp.

Below: A Swedish White Bus, a truck from the ICRC and a Swedish commercial ship, probably SS Lillie Mathiesen, *at the port of Lübeck, photographed from the Swedish legation on 29 or 30 April 1945. The SS* Lillie Mathiesen *and her sister ship SS* Magdalena *were about to take the last freed concentration camp prisoners to Sweden.*

*Women rescued from Ravensbrück concentration camp by International Red Cross trucks, waiting for repatriation to Sweden, late April 1945. Food was supplied by the Swedish legation at Lübeck (**above**). White crosses were painted on the inmates (**below**) to help the guards to shoot them down if they tried to escape.*

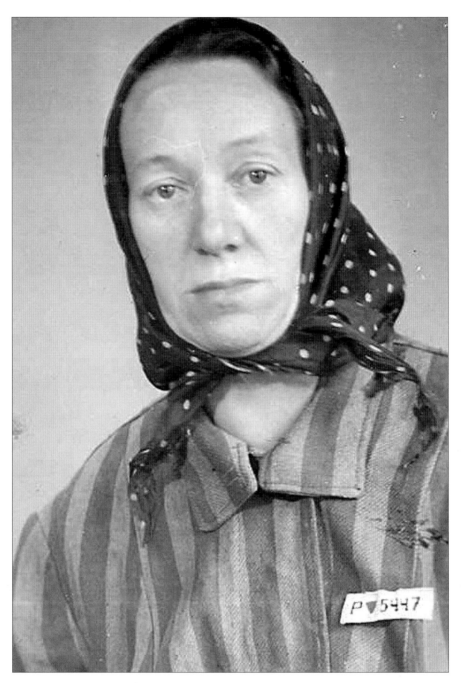

A Polish woman, known only as P 5447, rescued from Ravensbrück concentration camp by the Swedish Red Cross expedition, and photographed at the port of Lübeck, late April 1945.

personnel trying to stop our progress. They called us murderers and bandits, and reminded us that the first enemy planes could already be heard above us . . .

At five minutes to five we reached the camp. As we got out of the buses we were met by the commandant just leaving the officers' casino, and the loading on board of the 280 Scandinavians could start. It was curious to see the prisoners marching through the archway, the gates of which opened just as the head of the file reached them and closed as the last man went through. They marched in perfect time; they reminded me of drill time back at home. The allocation of different bus teams was completed in a rapid, military fashion. The sick were taken on board special buses, with doctors and nurses to care for them. The luggage was packed on the roof, and the prisoners stormed into the buses with a precision as if it were all a demonstration exercise. At half past five all was reported ready for departure and the convoy set off for Neuengamme. A first break was had after an hour's drive, and it was now we were able to take a closer look at our fellow Scandinavians. They were generally in fairly good condition compared to other prisoners I've seen, and as far as personal hygiene was concerned there were no complaints. They told us that the food parcels they had got from Norway and Denmark had kept them going, and recently the treatment had improved considerably. They were all touchingly grateful and happy. I believe that all of us who've had the privilege of being able to help these poor people in Germany have experienced such an enormous gratitude that it's enough to last us for the rest of our lives . . .

Around ten-thirty the buses reached the gates of the Neuengamme camp and we disembarked. 'Lovely trip's over now', said a Norwegian. 'But if I'm not mistaken, you'll be coming back to take us all home, right?' However much we would like to have given him an affirmative reply, at that moment things looked pretty uncertain for carrying out further action. Nothing, however, was impossible for Count Bernadotte, and one month later we had the privilege of being able to complete the action. It was heart-rending to see our fellow Scandinavians, gazing intently at us Swedes, being taken charge of by the rough individuals who came streaming out of this horror camp.[20]

Sachsenhausen had been a horror camp, although the Scandinavians had seen their situation improved at the camp. One of those rescued, a Danish doctor called Henry Mayer, gave this account:

It was night-time when we arrived at the dreaded Sachsenhausen, and what we saw and went through at that concentration camp belies description. I can tell of all the nasty methods these Nazi minds concocted to make their victims suffer. I can tell of how, with devilish inventiveness, they made use of technical equipment in torturing their victims. The Middle Ages and the Jesuits' beds of torment were a playground compared to the altars of sacrifice these Nazi scoundrels thought up. But I'd never be able to put down on paper the sound of the death rattle in the throats of the dying or the shrieks of those being beaten. The cries to heaven for help will never resound from the articles and books presently to be written by those who have survived these horrors – Hell's purgatory would seem a holiday jaunt by comparison . . .

Corruption became more and more rife as time went on and the Allies approached from every quarter. Soon it was possible to steal anything, as long as you weren't found out – if so, it was a sure death after indescribable torture. All the officials could be bribed if you could get hold of some food, while those who had access to the Red Cross food parcels belonged to the camp's aristocracy. Otherwise the veteran prisoners had lost all sense of human feeling: if a fellow prisoner was kicked or whipped to death it had no effect on them.

In March 1945 rumours began to circulate among the Scandinavian prisoners of an evacuation of the camp. Sweden was mentioned, but it didn't seem credible. It had to be the same figment of imagination that turned our mouldy lump of bread into a roasted chicken. Yet one fine day there they stood outside the camp, thirty white-painted Swedish buses, and we got orders to take our seats. Kindly Swedish Red Cross workers and members of the Swedish women's service, smiling at us and treating us not only as human beings but with friendliness and loving care. How could such a thing be possible? It had to be a dream![21]

The Swedes had no success in getting one Norwegian out of Sachsenhausen – Arne Daehli, who had been sentenced to death. On 9 April 1940 he had been in charge of the shore battery in Oslo fiord which sank a big German troopship with nine thousand men on board. At first the Germans reported that Daehli had fallen seriously ill, and later that he was no longer at the camp. Aksel Larsen, communist member of the Danish parliament, had better luck. He was in serious condition after years of internment in a special prison without contact with the other Scandinavian prisoners. In Neuengamme, Larsen was put in a special bunker. Only after a specific request had been made by Bernadotte among others was Larsen released to join the other Danes.

As the Norwegian prisoners were being transferred to Neuengamme the Norwegian 'committee' at Gross Kreutz was crossing them off their files and checking that no one had been forgotten at Sachsenhausen. As for Arne Daehli, he had been shipped away from Sachsenhausen once more, but was rescued on 28 April by the US army in the south Tyrol, on the border between Austria and Italy.[22]

The task facing the detachment's second and third platoons was to bring Scandinavian prisoners from concentration camps in the south of Germany to Neuengamme. It included the notorious Dachau camp north of Munich, where an estimated 519 Scandinavians were imprisoned, and a smaller number at the camps at Schömberg, eighty kilometres south of Stuttgart, and Mauthausen, twelve kilometres east of Linz in what is now Austria. These journeys were considerably longer – a distance of 950 kilometres, for instance, to Mauthausen. They could not therefore be started until fuel had been unloaded from the *Lillie Matthiessen*. The convoy did not set off until 19 March. It consisted of thirty-five vehicles under the command of detachment head Colonel Björck. Five days went by before the convoy returned to Neuengamme, on 24 March. Of the 640 Scandinavians expected to be rescued, forty had to be left behind at Dachau as they were in too bad a shape to be moved. The Swedish contingent made repeated attempts to hand over foodstuff to these forty people so that they could cope with their situation until such time as they could be fetched later on. The Germans refused, however, to allow such direct transactions, and the only way out was to bribe the official who was in charge of the distribution of food parcels at the camp. Mauthausen had the reputation of being one of the very worst concentration camps. There was next to no hope of survival for those sent there, and most were up for sentence of death. The Norwegian and Danish 'intelligence services' in Germany, otherwise so well informed, could only report that there should be fifty-four Scandinavians at the camp. The senior medical officer attached to the White Bus unit, Hans Arnoldsson, who took part in the transfer of these prisoners to Neuengamme, gave this account of the horror camp:

> At five in the morning the camp came to life again. Amid howls and shrieks the prisoners were aroused from their beds and driven to work in groups at the limestone quarries.
>
> It was tough work, leading to certain death for many of them, as one of the Norwegians we had fetched was to tell me later on. As long as the prisoners were able to move they were forced to the quarries every morning, returning late in the evening. Those who were unable to walk had to be carried by their fellow prisoners to the place of work where the weak and seriously ill were given a sledgehammer and made to work, sitting or crawling, as long as there was any strength left in their bodies. The food given for this work was 350 grams of bread a day and a litre of weak soup cooked from dried vegetables, turnips and suchlike. Those charged with the heaviest work were offered an extra ration of 150 grams of bread. Margarine and meat were available on rare occasions – meat, however, hardly ever. When anybody was unable to cope with the work any longer, the ration was lowered to 200 grams of bread. All the rations had been severely cut of late.
>
> The death rate rose considerably owing to the shortage of clothes and footwear. Prisoners often had to wear the same underclothes for five months at a stretch. Nor were they given any opportunity to wash their clothes themselves. Corporal punishment was meted

out if the Block Senior found lice in any of their garments during a check-up. Flogging was the most common punishment for lesser offences. Any amount of lashes could be dealt out at Mauthausen, but prisoners seldom survived more than thirty or forty. Another form of punishment was being bound to an electrified barbed wire fence or to a wall, often several days in a row in all weathers and starved of food. Hanging by their wrists, arms tied behind their back, was another common punishment. Public hanging was also practised to a large extent. Punishment was carried out in a variety of ways with astounding ingenuity and in devilish detail.[23]

After a series of tough discussions with the camp commandant Seydlitz the Swedes managed to take along with them all the fifty-four Scandinavians at Mauthausen. On the way to Neuengamme, however, one of the prisoners revealed that there were a further eleven Norwegians at the camp hidden away by the Germans, as well as sixteen Norwegian women who had just been brought there from Ravensbrück. The return journey of the Red Cross convoy from the south of Germany was one long nightmare. One of the nurses travelling with the convoy, Margareta Björcke, related the following story:

> We made a first stop during the morning when we had got as far as the motorway. Fortunately enough the weather was fine, and when we stopped everybody got out of the buses immediately – that is, all those who were able to – and threw themselves on to the grassy slopes and pulled off their clothes to be helped with fresh bandages. In all my twelve years of nursing I've never seen so much distress as I saw here at one and the same time. Legs, backs, necks full of carbuncles, such as would cause a Swede to go on sick leave for a week for just one of them – on his neck, for example. I counted about twenty on one man alone, and he didn't breathe a word of complaint. In passing I can mention the fact that this very man was on a later transport to Denmark, recognized me, and came up to me to thank me for helping him. He had now recovered, had a round and healthy face and shone with happiness at being free.

Most had clean bandages, more often than not made of paper, but with a black tarry ointment which they hated. You just had to remove the dressing, apply a little white ointment and replace with proper bandages, and they were utterly delighted. The gratitude they showed for the most minor detail was something you'd never forget.

But a Swedish nurse's sense of the need to sterilize equipment was almost dealt a death-blow. There we were, kneeling in the roadway in the midst of dust and dirt, bandaging the most terrible wounds and opening boils. We had scissors and a pair of tweezers we could just about clean with alcohol and sometimes by burning, but which had to be used by one after another. There was quite simply neither enough time nor the opportunity if we were to cope with the most essential. And strangest of all was the fact that it evidently made very little difference. From eleven o'clock in the morning until late in the evening there were five of us working – two doctors, two nurses and a medical orderly. We had people running temperatures of 40° Centigrade and higher, and after consuming the contents of their gift parcels everybody was more or less afflicted with diarrhoea. It was dreadful to see them sitting in row upon row along the side of the road. But yet they were so terribly hungry. I watched them tear open the parcels and gobble down the dried milk with a spoon. What did it matter if half landed anywhere but in their mouths! We warned them about eating too much all at once, but what good did that do! And we didn't have the heart to take the parcels away from them, even though we realised what misery it would cause. All the time our store of opium and bismuth was shrinking.[24]

The prisoners' continual attacks of diarrhoea were a big problem during the transport. Johannes Holm, a Danish doctor, was attached to the Swedish Red Cross expedition from 13 March, representing the Danish Foreign Ministry. In his book written in Danish entitled *The Truth about the White Buses*, he expresses his warm appreciation of the Swedish officers' rôle but portrays Bernadotte in an unfavourable light. From 14 March Holm was able to participate in Swedish staff meetings where transport plans were laid. Holm's book gives accounts of these meetings, although Swedish primary sources are missing. Already after the first transport from Sachsenhausen, according to Holm, the Swedes complained of all the stoppages caused by the diarrhoea problem. Holm had had similar experiences on the first Danish transports and told the staff meeting that the Danes subsequently always included on board every bus special 'emergency toilets'. He then offered the Swedes a sufficient number of these units but the offer was turned down by Bernadotte 'with force and determination'. Following the first long and difficult journeys from the south of Germany, however, Colonel Björck requested delivery of these toilets from the Danes. Two days later the Danes supplied Björck with fifty such units. This was the first contribution the Swedish contingent accepted from Denmark.

Juel Henningsen, the Danish medical officer mentioned earlier, has also told of how, before the transport process had begun, the Swedes refused to believe Danish information concerning the situation in Germany – for example, the fact that ordinary drinking water would not always be available during a long day's march. 'In their favour', remarked Henningsen, 'it should be said that when they had completed the first transport they came up to us and said you were absolutely right . . .'

According to Greayer/Sjöstrand's specification, a total of 559 prisoners were brought to Neuengamme from the camps at Dachau, Schömberg, Mauthausen and Natzweiler in the south of Germany, while 67 seriously ill Scandinavians were forced to remain.

The Neuengamme Camp
Neuengamme was considered one of the most terrible of the German concentration camps.[25] It belonged to the so-called 'second category' camps – the toughest sort – apart, that is, from the extermination camps. The camp lay eighteen kilometres south-east of the centre of the city of Hamburg in low-lying land north of the River Elbe. The area was humid, difficult to drain and unhealthy. The camp was surrounded by a double row of two-metre-high electrified barbed wire fencing, the upper part of which was curved inwards. Guards were posted at one hundred-metre intervals in watch towers. There were even patrols accompanied by fierce dogs in the surrounding terrain, reducing chances of escape to a minimum.

You had to pass seven sentry boxes before you could reach the first entrance gate in the vicinity of the gas chambers and where all cargoes were unloaded. To collect prisoners you continued along a broad avenue full of guard personnel and concrete bunkers and teeming with automatic weapons. Rows of electrified barbed wire encircled the camp. Prison guards went along bawling at their prey as they herded them together. Every time one of these unfortunate individuals passed a Gestapo officer he was expected to snatch off his cap and make a smart salute with a turn of his head. Woe betide any who failed to obey such orders! The barracks were crammed tight with people, and in some places there was so little room that these tormented creatures had no choice but to lie on their sides. The official bed space was a width of 30–40 centimetres per man. Healthy and sick had to lie the one next to the other. Those poor people who couldn't raise their bodies were forced to relieve themselves indoors and the stink was overpowering.

The camp commandant, SS-Obersturmbannführer Max Pauly, had previously gained his reputation in charge of gas chambers at extermination camps. He was, just like his closest subordinate SS-Obersturmführer Anton Thumann, a dreaded and hated man. Thuman has been characterised by the Danish medical officer Henry Meyer as a pure sadist, one hundred per cent, and had now been sent to Neuengamme after completing his work in the extermination of close to 400,000 people at Auschwitz. Discipline at Neuengamme was rigid. The guards frequently dealt out punches, lashes and kicks. Worse still, however, was being ordered to work in the more than thirty-five *Aussenkommandon* (external work units) outside the camp. Some people were made to work risking their lives clearing areas where the Allies had made bomb raids, even in Hamburg itself. Prisoners were completely at the mercy of employers or commando chiefs in these *Aussenkommandon*. No mail or gift parcels would normally reach these prisoners. The mortality rate was higher among these people, and when they returned to the camp they were not much more than human wrecks and were dubbed 'Muslims'.[26] Medical officer Rundberg decribed them in his book as 'physically and mentally on their way into another world'.

They were excessively lean, hollow-eyed, their skin was ash-grey in colour and their postures shrunken and legs and feet swollen – the majority suffered from uncontrollable diarrhoea.

Conditions worsened at Neuengamme in the final stages of the war. Jörgen Barfod estimated that approximately 52,000 out of perhaps a total of 87,000 prisoners at Neuengamme lost their lives. Out of these, 28,000 died during the last six months, in part as a result of executions carried out in an attempt to wipe out signs of war crimes, but also as a consequence of the terrible death marches from the camps and the British bombing of Lübeck on 3 May.

The Scandinavian prisoners had already enjoyed privileged status at Neuengamme – partly in the guise of 'Aryans' and partly through the arrival of Red Cross gift parcels. Bernadotte's negotiations were intended to lead to a special Scandinavian section being set up with access for the staff of the Swedish Red Cross. Developments were slow on this front, however, and the Germans were continually putting forward counter-proposals. Rundberg and his Red Cross staff spent two weeks at Friedrichsruh unoccupied, without as much as getting near the vicinity of Neuengamme. As late as 23 March the Germans were suggesting the Swedes build a completely new camp on the outskirts of Neuengamme, using Swedish building materials and prefabricated barracks. This totally unrealistic proposal was naturally rejected. Not until 25 March were Rundberg and the delegation's official clergyman, the Reverend Sparrstedt, able to hand over a consignment of medical supplies, bandages and delousing equipment to two of the prisoners at Neuengamme, a Danish and a Norwegian doctor. The Swedes were back again on 27 March with a truck loaded with medicine, blankets, toilet paper, etc. The Germans then raised fresh demands. In order for another batch of thousands of Scandinavian internees to be found room at the camp, the Germans insisted on the Swedish buses transferring two thousand prisoners of other nationalities to other concentration camps in Hannover and Braunschweig.

As more and more Scandinavians arrived at Neuengamme the already pitiful conditions grew worse and worse. The cramped accommodation was abominable – in many of the barracks the Scandinavians were forced to huddle together three, four or five to a bed. Still the Germans refused to set up a separate Scandinavian section and allow in a Swedish delegation until prisoners of other nationalities had been transferred in the Swedish buses. And this is what did finally happen, on 27 and 28 March. The head of the Swedish detachment, Colonel Björck, was extremely reluctant to agree to this German demand and flew into a rage, but yielded in the end. There was a sunny side to this outcome, however, inasmuch as the Swedish bus transport was a much more endurable affair than if the Germans had used their cattle trucks and goods wagons.

The transfer of prisoners to other German concentration camps in the Swedish buses is a sad, controversial story.[27] Swedish primary sources do not allow us an exact reconstruction after the event of the discussions which led to the Swedes yielding to the German demand. The Danish minister in Berlin reported on 21 March that Schellenberg had been put in charge of a special section to be set up at Neuengamme for Scandinavians. On 24 March Bernadotte asked the Swedish legation in Berlin to convey to Schellenberg his indignation at the fact that no measures had been taken at Neuengamme – no special Scandinavian section had been created, the Swedish delegates had not been allowed to begin their work, and no orders had been issued for the transfer of the Danish policemen or the Scandinavian Jews. 'Thus Swedish detachment now inactive.'

Bernadotte sent orders by telephone to Dr Rennau on 26 March insisting that these matters be resolved, and Rennau gave assurances that it would all be settled in two or three days. Subsequently, up until Bernadotte's return to Germany on the evening of the 28th, the problems seemed to have been solved both in Berlin (where Brandel was Bernadotte's contact in his absence) and in Friedrichsruh. According to Svenson Rennau was summoned to Berlin where he 'was invested with authority by Himmler or Schellenberg' to set up the necessary devices at Neuengamme. The version given by Holm, who can give a more detailed account of events, was that Rennau was forced to admit to Colonel Björck that he had no authority whatsoever over camp commandant Pauly. The latter was under the jurisdiction of Reichssicherheitshauptamt, the head of which was Kaltenbrunner. Admittedly Schellenberg was head of the intelligence services under Kaltenbrunner, but the Gestapo chief was Gruppenführer Müller.

Schellenberg's pledges to Bernadotte were therefore as good as worthless in Rennau's opinion, as Kaltenbrunner had scarcely approved them. Pauly's immediate supervisor was Müller and in Rennau's eyes the necessary orders to Pauly could only proceed from Müller. Holm, however, had acquired for himself a favourable position with Dr Rennau. Colonel Björck had previously rejected Rennau's request for a car of his own with a chauffeur but allowed Holm to give Rennau a lift in Holm's own smart Humber. Holm described how he and Rennau drove to Berlin on 29 March. In the Gestapo headquarters Rennau then obtained the necessary orders in writing for Pauly. At the same time Holm seized the opportunity to arrange a meeting with Müller, supply him with a bumper Danish food parcel and secure permission for the Swedes to bring Aksel Larsen from Sachsenhausen to Neuengamme.

Meanwhile German soldiers at Neuengamme violently packed the Swedish buses brimful with prisoners. The transports that were about to take place turned into the grimmest experience of all for the Swedish expedition personnel. Lieutenant Åke Svenson wept at the spectacle:

We were now able to see how the Germans treated their internees in general: Frenchmen, Dutch, Belgians, Poles and Russians. It was something terrible. This time the Germans had to allow us to drive into the camp proper as most of the prisoners were unable to walk the very short distance from the barracks to the road. Out of these barracks were hounded, pushed and led a herd of creatures who barely resembled human beings. These people stumbled and crawled into our buses, emaciated to a degree scarcely credible and further debilitated by high-level dysentery and other ailments. Many people in Sweden who have seen films from Buchenwald and other camps have asked us after our return whether it was possible for such human skeletons as were shown to exist. A number of doubting Thomases believed that some of the scenes had been introduced using trick photography to promote Allied propaganda. We can give full confirmation – those of us who went with the buses – that it was not only possible but quite common. There were fully-grown men of medium height or more who weighed a mere thirty kilos. There were persons who didn't have the strength to hold a slice of bread . . .[28]

The prisoners were driven to camps in the vicinity of Hannover and Braunschweig. The journeys were sheer nightmares. Many prisoners died during the transport. The dysentery made long and frequent stops inevitable, during which the Swedes had to hold the prisoners up while they relieved themselves. It was at this point that the Swedes began to lose any respect for the Germans that they may up until then have had. Clashes between the unarmed Swedish soldiers and the Gestapo people now occurred more often.

The journeys did, however, produce an unforeseen result. Before the very last trip the German commandant revealed that at his camp there were seventy-three Danes who would soon be transferred by rail. This was totally unexpected news: these persons had not appeared on any list of Danish prisoners. Svenson seized the chance and with the aid of a hundred American cigarettes, among other things, he managed to bring all the Danes back with him to Neuengamme. They had been confined to the *Aussenkommando* at Hannover-Stöcken, the majority of them in lamentable shape.

The head of each of the Swedish bus convoys always carried a reserve store of cigarettes in case a bribe or two was called for. They came to great use. German morale was then at such a low ebb that practically anything could be traded for cigarettes, chocolate or vodka. According to Rundberg, the doctor, on his arrival in March half a kilo of coffee cost around 4,000 German Reichsmark, and by the end of April two kilos of coffee was said to be worth the price of a DKW car in fine fettle. Captain Folke has described how, in a camp for women, he was able to pay for the release of three Scandinavian women who had been sentenced to death with a half-litre bottle of Scandinavian vodka. We should perhaps add that the fact that Swedish goods were so much in demand on the German black market created a number of moral dilemmas for some of the Swedish personnel!

There were more transport missions between 30 March and 2 April from the camps at Torgau, Mühlberg and Oschatz in eastern Germany in the vicinity of Leipzig, in which the Swedish buses fetched most of the

Danish policemen and a further number of Norwegians. These journeys brought in total 1,251 prisoners to Neuengamme. Various Swedish memos estimated that the number of Danish policemen stood at 1,610, and of these the Danes themselves would be transporting home some 200 while the Swedes would take the remaining 1,400 policemen to Neuengamme. Between 3 and 5 April two Danish convoys were able to move 1,044 members of the Danish police corps from Neuengamme home to Denmark for internment at Frøslev.

The Swedish Red Cross delegates finally obtained access to the Neuengamme camp on 29 March. Supplies were now rapidly handed over in the form of medication, bandages, blankets, washing detergent, toilet paper, gift parcels and the like. Naturally the Swedish contingent could now establish close contact with the twenty-three Scandinavian doctors (thirteen Norwegian and ten Danish) who were already at Neuengamme. Bernadotte was able to visit the camp on 30 March when he requested various kinds of improvement from the Germans. An intensive delousing campaign was initiated to combat lice and spotted fever – this involved all and everyone being systematically drenched in DDT. After the second week no new cases of spotted fever were reported, and the internees were vaccinated against this and other diseases. The Scandinavian prisoners inhabited a large brick building and a dozen or so smaller barracks which together constituted a special 'Scandinavian section'. Gradually the Danes were to supply medical equipment for full-scale hospital barracks, but these barracks were never to be constructed before the camp was eventually evacuated. Towards the end the supply of gift parcels had improved the Norwegian and Danish prisoners' situation to the extent that, at least as far as food (and tobacco) was concerned, their nutritional level was probably higher than that of many Norwegians back home in Norway! A camouflage net was now thrown over the whole of this section of the camp to keep prying eyes out – prisoners in other parts of the Neuengamme camp had begun to show animosity towards the favoured Scandinavian internees.

Thus it was that by the beginning of April 1945 the first task of the Swedish detachment – gathering the Scandinavian prisoners at the Neuengamme camp – had practically been fulfilled. About 7,000

Danish and Norwegian prisoners were interned there at this stage. Of these, approximately 1,700 had been there from the start, about 600 had been taken there by the Germans, and the White Buses were responsible for the transport of some 4,700 persons. The statement in the *Swedish Foreign Office White Book 1956* to the effect that 'the transports were now to a large extent concluded', however, is far from being the whole truth. Still to be moved to Neuengamme were a number of Danish policemen, all the Norwegian and Danish Jews, and a thousand or so prisoners in a number of hard labour camps. Furthermore, the ultimate purpose of the entire expedition was still to be achieved – bringing all the Scandinavians to Sweden!

At this stage those responsible for the expedition were on the horns of a dilemma. It was originally planned to last three or four weeks, and most people had adjusted their work to fit this schedule. The military personnel had been given a month's leave. A breaking-up mood began therefore to prevail within the detachment. Colonel Björck, the head of the detachment, was summoned back to Stockholm for fresh assignments. He returned with little enthusiasm – he knew he left behind 'a job half done'.[29]

Command of the detachment was taken over on 5 April 1945 by Major Sven Frykman. In the meantime Bernadotte continued his discussions with the German authorities so that at any moment a fresh call for transport might arrive, even to the extent of bringing all the Scandinavians home to Sweden. Powers of persuasion were now brought to bear on the personnel within the detachment. Bernadotte managed to elicit a doubling of the wages paid – the ordinary soldier would now receive five Swedish kronor a day. Colonel Björck promised that none who stayed on with the detachment would lose his job later in Sweden, and that the time employed in Germany would count as full emergency military service back in Sweden. In the end just over half (some 130 people) volunteered to stay. This was sufficient to man the vehicles, which had now been reorganised into two bus platoons, as well as to operate all the other engineering and army supply corps services. The need for assistance from the Danes, however, previously rejected, had now become acute.

9

The White Buses: Night and Fog

The Dachau concentration camp, 23 March 1945:

Out of the twilight appeared a procession of white buses, one
after another. The prisoners counted: one, two, three . . . sixteen,
seventeen, eighteen. This was almost more than we could believe.
More than twenty buses cruised slowly up in front of the long row of
Scandinavian prisoners standing there waiting, not knowing what
they were waiting for. A big sturdy fellow stepped out of the first bus
– Colonel Björck, head of the entire expedition. For a moment he
ran his eye over the congregation. Then, in a clear, ringing voice, he
said in Swedish: 'Well, well, so these are all the fellows.' Never in the
annals of modern Scandinavian history has the Swedish language
sounded more beautiful to Danish and Norwegian ears.

But neither the Norwegians nor the Danes had time to react.
Hardly had Colonel Björck uttered his words than he marched
straight up to the camp commandant, surrounded by his closest
colleagues. Colonel Björck then spoke, after introducing himself
and his colleagues, in good German: '*Und de Skandinavische Häftlinge
– sind sie alle da?* (And are all of the Scandinavian prisoners here?)'
The commandant gave a stiff salute and replied: '*Jawohl*, Herr
Oberst.' Then something unexpected happened. The prisoners'
spokesman, Waldemar Aune, stepped forward and he, too, in a
clear, ringing voice, said: 'No, all are not here.' Confusion arose for a
brief moment. Colonel Björck himself had to translate for the camp

129

commandant what Waldemar Aune had said. The commandant burst out: '*Verflucht. Sie sind ja alle da.* (They are *all* here.) See that you get them on board.' Björck gave Aune a questioning look. Aune stood his ground. 'There are two Norwegians in a cell in the main building,' he said calmly and without trepidation. 'We have to have them with us.' The commandant was on the point of aiming his revolver at Aune. Björck grasped the situation at once. 'Where's the nearest telephone for Berlin?' he asked. 'I'll have to call Berlin.' When the commandant heard the word 'Berlin', he suddenly calmed down. '*Einen augenblick, bitte,*' he said. Less than half an hour had elapsed before two Norwegians appeared through the Dachau prison camp gates. They were shipowners Wilhelm Klaveness and Arne Bjørn-Hansen. They'd been detained as hostages at Dachau for quite some time.[1]

Nacht und Nebel: The Prisoners trapped in Night and Fog

The German death sentences and executions of men and women of the resistance in the occupied countries caused great alarm and commotion, and in the neutral countries as well. Those executed were made martyrs and heroes in countries under occupation. The executions carried out in Norway gave rise in Sweden to an increasingly strong protest movement against German policies not only in Norway but also the Nazi regime as such.

The Germans' counter-move was the *Nacht und Nebel* (NN; Night and Fog) decree signed by Hitler Germany's top military officer, Field Marshal Wilhelm Keitel on 7 December 1941, on the orders of the Führer. The decree came into force in Norway, Belgium, the Netherlands and France – though not in Denmark. Instead of being publicly sentenced and executed, people of the resistance were dispatched to Germany in all secrecy. There they would work themselves to death under the slogan of *Vernichtung durch Arbeit*. Their existence in Germany was kept secret and their death was never reported to family and relatives. They were not allowed to write home and were not allowed gift parcels either. Male NN prisoners, as they came to be called, were sent to the special camp Natzweiler, near Strasbourg in France. Most of them were French. At Natzweiler they were put to work in stone quarries. There was also a small gas chamber where experiments were carried out using a variety of gases, later to be employed at other camps. Test material were gypsies. Many Romas were sent to Natzweiler; and few would leave it alive.

During 1943 and 1944 504 Norwegian men were transported to Natzweiler, and half of them were to die there. A fourteen-hour working day at the stone quarry in rain, snow and freezing weather, miserably clad, saw to it that Hitler's aim was achieved – working the prisoners to death. It was a long time before these prisoners obtained assistance from international quarters. On only two occasions did the Norwegian prisoners receive a small number of food parcels.

Following the Allies' landing in Normandy in June 1944 and the liberation of Paris in August, there was a noticeable change in the conduct of the German camp authorities as the Allied forces under General Patton got closer to Natzweiler. The slave drudgery at the quarry came to a halt. Machine guns were mounted instead around the camp, pointing inwards. The approximately six thousand prisoners had dismal premonitions of what the future held for them. Natzweiler was evacuated in September and the prisoners put 'under transport', as the expression went. About half of the Norwegians who were still alive were sent to Dachau, from where many travelled on to other camps : Mauthausen, Ottobrunn, Gotenhafen, Leonberg and Neuengamme. Dachau remained, however, the main base. Between 22 and 24 March the White Buses fetched seventy-seven Norwegians from Dachau. Colonel Björck was leader of the expedition.

Thirty-five Norwegian NN prisoners had already been sent from Natzweiler to the *Aussenkommando* at Erzingen on Midsummer Eve in June 1944. This came under the supervision of Organisation Todt, led by the minister of armaments Albert Speer, and formed part of Operation Wüste (Operation Desert) with the object of extracting oil from German lignite or brown-coloured coal. The Erzingen camp, however, was run by a former hotel proprietor, commander Lettner, who had been coerced into joining the SS and who was opposed to Hitler's war. His Norwegian 'hotel guests' at Erzingen all survived the winter of 1944–5.

The same fate was not to await the sixty-one Norwegian Natzweiler prisoners who arrived at the recently set up camp at Dautmergen in

September 1944. There were no proper dormitories, dining rooms or toilets, nor was there clean water. Hardly had a week gone by and the first Norwegian, Øystein Jahren from Rjukan, had died. More and more Norwegians died as time went on, or were sent on to Dachau or the camp at Vaihingen. When the White Buses reached Dautmergen only three of these Norwegian prisoners were still alive and all of them were desperately ill. Seven had recently died. During what is termed in the Swedish files the Schömberg–Dachau transport, the White Buses were able to rescue the Norwegians from the *Aussenkommandon* at Erzingen (twenty-one Norwegians and a Dane) and from Dautmergen.

A total number of twenty-nine Norwegian prisoners were transferred between November 1944 and January 1945 from various camps (mostly Dautmergen) to Vaihingen an der Enz, situated between Karlsruhe and Stuttgart. They had all been detained at either the Natzweiler or the Dachau camp. Vaihingen was a small concentration camp where foreign prisoners were engaged in building an underground aircraft factory. Speer had sent three thousand work slaves here from Auschwitz, most of them Polish Jews. The Allies' advance, however, had brought work on the factory to a halt. Instead, Norwegians and others were sent here, people incapable of further work on Operation Wüste – sick people, the worn-out and the frost-bitten. Spotted fever was rife and the Norwegians died, one after another. Björck's March expedition to the south of Germany had missed Vaihingen – the camp was unknown to Swedes and Norwegians alike. In the middle of March there were only sixteen Norwegians still alive. On 2 April, however, a fresh Swedish expedition started off for southern Germany from Friedrichsruh, comprising four buses, a truck and a motorcycle. One of the buses was under the charge of Hans Arnoldsson and was to fetch the remaining Norwegians from Mauthausen. Two buses would rescue the remaining forty sick Scandinavians at Dachau. The fourth bus, supervised by Group Chief Axel Molin and accompanied by a Norwegian doctor, Bjørn Heger, was to hunt around Schömberg for what at Gross Kreutz were supposed to be about thirty 'missing' Norwegians. Molin later gave this account:

. . . on the way to Schömberg there was quite a bit of movement in the air and Allied fighter planes often flew over us, though they didn't attempt to shoot at us. On either side of the autobahn lay lots of cars riddled with bullets and shells, as well as badly injured people. In some places, in a state of chaos, we just couldn't drive past with our Red Cross-marked White Bus but had to stop and help out with first aid. Some of the injuries were dreadful. We finally got to Stuttgart where the Gestapo officer, Dr Bjørn Heger and I requested information of a prisoner commando unit as to where we could find the remaining prisoners from Schömberg. The Gestapo officers were in a fair state of confusion and nervousness and unable to give us any proper information. We were close to the war front and could hear bombs exploding not far away. We discovered, however, that there were a number of smaller work camps in the vicinity, but where the Norwegians were was anybody's guess. We were told there was a camp called Vaihingen, and they might possibly be there. During the last few days there had been a huge amount of prisoner transfer between camps, and it was very difficult to obtain more precise information.

We drove on towards the camp we'd been indicated, but to find our way there we had to make a number of enquiries. After combing the district we finally arrived at the camp where the Norwegians were detained. Up until then our Gestapo officers had tried to impede our search, but we stood up to them and continued our search until it produced results. It looked hopeless, but our stubbornness won through in the end. On meeting the Norwegians we were told they'd given up all hope of ever being rescued since all those who were able to walk or crawl had been ordered to leave the camp and make for Dachau. The Allied front was getting closer and closer, and fast. As soon as we'd got hold of all the Norwegians who were still alive and were still at the camp, we counted up to sixteen men. Some had died of spotted fever the week before. Those we were able to take with us were very ill, but we took them anyway. Otherwise they were sure to have met a certain death. There were stretchers in the bus, though not as many as we needed. The worst cases were given a stretcher each, while those who were not deathly ill had to take turns on the remaining stretchers.[2]

At the Vaihingen camp Bjørn Heger, formerly Sachsenhausen prisoner no. 41,464, dressed in Swedish Red Cross uniform, confronted the Norwegian spokesman, Kristian Ottosen, formerly Sachsenhausen prisoner no. 54,266:

> 'How many Norwegians have you there?'
> 'Sixteen', was the reply.
> 'We're looking for something like thirty,' said Bjørn.
> 'The others are dead,' answered Kristian. 'They're over there.'
> He pointed to a mass grave. Bjørn was visibly shaken.
> 'And Danes?'
> 'None.'[3]

The journey back to Neuengamme was even worse. Molin will never forget that trip. Even today, in the year 2001, it comes back to him and gives him nightmares. With his heart in his mouth on many occasions during that 'journey of horror and tension', he found himself consuming a large amount of amphetamine tablets and chocolate. Molin had the honour, however, of driving his bus into Neuengamme.[4] Altogether this Swedish mini-expedition to the south of Germany between 2 and 6 April rescued seventy-five prisoners – the sixteen from Vaihingen, sixteen NN women from Mauthausen, and forty-three seriously ill men from Dachau.

When the first Neuengamme prisoners were subsequently sent off to Sweden the prisoners from Vaihingen were allocated the first sixteen places. They included people from embargoed vessels from the west of Sweden as well as a man who would later become prime minister of Norway, Trygve Bratteli:

> A storm of rejoicing broke out at the news – not only among the sixteen of us, but also among all the others present. They weren't going to begrudge their fellow-prisoners this favour. Each of the sixteen was given a towel and led into the shower – it was as if nobody would let go of us. While he was drying himself, Trygve

Bratteli discovered he hadn't got all the dirt out of his finger nails. He therefore quite naturally threw the towel between his legs to hold it there while he gave his finger nails one more going over. But the towel fell straight to the floor. Trygve bent down, put the towel between his legs again, and the same thing happened – the towel fell to the floor. Then it was that he realised what his two legs had turned into. His thighs, which used to be strong and sturdy, now looked like two bamboo canes.[5]

The following day the Vaihingen people were driven into the spa town of Ramlösa-Brunn in the Swedish province of Skåne. Vaihingen still haunted rescued and rescuers, however: on 27 April 1945 one more of them, the Norwegian lawyer Leif Hallesby, died at a hospital in the south of Sweden.

Norwegian women had also been made prisoner by the *Nacht und Nebel* decree, and had all been placed in the women's camp at Ravensbrück. They had, however, been mixed with 'common' concentration camp prisoners, which turned out to be a serious mistake on the part of the camp commandant, SS-Sturmbannführer Suhren. At the beginning of March the eighteen Norwegian NN women were therefore dispatched to Mauthausen. Later in March Dr Arnoldsson fetched the Scandinavians from Mauthausen that he had on his list. On his way back to Neuengamme, however, he discovered he had been taken in by the camp commandant: Mauthausen also housed the eighteen Norwegian female prisoners the Germans had concealed.

During the journey back to Neuengamme a prisoner named Fredrik Dietrichson gave Arnoldsson a list of the names of the eighteen women. The list had been put together by Sylvia Salvesen, whom we shall meet later on in the chapter dealing with Ravensbrück. Arnoldsson realised he had been the victim of the camp commandant's deceit and swore that he would be back (see p.119).

Three weeks later, in fact, a Swedish White Bus was back at Mauthausen with Arnoldsson in charge. The camp commandant at first adopted an unsympathetic attitude to the new Swedish demands, but when confronted with Arnoldsson's complete list of names – as well as with an attractive supply of cigarettes and foodstuffs – he softened up and promised to get back with fresh information in three days' time. Arnoldsson duly returned with his White Bus when the time had elapsed. The eleven Norwegian men in the *Aussenkommandon* were not to be found anywhere (they had probably been sent off on a march) and Arnoldsson had to leave without them.

He did, however, prevail upon the camp commandant to surrender sixteen of the NN women. The two others, Solveig Hofmo Smedsrud and Gudbjørg Skaug, had been 'transported' a few days before to Bergen-Belsen. They died on their way there. But as to the other sixteen women:

> . . . their joy at seeing us was undisguised and indescribable. They'd abandoned all hope of ever being liberated, and as late as one hour before our departure had been totally ignorant of what was brewing. I greeted them in Swedish, much to the exasperation of the Gestapo gentlemen. They immediately commanded me to use German, and were unable to appreciate the fact that I called the prisoners ladies, something they oddly enough considered showed disrespect for Germany. They were even cynical enough to suggest that, although these women might once have been ladies, they would never be again after spending a few months in a concentration camp. We carried on calling these women ladies all the same, and we even got some pleasure out of seeing the Gestapo officers' looks of disgust every time we used this form of address![6]

How, then, had the Norwegian 'Centre of Intelligence' in Germany been able to get wind of the existence of the secret Natzweiler NN camp? It is a tale almost as fantastic as the rescue of prisoners from the hellish NN camp. The Norwegian community at Gross Kreutz had had a nasty suspicion that Germany housed secret concentration camps. Some Norwegian prisoners – such as Kristian Ottosen and Trygve Bratteli – disappeared 'under transport' without trace. Parcels addressed to Sachsenhausen started to be returned to Norway, unopened. The fearless young woman Wanda Hjort (subsequently married to Bjørn Heger) managed, however, to persuade a thoughtless German soldier at Sachsenhausen to blab and reveal that a Norwegian prisoner called Kolderup had been sent to a camp known as Natzweiler in Alsatia. He regretted his slip too late. An unsuspecting employee at the little post office at Gross Kreutz helped Wanda locate Natzweiler. At about the same time, in December 1943, seamen's chaplain Vogt-Svendsen had also located Kolderup at Natzweiler. Neither his nor the ICRC's attempts to establish contact with the prisoners at Natzweiler would succeed, however. Wanda Hjort's two attempts to reach the Norwegians at Natzweiler were also doomed to failure. Wanda had to rest content with the Swedish Dr Arnoldsson's words of consolation: 'We'll follow your information and go and search!' And so it was – the Norwegian and Danish sources of information were decisive in crowning the Swedish expedition with success.

10

The White Buses: Theresienstadt

A Danish visit to Theresienstadt in 1944:

> Summing up the numerous impressions we received in the course of our tour of Theresienstadt, and adding those of Dr Epstein together with information supplied by the German authorities, our conclusion is that inside this community, isolated from the rest of the world, considerable organisational progress has been made, particularly during the last six months, and that much good work is continually being carried out, wherever it is possible.
>
> In regard to hygiene, health risks are mainly linked to the excessive overpopulation. In this respect there can be no doubt at the present moment that the Jewish management, using material supplied by the Germans, has succeeded in compensating for the inconveniences and risks in an admirable way.
>
> As regards nutrition, the internees should not suffer any risks as long as they are able to receive food additional to existing rations through the delivery of food parcels.[1]

Camouflaging Theresienstadt as a model Jewish ghetto:

> When the Danish commission – and on one occasion a commission from the International Red Cross too – visited the camp in the summer of 1944, the head of camp administration, a Dr Epstein from Berlin, was able to talk to the visitors alone without the presence of the SS or Gestapo officers. He showed the gentlemen around and

they could go wherever they pleased. He had previously, however, been given instructions by the Gestapo as to what he was to say, and according to reports he had been threatened that any breach of these instructions would lead to the severest reprimand, even including capital punishment.[2]

Further Instructions for Folke Bernadotte from the Swedish Foreign Office

As we have already seen, Bernadotte returned to Stockholm on 22 March. Before he hurried back to Berlin on 27 March, a glance at his private diary tells us that he only had time for a meeting with Kersten on the 26th and a further meeting with foreign minister Günther the same day. What took place during these meetings we do not know.

Of vital importance, however, was a conference held the same day, which was attended by Boheman (Swedish under-secretary of state for foreign affairs), von Post (head of political affairs at the Foreign Office) and Bernadotte. They sketched out the general outline for Bernadotte's planned conversations with Himmler. As these are the only instructions Bernadotte received from the Swedish Foreign Office, and since his continued action in Germany clearly followed these lines, the memo referring to this conference is reproduced here in its entirety:

> First of all a request is now once more to be made for permission to transfer to Sweden all the Danish and Norwegian men and women interned in Germany (Neuengamme).
> Subsidiary issues:
> 1   Request presence of Swedish Red Cross personnel in entire Neuengamme camp (approx. 50,000 internees).
> 2   Offer of Swedish Red Cross buses for use as transport to Neuengamme camp or to other suitable camp of non-Scandinavian internees in Germany. Should mainly concern approx. 25,000 French women, who in conjunction with the German retreat from France were removed to Germany and placed in a camp there.
>
> The above has been supplemented today with a communication to Bernadotte whereby, inasmuch as it is convenient and no

139

impediment is to be feared for the tasks mentioned above, he request the transfer to Sweden of a number of Jews.[3]

Bernadotte's mission to Himmler, then, still concerned first and foremost getting all the Danish and Norwegian prisoners out of Germany, including Jewish ones. In Boheman's judgement, in 1953, among the Foreign Office priorities lay a rescue operation for those people 'closest at hand'. Himmler was seen to be most well disposed to Danes and Norwegians, who 'were of course considered as belonging to a better race of people than many others'.

Bernadotte was to repeat the demand that Swedish Red Cross personnel be admitted to Neuengamme, this time to the whole of the camp. Bernadotte was, furthermore, to push for the transport to Neuengamme of no fewer than 25,000 French women. Boheman, who had been appointed Swedish envoy in Paris in December 1944 but who was still under-secretary in Stockholm in March 1945, later assumed that the attempt to come to the French women's aid stemmed from his own initiative. Repeated appeals had reached the Foreign Office from French quarters. As we saw earlier, however, Bernadotte had himself received similar proposals as early as in November 1944 from consul general Nordling in Paris. That time it expressly concerned French women at the Ravensbrück camp.

Bernadotte was now authorised to include in his mission the rescue of 'a number of Jews', with the implicit understanding that they were non-Scandinavian ones. This mandate was not given until the following day and for no known reasons. A prerequisite was that it did not jeopardise the task of transporting Danes, Norwegians and French women. Plainly, it was Bernadotte personally who was to decide whether it was 'convenient' to request of Himmler that non-Scandinavian Jews be included in the rescue operation.

Bernadotte and the Rescue of Jews

After the war Bernadotte was accused of not having shown interest in rescuing Jews – not even Danish and Norwegian ones – from the German concentration camps. One of Bernadotte's critics was Felix Kersten, who in a letter to Storch claimed that: 'There was no doubt that Bernadotte had actually refused to transport Jews in March 1945. Several SS men can bear witness.'[4] Letters sent by Kersten to others at the same time, however, showed a different story. As we have already seen Kersten had merely elicited a promise from Himmler to negotiate the release of the Jews with Bernadotte. Writing to Storch on 29 March, Kersten announced that Himmler would receive Bernadotte for more talks, mainly concerning the Norwegian and Danish Jews.

Actually both Bernadotte and the Swedish Foreign Office had been doing what they could for a long time so that the Norwegian and Danish Jews in any case would be rescued and taken to Sweden. The Foreign Office had also had discussions with the Germans in respect of the rescue of other Jews, not just Scandinavian. On 26 March, moreover, Nylander reported from Berlin that the homeward journey planned for the Swedish Jews had come a stage further with the German acknowledgement of their Swedish citizenship. This concerned, though, only a few dozen cases. Nylander had also discussed 'a larger Jewish action' with the Swedes' liaison officer on the German side, Dr Kleist, in which Stockholm 'offered in return a package including clothes, blankets, child-care equipment, etc.' Kleist had welcomed this proposition with the greatest of interest and suggested calling the Swedish compensation '*zur Humanisierung des Krieges*'.

There were no reports from Bernadotte, on the other hand, which indicate that up to 27 March he had had talks with the Germans about any Jews other than the Scandinavian. The Red Cross expedition had come up against the serious problem of where to locate the Jews. That the Danish Jews were detained at Theresienstadt was known by the Swedes. On 9 March the Jewish Community in Stockholm had delivered a list to the Foreign Office enumerating 1,710 Jews at Theresienstadt. On 28 March a welfare officer in Gothenburg, Dr Otto Schütz, signed a detailed report of the conditions prevailing at Theresienstadt. This was based on the testimony of six Turkish Jews who had been at Theresienstadt until September 1944 but had reached Gothenburg on 15 March on the *Drottningholm*, a ship carrying exchange prisoners.

As for the fate of the Norwegian Jews in Germany, the Norwegian liaison people working with the Swedes could only confirm time and time again that there was no information available. Bernadotte perse-vered, however, in his endeavour to bring Norwegian and Danish Jews to Neuengamme. Brandel reported on 19 March that Kaltenbrunner was in accordance with this: 'Most of them are coming from Theresienstadt. Some are trekking it. Göring's trying to locate.' Leaving Germany on 20 March, Bernadotte had given orders for eight hundred Scandinavian Jews 'to be brought to Neuengamme from sites as yet unknown'. The following day the Danish minister Mohr informed his Foreign Ministry that nobody knew where the Danish Jews from Theresienstadt were at that moment but Bernadotte had promised that 'transport facilities would soon be available to take them on to Neuengamme'.

Storch has subsequently on a number of occasions given Bernadotte all the credit for the rescue of the Danish Jews.[5] Regarding Kersten's refer-ence to what various SS officers had had to say, Storch countered that not too much attention should be paid to these statements: many high-ranking Nazi officials had, for example, produced various documents for Kersten in exchange for money.[6] It was Günther, anyway, and not Bernadotte who was opposed to the mission being extended to include Jews – Günther was eager for the Swedish rescue operation to concentrate on Norwegians and Danes.[7]

As under-secretary of state Boheman was later to describe the Foreign Office's assessment of the situation: 'Any action in aid of the Jews had for a long time been rated hopeless.' In Boheman's opinion the mandate had been extended after the Foreign Office had heard that the Swiss had man-aged to get a number of Jews over to Switzerland. In 1953 he said: 'I can vouch for Bernadotte being as eager as anyone else to rescue the Jews, and also for the fact that priorities in the rescue operation were solely gauged by the desire to achieve the best possible results within the limited circum-stances prevailing.'

The person at the Swedish Foreign Office who did most in 1945 to rescue Jews was Gösta Engzell. In 1953 he assumed that Bernadotte's extended mandate to rescue 'a further number of Jews' was the result of Storch's and Kersten's discussions to this end, talks about which the For-eign Office had been informed. He stressed Kersten's 'important rôle', and considered Bernadotte at first suspicious of Kersten and reluctant to collaborate with him. He pointed to the fact that there was displeasure among Jews active in Sweden over what they saw as back-pedalling their requests in the Bernadotte operation. He also observed that Storch had confided in a report, probably stemming from New York, that Bernadotte had expressed himself unfavourably on actions in aid of the Jews.

Exactly what was meant by the extension of the mandate on 27 March for Bernadotte to rescue 'a number of Jews' we supposedly will never find out. It is plain, however, that Bernadotte was not himself part of the decision but that the broader task was 'communicated' to him later. Storch's and Kersten's insistent work together with the host of petitions from various Jewish organisations and individual Jews were probably the deciding factors. What is clear is that Himmler's and Brandt's benevolent letters to Kersten were passed on to the Foreign Office on 23 March and to Storch on 24 March by Kersten himself, and that Kersten in meeting Bernadotte on 26 March presumably showed him the letters. Himmler had boasted in his letter of having saved the lives of 2,700 Jews by allowing them into Switzerland.

On 27 March a happy Kersten was able to announce to Storch that he had succeeded in obtaining the release of 5,000 Jews to Sweden and Switzerland, and that this number could surely be doubled through talks with Himmler. The impulsive Storch immediately dispatched a telegram to the US secretary of state Stettinius stating that Himmler was prepared to liberate about 10,000 Jews to Sweden or Switzerland. 'Count Bernadotte . . . will also negotiate regarding our question but he also considered I must definitely go Berlin stop Kersten declared he supposes Himmler wishes procure alibi.' The *White Book* assumed that Storch had also informed the Swedish Foreign Office that Himmler was now prepared to release up to 10,000 Jews, which probably also gave rise to the additional instructions to Bernadotte on that day.

The Swedes Accept Danish Aid

The Swedish Foreign Office drew up a strictly confidential memo on 27 March when Bernadotte returned to Germany. In it the Foreign Office estimated the total number of Norwegians and Danes at 9,000, a much lower figure than the 13,000 previously reported by Norwegian and Danish sources but considerably higher than the barely 3,000 prisoners alleged by the Germans. At Neuengamme there were now about 4,800 Scandinavian prisoners, of whom the White Buses had fetched only 2,483 by then. The 1,000 Scandinavian internees at Stutthof were reckoned to be 'at an unknown site' and were evidently no longer included in the Swedish estimate. There were still 3,200 Scandinavian prisoners to bring back – 1,400 Danish policemen, 800 Jews and close on 1,000 hard labour camp inmates. Permission to fetch the last had not yet been forthcoming. In addition, there remained sixty-seven seriously ill and infectious people in the south of Germany.

With the Swedish detachment's imminent final journey home the Danes grew anxious that the Swedes would not bring back all the Scandinavians in time. The Swedish legation in Berlin issued a report on 24 March of a new Danish feeler. The Danish Red Cross asked the German Foreign Ministry about the possibility of participating in the Swedish Red Cross operation. The matter was discussed on the German side between Schellenberg and Auswärtiges Amt. Barely four hours later Bernadotte gave his reply from the Swedish Foreign Office – it was desirable to accept the Danish offer should the German authorities agree. The operation might still remain perhaps under Swedish Red Cross administration. Günther did not, however, authorise the collaboration until two days later, and then with a proviso: 'We should not take any initiative in the matter. His Excellency is anxious for the operation to remain and not split up merely because a number of people wish to return home.'

So that was what happened: the Foreign Office in Stockholm had at long last perceived the need for assistance from the Danes. When about half of the Swedish detachment made for home on 5 April it was replaced by a large Danish convoy. During the Easter weekend two convoys had been equipped in Denmark consisting of thirty-three buses, fourteen ambulances, seven trucks and four cars. They had been furnished with equipment at the Danish State Serum Institute in Copenhagen, but their base for mechanical equipment, etc., was now transferred to the quarantine station at Padborg on the German–Danish border. The first Danish convoy reached Friedrichsruh on 4 April. It was commanded by Frants Hvass, head of the politico-legal department at Denmark's Ministry of Foreign Affairs. In March he had been part of the negotiations for transporting the Danish policemen home to Denmark. Hvass was now invested with responsibility for the negotiations at Friedrichsruh together with Swedes and Germans, as well as for all telephone connections with the Danish ministries for foreign and social affairs in Copenhagen by way of Denmark's general-consulate in Hamburg. Tasks of a practical nature were under the charge of Bjarne Paulson, secretary at the Foreign Ministry, and Finn Nielsen, secretary at the Ministry for Social Affairs. Nielsen headed the section for personnel and vehicles. The medical officer, Johannes Holm, remained as 'information officer' in cooperation with Swedes and Germans.

Between 7 and 8 April, fourteen Danish ambulances and about thirty-five buses were formally incorporated into the Swedish detachment's organisation. As from that date the White Buses and the entire Red Cross expedition were to all intents and purposes a combined Swedish–Danish operation, approximately half of which was Danish but under Swedish command. The Danish vehicles, too, were painted white but were decorated with the Danish flag instead of the Swedish one. Cooperation on a practical level between Swedes and Danes appears to have been very good. Captain Sigurd Melin admired the Danes for their 'sparkling good humour and their spirit of optimism'. Whatever they were asked to do, however difficult and dreary the task, the reply was always: 'No trouble, we'll manage it.' In this respect Hans Arnoldsson wrote that Johannes Holm 'was of great help to us in producing reliable information on prisoners in different camps', and that Hvass, Paulsson and Nielsen 'were men capable of tackling and solving any organisational problem whatever'. Holm, from the Danish side, was very positive about his cooperation with the Swedish officers Arnoldsson, Folke and Frykman. Highest praise from the Danes was showered on senior physician Hans Arnoldsson from Gothenburg: 'Night and day he kept active, always charming, never tired or exhausted . . . He gave you the feeling that he was harnessing all his energy and every nerve to the task of making sure that as many people as possible could be rescued to Sweden.' But then, Arnoldsson was also married to a Danish woman!

Swedish sources have nothing to tell us about what really went on, between the time Bernadotte accepted Danish assistance on 24 March, the reluctant attitude shown by Günther with his 'no Swedish initiatives, please', and the Danish convoy's departure on 3 April. The Danish side of the story, however, has some less pleasant tales to tell.

Denmark's minister in Berlin, Otto Carl Mohr, revealed that on 26 March he received a telephone report from Holm to the effect that the Swedish transports were heavily delayed and that they would not be completed until May. Holm further reported that the Swedes intended fetching the Danish policemen from Mühlberg and the Jews from Theresienstadt last of all – in spite of the fact that these camps were situated farthest away from Neuengamme and very close to the war front. Mohr's interpretation of Holm's communication was that Bernadotte's plans were about to come unstuck – by May most of the concentration camps would have been over-run by the theatre of war and the prisoners either killed or persecuted out on the country roads. Mohr suggested to Copenhagen that the agreement with the Swedes be annulled, and that the Danes themselves take charge of the transport of the Danish policemen and the Jews – the Swedes could see to the rest! Mohr and Bernadotte met in Berlin on 29 March, however, when Bernadotte was able to set Mohr's mind at rest to some extent: the delays were not as serious as Holm's reports had seemed to imply, the Swedish detachment's equipment would be remaining at Friedrichsruh, and a Swedish convoy was in fact already on its way to Mühlberg.

Bernadotte was very reluctant to accept the idea of the Danes bringing the Jews back from Theresienstadt. He very much wanted assistance from the Danish Red Cross, on the other hand, and requested buses and ambulances with a capacity of transporting 200–300 and sixty-five people, respectively. Mohr was able to inform Bernadotte that a convoy having double this capacity would be ready for departure from Denmark within a couple of days. This convoy, Mohr urged, should first transport home about 1,000 Danish policemen from Neuengamme to the concentration camp at Frøslev in Denmark, and not until later should the vehicles be put at Bernadotte's disposal. Transport arrangements for the policemen would follow previous Danish agreements with Kaltenbrunner. What is more, any Danish participation in Bernadotte's bus transports to Neuengamme required German consent. Bernadotte's response was that Mohr's proposals only complicated Bernadotte's work all the more, and that he preferred to settle the matter himself with Schellenberg: Danish convoys were to come under Swedish command. On this issue, then, Mohr and Bernadotte were at variance with each other – we shall later return to the differences between these two men concerning the transport back home of the Danish policemen.

The Danish liaison officer working with the Swedes at Friedrichsruh, Johannes Holm, offered an even sourer picture of Bernadotte. Holm quoted a staff meeting of 30 March, with Bernadotte present, where Björck presented a gloomy picture of the expedition's situation and lamented the fact that he was now compelled to hand over a well-nigh hopeless situation to his successor, whereon Holm once more offered aid: fifty or so Danish buses would be available within twenty-four hours, together with ambulances, trucks, Danish drivers and Danish equipment. Bernadotte's reply was something of a sneer: such ready-for-use resources were hardly available in Denmark! Several Swedish officers, headed by captains Arnoldsson and Folke, however, adopted a positive attitude and understood the need for Danish assistance. Captain Melin later wrote that the Swedish expedition wouldn't have had 'the slightest chance of success' without resorting to Danish aid.

At the staff meeting the following day Bernadotte revealed that he had spent an uncomfortable night and asked Holm to give further details. Holm explained about all the secret Danish preparations which formed part of the so-called *Det Danske Hjelpekorps* (Danish Aid Corps). Bernadotte listened and then requested the Swedish officers' opinions. The result was a resounding 'Yes!' in favour of Danish aid. Bernadotte gave Holm the task of making the necessary contacts with the Danish ministries of foreign and social affairs. Acceptance of Danish aid was, however, conditional upon the transport of the prisoners remaining a Swedish operation, but with Danish participation. All Danish transports were to have a Swedish commander, all negotiations concerning release from prisons and camps were to be conducted by Swedes, and it was not until half of the Swedish detachment had left Friedrichsruh that a corresponding number of Danish buses were to be brought in.

Folke Bernadotte and His Talks in Germany: Round Three

Bernadotte was back in Berlin on 28 March. The following day he spoke to the Swedish minister and to Mohr and Schellenberg as well. These conversations were followed on 30 March by a visit to the Scandinavian section at Neuengamme. In his own view he was the first representative of a neutral international humanitarian organisation able to visit a German concentration camp.[8] This is stretching the truth. The previous day Gerhard Rundberg, a Red Cross doctor, had obtained permission for daily visits to Neuengamme, while Captain Folke reported that he had been there before Bernadotte – after having bribed the guards with cigarettes and chocolate.

Bernadotte inspected the camp in the company of its notorious commandant, Obersturmbannführer Pauly:

> I'd much rather have greeted the Norwegians and Danes more heartily at my first meeting with them, but caution dictated that I keep my emotions to myself and instead in the company of the camp commandant I inspected the various barracks and spoke to the Norwegians and Danes only fleetingly. I'd heard, however, that some people I knew before had been transferred to Neuengamme, and I asked the commandant if I could see them personally – particularly one of them I was anxious to meet: Fridtjof Nansen's son, the architect Odd Nansen, who I'd worked together with in 1940 in America. It was quite strange to see him now as just a number among this infinitely large band of prisoners . . .
>
> Conditions at the camp were naturally far from satisfactory, which the German authorities willingly conceded. The prisoners' living space was exceptionally cramped. In most of the barracks sleeping bunks had been placed on the floor with sacks on top, on which the prisoners could rest. I worried at the thought of what would happen if an epidemic broke out and diseases were to spread through the camp as the Scandinavian section only disposed of two hospital barracks with 200 beds in all. Norwegian and Danish doctors worked in these barracks, doctors who had also been brought to Germany from their home country as prisoners, and we immediately started to formulate a

plan for how the activity at the camp and the hospital barracks could be improved. The Swedish Red Cross had namely got permission to send from Sweden a number of Red Cross delegates using the camp itself as their base – these people, under the Swedish doctor Prof. Rundberg, at once began to work on improving hygienic conditions. Odd Nansen had already made out a plan for rebuilding the hospital barracks, and we had received a promise from Denmark that hospital equipment, new barracks and medical supplies would immediately be sent to Neuengamme.

The discipline at a German concentration camp is of course exceptionally tough, and I must admit that it made my blood boil as I walked around among the Norwegians and the Danes to see how, in accordance with prevailing camp regulations, they were obliged to snatch off their caps and come to attention whenever a German officer came near them. I did notice, however, that they felt very happy and calm that the Swedish Red Cross was now going to be present at the camp.[9]

One of the prisoners at Neuengamme, J.B. Holmgård from Denmark, remembered Bernadotte's visit that memorable Good Friday in 1945:

Bernadotte was not afraid of typhus. When together with two Germans he crossed the threshold of our isolation ward, a murmur went through the locale. We all stood up, but not hurriedly as stipulated by camp regulations, standing strictly to attention for a German *Achtung* command or the presence of an SS officer. No, we stood up respectfully to honour the man who had brought us better tidings. Those of us wearing caps on our crew-cut heads slowly removed them, and as Bernadotte, smiling at us and greeting us, moved down the barracks and passed the line of triple bunks, hearty Danish and Norwegian greetings were heard in return – some healthy and cheerful, others slower and uttered with a lump in their throat. It wasn't a 'off with the cap!' with a slap on the thigh – it was a friendly and companionable greeting.

For the first time in Neuengamme's history the Nazi executioners Pauly and Thumann ceased to be two swaggering representatives of the master race swinging their whips around. They humbly followed in Bernadotte's footsteps, suddenly accommodating, receptive and obliging to a sickening degree, with the sweet talk typical of the master race executioners when it finally came home to them that their days were numbered. We were now convinced that we were on the way home. Our days of overcrowding were over. A year and a half of torment was nearing its end.[10]

Holmgård had previously been an inmate of the notorious Dora concentration camp where V2 rockets were being assembled underground. He had been isolated at Neuengamme in barracks set aside for cases of typhus, where the Germans until then had not dared set foot.

After a further three visits to Neuengamme and the ensuing talks with Pauly, Bernadotte was able to give a report of his agreements with the camp commandant when he got back home to Sweden. The Swedish Red Cross delegates would enjoy free access to the camp 'at all time' and some of them would also stay the night there. These delegates would act in accordance with instructions issued by Prince Carl of Sweden. The Danish hospital equipment accompanying the Danish hospital barracks would be transferred to the permanent sick bay installations in the Scandinavian section of the camp, which would be tidied up and fitted out following proposals by Odd Nansen. During the day all the prisoners would have access to the entire barrack complex, which would facilitate the organisation of study courses, entertainment and suchlike. No Scandinavian prisoners – with the exception of 'professional criminals' – would be forced to work outside the camp. Every prisoner would have the right to write a letter to his or her family or relatives advising of their arrival at Neuengamme. In the event of an evacuation, the Scandinavian internees would be moved north into Denmark. This would be mainly carried out by the Swedish detachment, requesting help with transport from Denmark. Hvass had been informed of this and was keeping the Danish Jyllandkorps on the alert. In other words, if an evacuation was necessary, the Scandinavian prisoners would not be forced out on a 'death march' but would be rescued by the White Buses and taken to Denmark. Bernadotte never gained admittance to the other areas of the Neuengamme camp but did catch sight of prisoners beyond the Scandinavian section: 'It was an exceptionally lamentable sight – some were absolutely living corpses, totally apathetic. The Russians in particular were treated in an extraordinarily brutal manner by the German guards.'[11]

Bernadotte's most important talks were with Himmler. They met now for the second time and at the same place as previously: the sanatorium at Hohenlychen, close to Himmler's headquarters. The meeting took place on Easter Monday, 2 April, and lasted for four hours. Bernadotte described the talks as 'very cordial'. Schellenberg was present the whole time and seized the opportunity to have a private chat with Bernadotte whenever Himmler was absent. From a military point of view, Germany was now in a serious position. The western Allies had crossed the Rhine while in the east the Russians were pressing forward and would be liberating Vienna within a few days. Quite recently – on 22 March – Himmler had been relieved of his position as commander-in-chief of the German Oder Front. Clearly Himmler had now given up all hope of a German victory. He said he no longer saw any way of preventing Germany's – and with it Europe's – Bolshevisation. Notwithstanding this, he continued to swear his loyalty to Hitler. Bernadotte's response was to point out that the western Allies were now close to the very heart of Germany and he doubted that the Germans would be able to hold both the Western and the Eastern fronts. 'Wouldn't it be more sensible', went Bernadotte's argument, 'to try and concentrate your defence on the Eastern Front in an effort to stem the Russian thrust, which was expected soon, and more or less open up the Western Front to the western Allies?' Himmler understood the logic of this thinking but saw no possibility of it obtaining Hitler's sanction. Bernadotte repeated once again the pointlessness of sacrificing thousands of German lives every day instead of concentrating on a British and American occupation, much more beneficial for the German people than a Russian one. Himmler agreed but made no further comment.[12]

Bernadotte changed the subject and spoke about the Danish–Norwegian internees, requesting once again the transfer of all the Scandinavians from Neuengamme to Sweden. Himmler's response was a fresh refusal, and Bernadotte's conclusion was that this again was due to Hitler's opposition. Himmler did, however, permit the transport home of a number of prisoners – if all were to leave at the same time it would draw too much attention. Bernadotte was given permission to transport to Sweden all the Danish and Norwegian women, all those who were ill and a small percentage of the 461 Norwegian students at Neuengamme. All these people would not have to be interned in Sweden but could be accommodated at boarding houses or hospitals. They would, however, have to pledge their word that they would remain in Sweden until the end of the war, during which time they would refrain from occupying any public office. Himmler released a number of Norwegian civilians under similar conditions, including the Hjort and Seip families as well as a few French citizens, probably the Countess de Fleurieu and the Countess de Rambuteau. In addition, all the Danish policemen were to return to Denmark, initially for internment at the Frøslev camp, although the majority would be released after a short time.

The talks returned to the issues concerning power politics. Himmler regretted Germany's policies towards Britain while Bernadotte recalled Hitler's threats to wipe out all British cities as well as the German bombing of Warsaw in 1939 and Rotterdam in 1940. Himmler then retired for discussions with Schellenberg.

Schellenberg did not beat about the bush. On their way back to Berlin he confided to Bernadotte that Himmler had later been prepared to ask Bernadotte to meet Eisenhower, the commander-in-chief of the Allied forces, to discuss a German surrender on the Western Front. Himmler was struggling, however, 'between his desire to save Germany from utter chaos and his loyalty to Hitler'. The following day Bernadotte consulted Richert, who advised against this request: Bernadotte would only be making things worse for himself, as Eisenhower's only response would be an unconditional German surrender. A few days later Bernadotte again met Schellenberg, who informed him that Himmler and the other German leaders were expected to move to the south of Germany in a day or two. Bernadotte urged Schellenberg to remain in the north of Germany and to acquire letters of authority from Himmler enabling the Swedes to transport the Danish and Norwegian prisoners to Sweden. In the event of a meeting with Eisenhower Bernadotte told Schellenberg he could only go ahead with such a proposal after Himmler had accepted the following four conditions:

1   Himmler at the same time announced that he had been appointed by Hitler (who, for example, was no longer able to remain in office owing to illness) to represent the German people;

2   he thereby disbanded the German National Socialist Party and dismissed all the party officials;

3   he issued instructions to the effect that the so-called *Werwolf* (i.e. guerrilla warfare) was to cease;

4   before my departure from Sweden I [Bernadotte] receive confirmation from Friedrichsruh that an order has been given for all the Danish and Norwegian prisoners to be transported to Sweden.[13]

Schellenberg undertook to urge Himmler to go along with these proposals, although Bernadotte himself doubted whether he would have any success in persuading Himmler. It would of course in practice imply Hitler's dethroning and a revolution directed against the entire Nazi party.

In conclusion, Schellenberg reported that Hitler had given orders for the concentration camps at Buchenwald, Bergen-Belsen and probably also Theresienstadt to be evacuated and the prisoners forced out on foot marches of up to three hundred kilometres. Schellenberg claimed to have protested against this and prevailed upon Himmler to issue a counterorder. The camps would instead be surrendered to the Allied troops in an orderly fashion. A similar order would be issued to the commandant of the Neuengamme camp.

Bernadotte returned from Berlin to Stockholm on 9 April. He had Professor Seip and his wife with him on board the plane.

Gilel Storch, Felix Kersten and the Concentration Camp Jews

When we left Storch and Kersten on 27 March 1945 Kersten had, according to his own documents, managed to extract a number of promises from Himmler. The German concentration camps would not be blown up but surrendered in an orderly manner to the Allies, and the Jews would no longer be killed but put on an equal footing with the other camp prisoners.

I have been unable to find any written confirmation of these undertakings. The question of the release of Jews, moreover, had been adjourned until talks were resumed with Bernadotte. Storch was justified in continuing to be anxious, and he requested written confirmation from Kersten of Himmler's *Zusicherungen* (assurances). Such a confirmation did arrive from Himmler, according to Kersten, but only over the phone. It may be noted that Himmler's supposed *Vereinbarung* (agreement) with Kersten of 12 March had now been reduced to a mere 'assurance', and that Storch realised that this agreement in its written form lacked Himmler's signature and was therefore non-binding. Storch wrote once again to Kersten on 31 March communicating the unpleasant news: during the last few days messages had arrived intimating that a new set of guards had been appointed to some of the concentration camps, with orders that boded no good for the internees.[14]

Kersten tried to calm Storch down in a new batch of letters. There was no basis for Storch's fears – in Kersten's experience, Himmler always kept his promises. Bergen-Belsen would not be evacuated at all but be handed over *ordnungsmässig* (in orderly fashion) before the Allies arrived, and the same applied to Theresienstadt and other concentration camps. Himmler had, what's more – wrote Kersten – confirmed his pledges to Bernadotte. From Germany Bernadotte was to take home with him a letter from Brandt, Himmler's adjutant, in which attention was expressly focused on the Bergen-Belsen camp.

The letter sent by Brandt to Kersten, dated 8 April – and in Storch's copy furnished with his handwritten note 'this letter received by Count Bernadotte after the count's intervention' – can hardly have calmed Storch down. Brandt wrote that he had no new information to add other than what was given on 21 March. Himmler had now, however, appointed a special Sonderkommissar (commissar) for the Bergen-Belsen camp, with detailed guiding principles prescribed by the Reichsführer-SS himself. Concerning Theresienstadt Brandt could only say that an interesting film had been made and that the International Red Cross would now be given an opportunity to see the conditions prevailing there.

Behind this scanty correspondence lurked a situation of dramatic proportions. According to Storch's later accounts, on 7 April he was informed by his German contacts in Stockholm, Dr Kleist and Edgar Klaus, that the following morning at 6 a.m. Bergen-Belsen would be blown up by Hungarian SS men on Kaltenbrunner's orders. Storch rushed to Kersten's flat in Stockholm (they lived close by one other), where he was able to hear Kersten get hold of Brandt on the phone, and Brandt confirmed Himmler's pledge not to blow up the concentration camps. Storch also established contact with Bernadotte, who was at that moment in Germany, and got him immediately to enter into contact with Brandt and other leading Nazis.[15]

Kersten sent Storch the original of Brandt's letter on 10 April. When Bernadotte the following day met Storch he assured him that he had received the letter from Brandt in person, and that Brandt had told him that the demolition of Bergen-Belsen had been halted. This was a major contributing factor to Bergen-Belsen not being destroyed so that it could be liberated intact by the British forces. Storch maintained in 1979 that the demolition of Bergen-Belsen was prevented due to a common effort by Kersten and Bernadotte. In previous addresses to the WJC, however, Storch granted Kersten alone the honour of seeing that the concentration camps were handed over and not blown up.[16]

Oddly enough, this dramatic episode is absent from Kersten's accounts – it is not mentioned, for instance, in his memoirs *Samtal med Himmler* (Conversations with Himmler) from 1947. Nor is anything said about the phone call in Kersten's twenty-five-page address to the Foreign Office of 12 June 1945. On the other hand Kersten in this address did state the fact that it was not until 21 April that he received a letter from Brandt, composed on Himmler's orders, with a written confirmation of Himmler's 'pledges' from 12 March, which Storch had been calling for over such a long time. By then Bergen-Belsen had been liberated by British troops (on 15 April), and Buchenwald on 11 April by the Americans, while the Swedish White Buses had successfully brought all the Scandinavian Jews from Theresienstadt to Sweden on 18 April.

A somewhat different version is supplied by Walter Schellenberg. His detailed account showed how he and the former president of the Swiss Confederation, Musy, successfully persuaded Himmler to spare the camps from evacuation, and how that decision was communicated to Musy on

7 April so that, in accordance with Himmler's express entreaty, it should be passed on to General Eisenhower as fast as possible. Schellenberg does admittedly mention Kersten as being helpful in this matter through his support from Stockholm. Schellenberg claimed, however, that it was rather he himself who intervened directly with Himmler and thus brought Kaltenbrunner's plans to a halt, saving countless lives. He wrote more about his talks with Musy and Burckhardt, president of the International Red Cross, than about Kersten and Bernadotte at this point in time. By then Burckhardt had been able to meet Kaltenbrunner. Nevertheless, Burckhardt's proposal for the International Red Cross to go and fetch a number of French women prisoners from Ravensbrück was stopped by Himmler. Schellenberg maintained, on the other hand, that in his talks with Bernadotte already at the beginning of April Himmler promised Bernadotte the concentration camps would not be evacuated but be handed over in their entirety, especially the camps at Bergen-Belsen, Buchenwald and Theresienstadt.[17]

Strangely enough, Bernadotte omitted all mention of this in *Last Days* . . . In submitting his confidential report of 16 April to Sweden's National Board of Information, however, Bernadotte gave a long account of his 2 April talks with Himmler on this very topic. Himmler had announced that several concentration camps, among them Buchenwald and Theresienstadt, would not be evacuated but instead handed over intact to the Allies:

> Such was the scene at a number of camps in Schlesien. There the commandants had summoned the prisoners' appointed representatives and explained that the enemy was expected to arrive within the hour and that these representatives were to take charge of the camp. Count Bernadotte considered these to be favourable signs. Previously it had been feared that a disaster would befall prisoners in camps within easy reach of the Allied troops. Now, at least, there was hope of avoiding mass slaughter . . . Schellenberg had discovered that Hitler had decided that prisoners in the camps most exposed would be evacuated on foot. When Schellenberg found this out he made a protest to Himmler, declaring that such

a measure was tantamount to murder. At first Himmler had been indignant at Schellenberg's objections, but after an hour or so had repented and issued a counter-order conceding that Schellenberg was right. Whatever the case we could be sure that no catastrophe would present itself at Neuengamme . . . Discussions emerged as to whether the Swedish Red Cross couldn't take care of the whole of the camp in the event of there not being time enough to evacuate Neuengamme before the arrival of the Allied troops. Proposals in this direction were also put forward by Allied ministers to SHAEF headquarters.

So where is the truth? We have to depend entirely on Storch's own accounts to find out what happened that dramatic night of 7–8 April at Kersten's flat in Stockholm. Storch's colleague at the WJC in Geneva, Gerhart Riegner, is not sure there really was any danger of Bergen-Belsen being blown up – it might have been a false alarm. After the end of the war Storch put a straight question to Schellenberg while he was still in residence at Trosa in central Sweden, asking whether it was true that there actually was an order 'to exterminate all Jews and prisoners of war at the concentration camps'. Schellenberg gave an evasive reply: Obergruppenführer Berger had told him about 'the evacuation without exception of all prisoner of war and concentration camps', but following consultation with Schellenberg had not executed the order.

The Israeli historian Dov Dinur is convinced, however, that the call from Kersten's flat the night of 7–8 April saved Bergen-Belsen and the lives of its 60,000 internees. He had seen at least eight depositions from prisoners at Bergen-Belsen stating that that very night dynamite was laid out beneath the barracks. Furthermore, said Dinur, we know who was the 'special commissar' sent by Himmler to Bergen-Belsen. It was SS-Obersturmbannführer Kurt Becher who arrived at the camp on 10 April [sic!] in the company of a Hungarian Jew, Rezsö Kasztner. Dinur claimed that it was Becher who subsequently persuaded the Bergen-Belsen commandant to hand the camp over intact to the British. Afterwards, Becher continued to rescue other concentration camps from demolition, including Neuengamme. Becher was to get his reward in due course – this arch-Nazi became an influential man in Bremen after the war and one of western Germany's wealthiest men. Reszö Kasztner's fate was worse: he was murdered in Israel in 1957 for his collaboration with the Germans during the war.[18]

It seems impossible now after the event to get a clear picture of what exactly was happening on the German side in this respect during the final months of the war. Plainly Hitler intended to wipe out the entire prison-camp population, but it is uncertain whether any formal order to this effect proceeded from his hand. Schellenberg and Berger gave evasive responses, and it is difficult to see why they would not confirm such an order at the end of the war and thus shift all blame on to the dead Führer. It would have been particularly convenient for Berger who, in addition to having been Hitler's chief of staff, had also been head of the entire German prisoner of war administration. It is reasonable to suppose, however, that Himmler's actions during the month of April were still determined in part by his loyalty to Hitler (treason was still being punished by death – Canaris being executed on 9 April) and partly by the war scenario and the Allies' advance. Himmler's verbal pledges to Bernadotte and Schellenberg and his *Vereinbarung* with Kersten were probably of no consequence at all.

Himmler hesitated. As recently as 20 April he had visited Hitler on the occasion of his birthday. There were reports, moreover, of Himmler having sent written orders to the commandants of Dachau and Flossenbürg during the month of April not to surrender the camps to the Allies under any circumstances, to evacuate the camps immediately, and not to allow any prisoners to fall into enemy hands. The charges against Kaltenbrunner in the sense that it was he who had pressed for the extermination of the camp prisoners came from Himmler himself and from one other first-hand source – Schellenberg. Schellenberg, however, is no witness to the truth, and after the war he had every reason to pile all the blame on Kaltenbrunner, thereby minimising Himmler's (and indirectly his own) responsibility.

We have seen how Kaltenbrunner had previously negotiated with both the Danes and the Swiss Red Cross representatives concerning the release of prisoners. Peter Black maintained in his biography of Kaltenbrunner that he spent April 1945 at his headquarters in Austria, which would have given him few opportunities to influence decision-making in Berlin and northern Germany. In reality, it was rather the case that the concentration camps under Kaltenbrunner's jurisdiction – Mauthausen, Dachau and Theresienstadt – actually came to be handed over to the Allies intact, while the prisoners at many camps in northern Germany, such as Neuengamme, Sachsenhausen and Ravensbrück, were evacuated in the most brutal manner. And it was here that Himmler had the ultimate responsibility.[19]

In Stockholm, meanwhile, Storch continued his frenzied work, unaware of the intrigues going on in Germany. He asked Bernadotte on 11 April if during his talks with Himmler he had managed to intervene to alleviate the treatment of the Jews, as well as to bring about a situation whereby the Jews at concentration camps near the war front were not forced to evacuate their camp. He referred to a letter to 'Dr K' concerning in particular the Jews at Bergen-Belsen not having to be evacuated. Didn't Bernadotte have any information regarding the fate of the Danish and Norwegian Jews? What otherwise took place at the meeting that day between Storch and Bernadotte is not known. On 17 April, however, Bernadotte replied in a letter that in his talks with Himmler he 'had got a clear understanding that the concentration camps for Jews in Germany will not be evacuated but be handed over, intact, to the competent Allied military authority'. As regards the Scandinavian Jews, Bernadotte had some good tidings: the following day 423 Jews were expected to land in Sweden – these made up the total number of Scandinavian Jews at Theresienstadt.

Storch now made preparations for his trip to Germany to have direct talks with Himmler, who had via Kersten promised Storch 'safe conduct' and 'every protection' during his visit to Germany. Kersten announced on 12 April, in visibly hurried handwriting, that Himmler expected them and that he and Storch must take a plane by the following Saturday at the latest. On 16 April Gösta Engzell at the Foreign Office legal department signed and issued a sort of 'emergency passport' for Felix Kersten and Gilel Storch for their hazardous journey to Germany.

This is to certify that Medical Counsellor Felix Kersten will be travelling to Berlin during the next few days for talks concerning the release of certain internees. He is travelling in conjunction with the Royal Swedish Ministry of Foreign Affairs, and the Swedish legation in Germany has been requested to give him due protection. All civil and military authorities are called upon to offer him, if necessary, every protection and assistance.

In the light of later controversies regarding Kersten and his intrinsic relationship with the Swedish authorities, we can establish the fact that, at least as far as Kersten's last journey to Germany is concerned, there can be no doubt that he travelled there at the express request of the Swedish government and its Foreign Office. When Kersten flew to Berlin on 19 April, it was not, however, Storch who was his travelling companion.

Two hours before departure for Berlin, Storch defected. What had happened? Storch's own version is that a precondition for his trip was that he could travel to Germany as a Swedish citizen. There were many other instances where it had been a quick and easy operation during the war for the Swedish government to grant Swedish citizenship, and with it a Swedish passport, to foreigners in need, not least Jews. In 1945 Storch only bore an alien's passport. He had now, however, received a promise of Swedish citizenship from both the Swedish prime minister, Per Albin Hansson, and those immediately responsible, minister of justice Bergquist, and the head of the legal department at the Foreign Office, Engzell. Nonetheless, at the last minute foreign minister Günther said 'no'. Günther did not want to deceive Himmler by giving Storch a false Swedish passport – the risk of discovery was too great to take. Furthermore, Storch's wife made a huge scene over her husband's trip. All things considered, both she, Anja, and he, Gilel, had lost almost all their relatives to the Nazi executioners in Latvia. On top of things Gilel was now going to meet the top executioner himself, Heinrich Himmler!

Naturally one can ponder over the reason, or reasons, for Günther refusing official sanction. According to Felix Kersten's son, Arno Kersten, the absence of a valid passport was merely a pretext. Everybody in Stockholm, from the Foreign Office to the Jewish Community, as well as in New York, was agreed that Storch was unsuitable to negotiate with Himmler. He was completely unaccustomed to diplomatic negotiations, and his hot temper could have been fatal in a face-to-face with Himmler. Koblik has pointed out that the Americans and the British, via their legations in Stockholm, right from the start were opposed to letting Storch travel. They considered Storch to be an unsuitable person in the rôle of negotiator. Mallet, the British minister, portrayed Storch as 'very rich, self-important and very nearly a lunatic in some aspects'. What is more, the western Allies were on principle opposed to all negotiation with Himmler. The order then came from the very top, prime minister Winston Churchill: 'No truck with Himmler!' Added to this came Storch's wife and her hysterical refusal to see her husband disappear into the executioners' Germany: 'I'll go and jump in the lake if you go there! I'll go and jump in the lake if you go there!'[20]

Thus it was that when on 19 April Kersten boarded a special swastika-marked German plane at Bromma airport outside Stockholm, he was accompanied instead by another representative of the WJC in Stockholm, a wholesale merchant Norbert Masur. Masur had been a naturalised Swedish citizen since 1931 and of course possessed a Swedish passport. The Foreign Office had had to issue a new protective document at literally the last minute, replacing Storch's name with Masur's. Gilel Storch would never forget how he was prevented by Günther at the last moment from completing his work of rescuing the Jews from the Germans' concentration camps. In a short space of time Storch and Masur were to become bitter enemies.

Transport of Danish and Norwegian Women and Those Who Were Sick to Sweden

After the Swedes' access to the Neuengamme camp Professor Rundberg was made head of medical matters among the Scandinavians while Captain Ankarcrona was in charge of other relations with the camp management. The Reverend Sparrstedt was made responsible for the prisoner of war parcels, social affairs and leisure activities. The latter was such a success that already on 15 April Rundberg was able to attend an entertainment in which the Norwegians and Danes offered 'excellent song and music as well as amusing sketches'. The show was checked by the German head pharmacist at the camp, who failed to understand much of it but did not appear to be particularly amused by some of the English ballads.

By then Bernadotte had secured permission to take all the Danish and Norwegian women plus a small number of Norwegian students to Sweden.

My sources have little to tell about these transports. This may be because of their small number; Bernadotte on 9 April estimated the number of women at around 175. Most of the Scandinavian prisoners at the camp were men. H.H. Koch's extremely accurate Danish statistics show, however, that the first transport of sick people to pass the German–Danish border on 8 April was made up only of women: seventy-four Norwegians, twenty-four Danes and two French women. The following day they were driven on to Sweden, with the exception of one Danish woman, who was released.

Once on the Swedish side the women were accommodated at the spa town of Ramlösa-Brunn, where a camp had been prepared for some time. Göte Friberg, a police inspector in Helsingborg, has told how the first transport comprising 132 women (119 Norwegians, eleven Danes and the two French women, all from Ravensbrück) reached Ramlösa on 9 April. Most of them were young women, 'in fairly good physical shape, dressed, though, in rags and presenting an unkempt appearance to say the least'. Reporting to the National Board of Information a little later, on 16 April, Bernadotte wrote that 200 Danish and Norwegian women had arrived in Sweden. Here Bernadotte expressly mentioned – for the first time among my sources – the fact that Himmler's consent also included Danish and Norwegian women 'of Jewish birth'.

Bernadotte's verbal agreement with Himmler concerning transport of 'sick people' to Sweden had evidently been defined more precisely in talks with Pauly as 'chronically ill'. Their total was estimated by Bernadotte at 300 (Danes?) plus 400 (Norwegians?). It was Professor Rundberg's task and responsibility, in excellent collaboration with his Scandinavian colleagues at Neuengamme, to select these 'chronically ill' people. To begin with, a lot of work was put into the selection process; not that there was any lack of suitable cases, but in order to be able to offer good reasons for each case when presenting them to the senior physician at the camp. Rundberg had of course full confidence in his Danish and Norwegian colleagues and their case records, but still used his stethoscope in duty bound to listen to one or another of the patients. The diagnoses in Latin were typed out by the female Red Cross delegates, whereupon Rundberg could call on the senior physician, Hauptsturmführer Dr Med. Scabinski, for approval.

Scabinski was, as Rundberg put it, a 'pasty type of person, who left an unpleasant impression on most of us'. Scabinski inspected the Scandinavian hospital barracks, performing the most disagreeable hospital round Rundberg had ever experienced. The Scandinavian doctors' medical diagnoses were completely rejected while Scabinski expressed his contempt for the laboratory methods used, blood sedimentation and the like. Instead he made use of 'leg diagnostics': the sick were to show their legs, and if they were swollen like logs or exceptionally thin the person was accepted for transportation under the diagnosis of *schlechter Allgemeinzustand* (poor general health). In time, however, Scabinski grew tired. Instead he demanded new lists and this time with diagnoses made out in German. Here was the Third Reich in its death throes, and new lists in five copies were having to be made out just for the Germans: one for the camp commandant, one for the senior physician, one for Rennau, one for the camp's political section and one for the section for the custody of clothes and other belongings. The political section was particularly troublesome and always crossed off several names.

The first convoy of chronically ill prisoners was able to leave Neuengamme on 9 April, according to Svenson. It consisted of twelve Swedish buses and eight Danish ambulances. It carried 153 internees, nineteen of whom had scarlet fever, thirty intestinal typhus, seventeen spotted typhus, forty tuberculosis, fifty-seven seriously emaciated so-called 'Muslims' with oedema, and a few cases of pneumonia. Most were bed-ridden. All transport of sick people was carried out under Swedish command, usually either Dr Arnoldsson or Lieutenant Svenson. Danish sources showed that it was almost always Danish vehicles which were used and Danish personnel. One member, a doctor called Harald Roesdahl, gave this account:

> The first sick prisoners to be transported were in a terrible state: cases of high-fever spotted typhus, tuberculosis with severe coughing, serious intestinal disease, people with huge open operation wounds in legs and arms, often in the case of so-called 'Muslims', the name given to people whose fat and muscle tissue almost all had disappeared or hung and flapped over visible bones, and whose eyes sunk into their cavities, presenting a glassy and almost fanatical

look. Chances of survival frequently seemed as good as hopeless, but our patients were bent upon leaving this German hell-on-earth at any price, and it might well be their only chance of surviving – but a journey by road of 12–16 hours at the best of times requires an enormous effort, and several times after chasing around the German horror camps Death caught up with us after our arrival at Padborg . . .

The magnificent Swedish buses were the best ones adapted for this type of transport; on either side you could fit three tiers of stretchers and still have room to move about.

As the war scene approached and transport operations proceeded, and with Professor Rundberg managing to get varicose veins and flat-footedness recognized as chronic illnesses (our good old Danish akvavit helped a lot!) and qualifying the patient for transport to Sweden via Denmark, most of the prisoners could be accommodated in a sitting position, and this increased transport capacity considerably.[21]

The sick internees were transferred to the quarantine camp on arrival at Padborg on the Danish side of the border. Here they were de-liced, bathed and fed, and allowed to rest. A hectic, pioneer atmosphere pervaded the frontier station as thousands of camp prisoners had to be taken care of. Barracks were constructed, and there was an invasion of doctors, nurses, women's corps workers and volunteers. Transport operations through Denmark were undertaken by the Danes, under the leadership of the Ministry of Social Affairs, enabling the Swedish White Buses to concentrate their transports in Germany. Soon railway traffic was being used for most of the transport. Danish Rail converted a number of its passenger carriages into ambulance coaches. There was a distinctly primitive air about these wagons with bed sheets made of paper, for example, but still a lot more comfortable than hitherto for the seriously ill. Transport by rail brought its own problems, however. The Danish resistance movement kept its eye on the railway line running south from Fredericia towards Padborg on the German border, and now and again this line was blown up. When these attacks took place, the internees had to be transferred to buses and sometimes travelled on improvised trains to Copenhagen, where they had a further meal, frequently in the so-called Free Port while awaiting the ferry to Malmö in Sweden. The journey ended with a short ferry trip and quarantine in liberty in Sweden. One problem the Danish Ministry of Social Affairs had to contend with was that quite a few of the internees chose to jump ship (or rather the bus or the train) while still in Denmark, in spite of the fact that all the transport operations were guarded.

As the Danish doctor remarked above, German control at Neuengamme grew slacker in step with the Allies' steady approach towards the camp. At the same time the internees became increasingly nervous, more and more of them applying to be qualified as 'chronically ill'. By the time 800 chronically ill prisoners had left the camp, Rundberg was ready to present the Germans with a fresh list of 336 names. Rundberg countered the German protests, explaining that he now defined 'chronically ill' as referring to all those prisoners who were troubled by complaints that could last longer than the duration of the war. As the war would soon be over most of the prisoners could safely be sent home. The Danish statistics for 18 April, carefully compiled, put the number at 1,216 sick men and women, both Danish and Norwegian, having been transported to Sweden. Two days later, on the 20th, all the remaining Scandinavian prisoners were evacuated from Neuengamme.

Danish Policemen are Brought Back to Denmark

The Danish policemen had been spread all around Germany in different camps and *Aussenkommandon*. A Danish Red Cross delegate, a cavalry officer called Zeilau, was able to report home in March 1945 that they 'were happy and satisfied with where they were' at most of the places, and that most of them were receiving their Red Cross parcels. At one camp their pantry contained half a pig and at another Zeilau was treated to first-class home-baked bread. Things were worse at the more southerly camps, however, and most of all at Grosszössen. No Red Cross parcels had reached there since January. The policemen here received poor and scanty fare, were brutally manhandled and made to quarry brown coal in the course of a twelve-hour working day. Not even at this camp, though, did the news of a move to Neuengamme arouse any enthusiasm. The Danish policemen preferred to remain at camps supervised by the Wehrmacht rather than fall into the hands of the Gestapo at Neuengamme. It was not until they realised they would be under Swedish control that they perceived the advantages of a move to Neuengamme.

The remaining Danish policemen had been fetched between 30 March and 2 April from various camps at Mühlberg, Torgau and Oschatz to be transported in the Swedish buses to Neuengamme. Following the Danish Red Cross detachment's arrival at Friedrichsruh at the beginning of April the Danes themselves were then in a position to drive their policemen home for internment at the Frøslev camp. The detailed notes compiled by head of detachment Koch quote the arrival in Denmark of 450 policemen on 3 April, 594 on 5 April and a further 473 on 10 April. The total would then amount to 1,517 policemen. Of these about 1,000 were transferred to Sweden on the 23rd. The remainder were to be ferried over to Malmö on 4 May when, immediately prior to the ferry's departure, they were released after the Danish Foreign Ministry had lodged a request with the German authorities.

Bernadotte had secured an undertaking from Himmler on 2 April that all the Danish policemen would be allowed to return to Denmark, first of all for internment at the Frøslev camp. As we saw earlier, however, the Danish minister in Berlin, Otto Carl Mohr, had already on 8 March been promised by Kaltenbrunner the transfer 'soon' to Frøslev of 1,000 policemen. The remainder would follow within the space of a month, on condition that a Danish police force was reinstated. After the end of the war Bernadotte and Mohr disagreed as to who should claim the honour of bringing the Danish policemen back home. Mohr's version was that their release was entirely thanks to him. What is important here is how we interpret Kaltenbrunner's 'intention' of restoring the Danish police force so that it could then combat Danish espionage. Mohr discussed this question in the notes he recorded after the war, and concluded that it was not a 'condition' for sending the policemen home to Denmark but rather an 'assumption' or 'expectation' on Kaltenbrunner's part. Mohr also referred to a meeting on 19 March at the German Foreign Ministry with its secretary of state and under-secretary to clarify the conditions under which the policemen would return home. Both these German officials then declared that the German 'assumptions' or 'expectations' had nothing to do with sending the policemen home but concerned only the release of the final 500 policemen from the Frøslev camp.

Most of the evidence points towards Mohr's version being the correct one. The man immediately responsible at the Danish Ministry of Social Affairs, H.H. Koch, stated in his account that the return of the Danish policemen was a result of the talks the Danish minister in Berlin had had with Kaltenbrunner, among other issues. Bernadotte himself notified the Swedish Foreign Office as early as 28 March that the Germans had consented to the transfer of 1,000 Danish policemen from Neuengamme to Frøslev. This message was sent, then, a full four days prior to Bernadotte's rendezvous with Himmler but the very same day that Bernadotte had met Richert, Mohr's colleague in Berlin. Bernadotte briefed the National Board of Information on 16 April about the release of some 1,200 Danish policemen following Danish–German talks, but not until the Danes had admitted to the Germans the involvement of 200 of the policemen in sabotage activities. Finally Mohr referred to a conversation he had with Bernadotte in May at the end of the war, in Copenhagen, in which Bernadotte conceded that it was due to Mohr that the policemen returned home. In return Mohr gave Bernadotte the credit for the release of all the other Danish deportees.

Mohr's and Bernadotte's division of labour and responsibilities are not all that clear, however. Mohr's notes date from *after Germany's surrender,* when many were eager to gain a share of the credit – this concerned both Mohr and Bernadotte. Contemporary Danish sources showed no evidence of Mohr's claim. On the other hand there does exist a communication from Mohr dated 4 April in which he reported to Hvass that 'Count Bernadotte has effected movement of all 1,500 policemen to Frøslev', and in which Mohr himself in handwriting has added that Bernadotte succeeded in getting 'everyone' moved there 'very soon'. In any case, the Germans' explanation to Mohr of 19 March had come from the Auswärtiges Amt, which had no authority over the concentration camps, whether under Wehrmacht or under SS control. Himmler's later pledge to Bernadotte, however, could easily be converted into a series of orders from the Reichsführer-SS addressed directly to the camp commandants.

Prisoners in Hard Labour Camps

Apart from all the Scandinavian prisoners at the German concentration camps, there were hundreds of Danes and Norwegians detained at different German prisons and hard labour camps. Following Bernadotte's first round of talks in Germany in February 1945, he was uncertain as to whether the pledges given him by the Germans were to include prisoners at these institutions. After his next two trips to Germany he reported that no progress had been made on this issue – moreover, he never seems to have met the German minister of justice who was responsible for these institutions. Vogt-Svendsen, the Norwegian seamen's chaplain, claimed that Bernadotte had handed over the negotiation tasks concerning these prisoners to him and Brandel. Vogt-Svendsen was a natural choice for this type of work owing to his frequent previous trips to these German institutions. The German Ministry of Justice maintained there were no more than thirty-six Danes and Norwegians in German prisons and hard labour camps, while Vogt-Svendsen and Brandel were able to present a list of more than a thousand Scandinavian names. At the beginning of April – presumably the 6th (as told by Vogt-Svendsen) – Bernadotte in Berlin personally demanded of Schellenberg and Göring that all (Scandinavian) detainees at prisons and hard labour camps be transferred to Neuengamme.

An unsigned report of talks on 8 April between Bernadotte and detective superintendent Göring showed that a transport convoy did leave Friedrichsruh the following day in order to fetch prisoners detained at hard labour camps. After Bernadotte's departure on the 9th Göring was to hand over the necessary documents to the Swedish legation, which in turn would provide the relief convoy with them.

The transport of prisoners from these institutions to Neuengamme was given a fairly scanty description by Vogt-Svendsen as well as in Swedish and Danish reports home. Captain Frykman's is the only coherent account. He related how on 9 April a special transport convoy left bound for Berlin with Captain Folke in charge. It was made up of both Swedish and Danish buses, vehicles adapted for conveying sick patients, and a number of trucks. The convoy's task was to bring back some two hundred

Danish and Norwegian prisoners at hard labour camps in the south of Germany. Vogt-Svendsen, the seamen's chaplain, had visited all of these places and had furnished the relief convoy with information about the Scandinavian prisoners. Captain Sigurd Melin has verified the fact that it was only due to the chaplain's complete lists of names that all the prisoners at the hard labour camps could be rescued. Lieutenant Hallqvist secured the necessary written order and delivered it after nightfall to the convoy's camp outside Berlin. In the order Dr Thierack, der Reichsminister der Justiz, requested that Danish and Norwegian prisoners sentenced by the SS, Polizei or Wehrmacht (including the so-called NN prisoners) be handed over to a Swedish Red Cross convoy. Furnished with this authorisation Frykman's convoy was then able to collect forty or so male and sixteen female prisoners from Waldheim, east of Dresden. This took place only after much resistance from most of the commandants.

There were also three Swedish women under sentence of death at Waldheim. They were not covered by Thierack's authorisation, it is true, but the commandant was persuaded to release them as well after he had been kindly offered a parcel that contained a bottle of Swedish akvavit (prime quality). A Swedish nurse, Margareta Björcke, described the scene when the female prisoners were collected at Waldheim:

> I got permission to enter the institution for women prisoners and help in dressing them. Our arrival was a total surprise for them – it's utterly impossible to describe their quite hysterical outbursts of joy. I quite literally had to plop them down on a chair, half-dressed, and hold them there while I was forced to swear to them that it was no joke, we had actually come to rescue them. There were young and old alike, and it was quite a picture to see a skinny old lady, her face radiant with happiness, eyes red with tears, dressed in a skimpy shirt – wearing a pair of cheap, large pearl ear-rings! These ear-rings she put on first from her parcel of clothes . . .

Work at this institution consisted of plucking feathers. 'Work well and slowly and make it last a long time' was the unusual exhortation these prisoners received. Treatment had been harsh, and they had been commanded to do all and everything, but the place was clean and they told us the food was nicely cooked even though there wasn't much of it.[22]

Frykman went on to describe how prisoners were brought from other institutions at Dresden, Cottbus, Luckau, Zeithin and Groitsch. At this stage transport operations began to get unpleasantly close to battle lines. At Cottbus it was with great difficulty that a prisoner was found – half the city was in the hands of the Germans, the other half was held by the Russians. When on the way home the convoy reached the Swedish legation's provisional quarters in the castle at Schönhausen, the Swedish blue and yellow flag was indeed still hoisted over the castle roof, but the Swedish legation had been evacuated the evening before, and a German field hospital was now being set up. Wounded German soldiers reported that the Americans were dangerously close to cutting off the road the Swedes would be using for their journey back.

On their way back to Neuengamme the Swedes saw a German vehicle almost identical to the Swedish Red Cross detachment's bus, painted white and furnished with a red cross – all that was missing was the Swedish flag. The Germans were evidently aware that the Swedish vehicles were being spared attacks by Allied aircraft. It was not long before more white-painted German vehicles appeared. The return trip went alright, however, and on 11 April the convoy was ready to drop off at Neuengamme its male prisoners from the hard labour camps. The female prisoners were accommodated at a camp outside Hamburg for further transport directly to Sweden, together with other Scandinavian women.

This first transport, which took place between 9 and 11 April, saw 211 prisoners fetched from different institutions in the Leipzig–Halle–Torgau area. It comprised the first Swedish platoon of twelve buses plus Danish reinforcement. There remained some 400 other prisoners detained at the Mecklenburg hard labour camp, to be collected later on, according to Captain Folke. This action was reported to have been carried out on the night of 15 April, when 524 prisoners were transported from Mecklenburg. This made a grand total of 735 prisoners, a figure that tallied well with the accurate Danish statistics, which showed 718 Scandinavians (479 Norwegians, 228 Danes and 11 Swedes) rescued from German jails and hard labour camps. Frykman's subsequent report summarising the situation mentioned a total of 600 prisoners proceeding from hard labour camps having been transported from all over Germany. As often is the case, the figures from different sources varied.

Theresienstadt

The town of Theresienstadt was founded *c.*1780 as a garrison town by the Austrian emperor Josef II and named after his mother the empress Maria Theresia. It lies on the main road between Dresden and Prague in the Czech Republic and nowadays goes under the name of Terezin. After the Germans annexed the Czechoslovak Sudetenland in 1938, the town came to lie in the German protectorate of Bohemia/Moravia. The head of the protectorate, Reinhard Heydrich, and the Gestapo head of Jewish affairs, SS-Obersturmbannführer Adolf Eichmann, decided in 1941 that Theresienstadt should be employed as a ghetto for the protectorate's roughly 90,000 Jews on their way to the extermination camps further east. At the Wannsee conference in 1942, however, the Germans determined that Theresienstadt would also be a 'senior ghetto' for Jews aged over sixty-five as well as for those who came from Altreich (Germany–Austria) and from the Ostland (Baltic states). Further measures included bringing here 'prominent Jews', such as eminent Jewish politicians, public officials, scientists, artists and other representatives of the cultural scene, as well as Jews who had distinguished themselves in the First World War. Theresienstadt was to be a model Jewish ghetto for the world and was to form part of Eichmann's propaganda offensive. The Jews' compulsory evacuation from their homes to reside here was known as *Wohnsitzverlegung* (relocation of living accommodation), the senior ghetto was renamed Senior Citizens Residence, and the Jews were granted formal self-administration.

There were only about four thousand people living in the town in 1941. The thirteen large barracks and about two hundred small dwellings were in a poor state of repair and almost all of them were without sanitary installation. Water was unhygienic, while gas and electricity had only been installed in the most recently renovated barracks. Close to the garrison district itself was a small fortress which even before the Gestapo had arrived was equipped with solitary cells, scaffolds and other methods of

171

execution. There was a rail connection, too, in the vicinity. In November 1941 the first work platoon of Jews from Prague began to convert garrison town Theresienstadt into a Jewish ghetto, and within a short time the goods wagons were arriving with their cargos of thousands of Czech Jews.

Formally, the self-administrating Theresienstadt was run by a *Judenälteste* (Jew Elder). He was appointed by Zentralstelle für jüdische Auswanderung (Eichmann's local Gestapo office), in Prague. A Jewish Elder Council of twenty people, also appointed by the Gestapo office, was responsible to the *Judenälteste*, and it was to this council that the Danish chief rabbi Friediger in time would belong as a member. The self-administrative structure encompassed such elements as its own Ghettowache (police force), a bank of its own (Bank der jüdischen Selbstverwaltung) and a currency of its own (Theresienstadt kronen). There is much evidence that the Jewish self-administration put in a lot of effort to improve conditions at the camp and turn it into a model ghetto. Water and electricity supply improved considerably owing to the presence of a highly qualified Jewish work force. The self-administrative process also led to a reduction in the SS administrative unit to some 10–15 people. When the Danes came to Theresienstadt there were about 45,000 Jews, squeezed into a town designed for some 10,000 inhabitants at the most. Out of Theresienstadt's total number of 141,000 prisoners, no more than thirty-one would be 'de-ghettonised', meaning sent home, before the Danish Jews could be rescued in April 1945.

All Danish Jews who had been arrested by the Germans from 1 October 1943 were sent to Theresienstadt. One exception has been recorded: a Danish Jew who died at Auschwitz on his way to Theresienstadt. A list compiled by the Danish Ministry of Social Affairs contained a total of 481, while the definition of 'Jew' and of 'Dane' could vary. Fifty-two of them were to die at Theresienstadt, although none owing to starvation or violence on the part of the SS or others. Causes of death were old age, illnesses and physical collapse. The Danish Jews at Theresienstadt were the smallest contingent, but were also a favoured minority on the strength of Denmark's special status in relation to the German state. As far back as October 1943 twenty 'mistakenly arrested' Danish Jews (half-Jews and Jews of mixed marriages) were allowed to leave Theresienstadt and return home. Right from the start the Danes were permitted to send clothes parcels to their compatriots – on 21 February 1944 the first food parcel was sent to them from Denmark.

Werner Best and Adolf Eichmann concluded an agreement on 4 November 1943 whereby all Danish Jews would remain at Theresienstadt and not proceed further east to the extermination camps. This same document stipulated that Danish authorities would be able to visit the Danish Jews at Theresienstadt. Such visits would form part of Eichmann's propaganda campaign proving that the rumours circulating about a German policy of extermination were groundless. After a lot of delays a Danish visit was planned and completed on 22 June 1944. Denmark was represented by department head Frants Hvass from the Ministry of Foreign Affairs and senior physician Eigil Juel Henningsen for the Danish Red Cross. Delegates from Germany's Red Cross and the International Red Cross in Geneva also took part in the visit.

The visit became a huge propaganda success for the Germans. The delegation left an overwhelmingly positive report, and a cynical view would be that the report produced successful results: the Danish Jews subsequently were allowed to keep their privileges, which were also extended to the 135 Danish Jews who had not been accepted by the Germans as Danish citizens. The essential Danish food parcels were limited to a single five-kilo parcel a month, one letter home a month was permitted, and books to the tune of a thousand copies could be sent to make up a small Danish library at Theresienstadt.

Irrespective of the happy result for the Danes, the exhibition of Theresienstadt on 22 June 1944 in reality was an enormous German propaganda bluff. Prior to the visit some 17,500 prisoners, mainly elderly people and cripples, had been sent to their deaths in the gas chambers in Poland. Thus the overpopulation was reduced and the inhabitants gave the place a more youthful appearance. A school was founded before the visit took place, even though in the course of the visit itself it happened to be 'closed for holidays'. The houses were given a fresh coat of paint, a dining-room was built, and a children's playground and a park resplendent with newly seeded lawns was inaugurated. A pavilion was built where a thirty-man orchestra under the baton of the Danish conductor Peter Deutsch [sic!] played merry music in honour of the Jewish 'health cure guests' and the visiting delegation. The streets were given proper names and the ghetto was renamed Jüdisches Siedlungsgebiet (Jewish Settlement District). More than anything else, the Danish Jews were made much of and courted. Some of them were able to move into real family homes, and the four 'Danish houses', as they came to be known, were even provided with furniture.

When the Danish delegation had gone home the façade was removed. First, however, the Germans shot a propaganda film: *Theresienstadt – ein Dokumentarfilm aus dem jüdischen Siedlungsgebiet*. Afterwards the mass deportation of Jews eastwards was resumed. All those who had taken part in Eichmann's campaign of embellishment disappeared with the exception of the Danish Jews. Morale then sank disastrously. Expectations born of the improvements undertaken up to 22 June had proved to be short-lived. 'Here the law of life is self-obsession', as the Danish Jew Rudi Freinsilber was later to write, based on his diary notes.

The Danish Jews are Rescued from Theresienstadt

We have already witnessed the fears expressed by the Danes that the Swedes would not be in time to rescue the Danish Jews. This apprehension was mainly shown by the Danes' liaison officer at Friedrichsruh, Johannes Holm. In his book *Sandheden om de vite busser* (The Truth about the White Buses), Holm presented a very unfavourable picture of Bernadotte's performance in particular. He maintained that he had been informed by Rennau that there existed an order issued from 'the highest German level' (Hitler?) to the effect that no Danish Jews were to be removed from Theresienstadt. Kaltenbrunner was of course opposed to the transports in general and would hardly have allowed any at all for the Jews. Moreover, Gruppenführer Müller had stressed that the Jews could not be allowed to mingle with the Norwegian and Danish Aryan prisoners at Neuengamme. In Rennau's opinion the only chance was to take the Jews straight to Sweden. The situation, then, was beginning to become urgent, very urgent. American troops were approaching Dresden from the west and the Russians were visible not far away to the east of Dresden. The two armies would be meeting very soon and the White Buses would find their transport path from Theresienstadt cut off.

Holm claimed that at the last staff meeting held before Bernadotte travelled back to Sweden on 8 April, no Swedish transport from Theresienstadt was planned. As he had done earlier, Holm reminded the Swedes that the Danish Jews had to be rescued and pointed to the urgent nature of the situation. Bernadotte then announced that he had given up on the transport of the Danish Jews. He had realised that fetching the Jews from Theresienstadt could very well jeopardise further transport operations involving Scandinavian prisoners, on account of the opposition posed by Kaltenbrunner and his Reichssicherheitshauptamt. Holm, Hvass and Nielsen, in great agitation, agreed upon a purely Danish rescue operation using the Danish buses and ambulances which were then stationed at Friedrichsruh. Transport of Jews to Sweden, however, necessitated a permit from the Gestapo in Berlin. The Danes decided to wait for Bernadotte to leave for Sweden on 9 April. In the meantime Hvass promised Rennau he would be granted a residence permit in Denmark after the war if he could see to it that all the Danish prisoners were home in Denmark before the end of the war.

The following day Holm drove Rennau to the RSHA headquarters in Berlin, but in vain. None of the people responsible was available, but with a mind to future necessities Holm dropped off a Danish food parcel for the staff at headquarters. He then notified the Swedish officers Arnoldsson and Folke on 11 April of the Danish plans for a Danish convoy to Theresienstadt. Folke pointed out the risks of using the producer-gas-powered Danish vehicles, which would require a journey lasting two whole days longer than if the petrol-driven Swedish vehicles were chosen. He could quite certainly arrange permission for this from Major Frykman if the convoy was put under Swedish leadership. Frykman did indeed place the buses at their disposal on condition that Captain Folke was made head of convoy. They set off for Theresienstadt on 12 April with Folke in command. There were twenty-three petrol-driven Swedish buses, twelve Swedish passenger cars and three motor-cycles, Swedish and Danish drivers, in addition to petrol-driven Danish ambulances with Danish doctors and nurses.

There is a lot of evidence to suggest that Holm's account, which does not exactly flatter Bernadotte, is not entirely truthful. In the first place, this is the version he gave in his book published in 1984, while in the report that he himself said was jotted down straight after the end of the war in 1945 he did not mention a word about Bernadotte or the Swedes having called off the rescue operation of the Danish Jews from Theresienstadt, or that a purely Danish convoy was being planned to go there. On the contrary, in that report Holm indicated that right from the end of March Hvass had brought up the subject of the Danish Jews with Dr Rennau and Count Bernadotte, who had both 'made as great an effort as possible'. Holm changed this wording in his 1984 book to 'Count Bernadotte has announced that in Sweden they would be very happy to receive the Danish Jews.'

In the second place, it is rather strange to imagine that the Gestapo should be in a position first to arrange for the Jews to be transported and then to have them welcomed by the Swedes in Sweden. All decisions concerning both the White Buses in Germany (including the Danish buses, since they formally lay under the Swedish detachment) and their reception in Sweden were of course the responsibility of the Swedish authorities and, in practice, of the leader of the expedition, Bernadotte. Schellenberg, sure enough, made no mention of this in his so-called 'Trosa notes', while Franz Göring, on the other hand, attributed the rescue of the Jews from Theresienstadt in fact to Schellenberg, and secondly to Kersten.[23]

A third point to consider is that neither in the Swedish accounts from 1945 – Bernadotte's, Arnoldsson's, Frykman's and Svenson's books and Melin's notes later – nor in Captain Folke's memoirs from 1999 was anything said about these Danish–Swedish differences prior to the Theresienstadt convoy's departure on 12 April. Frykman referred to the rescue of the Jews from Theresienstadt as that point of honour 'Bernadotte had so intensively worked for.' According to Folke it was indeed Bernadotte himself who had drawn up a plan to send Folke along with a transport of French prisoners from Neuengamme to the Swiss border and then, after having handed them over to the Swiss Red Cross, 'carry on to Theresienstadt and come back with all the Scandinavian Jews there'. The plan was presented to Rennau together with the proposal that the operation be put into practice 'at once'. Rennau, however, said 'No', day after day, in expectation of the go-ahead from Himmler's headquarters, until finally one morning he said 'Yes' – and by then 'we'd almost forgotten what we'd been planning!'[24]

In the fourth place the abundant Swedish and Danish primary sources from this period made no mention either of any Danish–Swedish antagonism or of any plans for a separate Danish expedition to Theresienstadt. On the contrary, the reports were fully in line with Folke's version. For instance, Paulson notified Copenhagen on 7 April that the mission to Theresienstadt would be 'hurried along as much as possible'. The same day Folke telephoned his Foreign Office that the Jews at Theresienstadt would be collected 'some time next week'. Planning procedures for 7–10 April included a transport of Jews (between 420 and 800) from Theresienstadt via Neuengamme to the Danish border marked down for 9 April – but, let it be noted, *with Danish buses*. All of this was taking place while Bernadotte was still in Germany. Bernadotte's talks with Göring on 8 April revealed, moreover, that 'Rennau has received instructions that the Danish Jews at Theresienstadt may be collected immediately'. Brandel reported on 9 April that on the same day Göring would be travelling to Theresienstadt to gather together all the Jews there so that they could be fetched on the 12th or 13th. But then something happened . . . Hvass notified the Danish Ministry of Foreign Affairs that concerning Theresienstadt 'a tricky situation has arisen. Dr Rennau and Dr Holm have driven up to Berlin today. Instructions are expected there tomorrow, and in any case a convoy is being sent as swiftly as possible to Theresienstadt.' Hvass made no reference to any Danish plans for a Danish convoy. Neither did Mohr, the Danish minister in Berlin (from 28 March) in his sixty-five-page report, or departmental head Koch in his briefer account.

It was certainly a tricky situation that was now evolving. Before the departure for Theresienstadt the Swedish personnel were lined up and told that the journey about to be undertaken would involve very considerable risks and anyone not wishing to take part was asked to step forward. Nobody moved – 'It was a moment to be proud of.' Right on time the convoy drove past the headquarters at Friedrichsruh. Richert, the minister, had established his provisional office there since the Swedish legation had been forced to leave Berlin for good. Just as the convoy was passing the castle Richert received a telephone call from the Foreign Office in Stockholm. They informed Richert that an expedition to Theresienstadt was now quite impossible as the Russians had already reached the highway between Dresden and Berlin. Richert was ordered to stop the whole operation. He coolly gave the reply that it was too late: the convoy was already on its way. Captain Folke was then given the order to set off at once.

The Swedes did, then, actually try to stop the whole operation, but it was certainly not Bernadotte who lay behind the decision; it was the Ministry of Foreign Affairs. That very day Bernadotte wrote a letter reassuring a family member and informing her that the day before a transport convoy had left to collect all the Danish and Norwegian internees at Theresienstadt. We might recall at this stage Storch's view that it was entirely to Bernadotte's credit that the Danish Jews were rescued, whereas it was Günther who opposed Jews as well being brought to Sweden.

Meanwhile Holm's fast car had taken him and Rennau straight to Berlin. Holm took along three Danish lists: Danish Jews imprisoned in Denmark, Danish Jews imprisoned in Germany, and stateless Jews – Jews, that is, who had fled to Denmark prior to 1940 and who had later been arrested in Denmark. Rennau's negotiations with the Reichssicherheitshauptamt in Berlin were slow and tedious, however. When there was a break to eat, Holm produced a few Danish food parcels and a couple of bottles of Danish akvavit. Once the bottles had been emptied, the necessary documents were duly signed and stamped. The RHSA undertook to communicate to both the governor of the Protectorate of Bohemia–Moravia and to the commandant at the Theresienstadt camp that the Danish Jews were to be handed over.

A day later Holm and Rennau reached Theresienstadt. After meeting the commandant, Holm was given the opportunity to speak to the Danish Jews' spokesman, chief rabbi Friediger, who gave this account:

> I was led into the commandant, who was sitting in his office together with a senior SS officer and a stranger. It was Dr Holm from Copenhagen! He it was who spoke and informed me that the Danes were to leave for Sweden and would be collected by Folke Bernadotte's buses. I imagine that if Heaven had opened up in front of me at that moment, the glory I would have witnessed could

hardly have caused a greater impression on me than this news. I sat on my chair petrified, and my face must have worn such an odd expression that Dr Holm was obliged to repeat his message and the camp commandant, in unusually mild voice, confirm it. Was this now but a dream, another of my flights of fancy? No – it was the real thing![25]

Holm and Friediger checked Holm's lists of names. It was not a simple matter. During their stay at Theresienstadt Danish Jews and Jews of other nationalities had entered into marriage. Children had been born. There were also formal engagements with Jews of other nationalities. For the sake of Danish and Jewish morals, four weddings were held at the camp that night. All of these Jews joined the main body for the journey home. For similar moral reasons, however, a number of Danish Jews, already married back in Denmark but who had entered into new relationships at the camp, were left behind. Two days later, on 15 April, the Danish Jews were ready for departure. Meanwhile, Holm and Rennau had been able to secure the necessary documents at the governor's headquarters in Prague. The city was basking in beautiful spring sunshine and Rennau was able to fetch his wife and daughter who now began a long flight from their splendid private residence in Brno.

The Swedish convoy had by then embarked on its slow journey, which was much longer and much less pleasant. Bernadotte had got Rennau to agree to the Swedes transporting 456 prominent French prisoners down to the Swiss border while on their way to Theresienstadt. The Gestapo had suggested the Flossenbürg camp in Bavaria as a meeting point, where the Swiss Red Cross would collect the French contingent. Initially the convoy drove along the main highway between Hamburg and Berlin via Potsdam, also resplendent in lovely spring weather and as yet undamaged by the trials and tribulations of warfare. The French were in high spirits and ate hungrily from the Swedish food parcels.

The journey then took a southerly direction and a more and more ominous turn. Flossenbürg turned out to be a concentration camp of the very worst type, where forced labour in stone quarries was driving prisoners to their deaths. The camp commandant knew nothing of any arrangement with the Swiss Red Cross. A four-hour, very unpleasant dialogue between Captain Folke and the camp commandant ended with Folke persuading him to sign a slip of paper confirming that he was unable to receive the French prisoners. The Swedes were without sufficient fuel to drive the French straight into Switzerland so they were obliged to take them with them to Theresienstadt. Later on they would learn that the legendary Admiral Canaris had been executed at Flossenbürg a few days before their arrival there, and that all the other prisoners had been murdered after their departure.

The following night the White Buses reached Theresienstadt where the friendly commandant had arranged board and lodging for the Swedish crew. The French passengers therefore had to be dumped there.

During the night of 15 April Germans and Jews packed 424 Danish Jews into the Swedish buses while the camp orchestra played:

> . . . The vehicles were then loaded with luggage and passengers. An incredible sight it was . . . The buses almost doubled their height, so much was packed on top of the roofs. Suitcases and parcels, children's prams, chairs and tables, cupboards and shelves. It was understandable that they wanted to bring along as much of their belongings as possible, but we wouldn't have had a chance in a million to manoeuvre all the viaducts and overhead tram wires. So the buses had to be reloaded amidst tearful protest and all bulky objects had to be left on the ground around. When we finally got going and could start our journey home we and our passengers were given a hearty cheer by masses of happy people who sang to the accompaniment of the brass band.[26]

At the last moment the band's Danish conductor handed over his baton to his successor and jumped into the passenger seat in Captain Folke's car.

The journey home to Sweden had started, making straight for Dresden. The Swedes were confronted with a city completely razed to the ground when they got there, and the German military governor told them that the motorway running from Dresden to Berlin had been cut off by the Russians. Folke held a council of war with the Swedish officers, told them he disbelieved the German governor and gave orders for the convoy to run the risk and continue the journey. It turned out that the Soviet war front was very close, some 10–15 kilometres away. At top speed – some eighty kilometres an hour – the entire expedition (save one solitary motor cycle dispatch rider) managed to drive along this autobahn in three to four hours and unharmed reached their night encampment outside Potsdam.

That night Potsdam was subjected to a devastating air raid at the same time as the Red Army began its final offensive on Berlin with intensive artillery attacks. The following morning, under cover of blacked-out windows, the White Buses passed long lines of German civilians fleeing bombed-out Potsdam. There remained an almost risk-free stretch northwest towards the border with Denmark. The rumble of cannon fire could be heard in the west, and this time it was the British war front. The expedition finally reached Padborg on 17 April, and the journey through Denmark was one long triumphal procession. One day later the Danish Jews were ferried over to Malmö in southern Sweden. All the passengers swarmed out of the buses onto the ferry amid chaotic scenes. The Gestapo officers on board were furious but were compelled to abandon control procedures. In the turmoil a further ten Danes were smuggled over to Sweden.

On 17 April Bernadotte was in a position to communicate to Storch that all the Scandinavian Jews – a total of 423 – had been rescued and would be brought to Sweden from Theresienstadt. The day before, however, the detachment had reported the number of Jews as being 429. Had six of them jumped boat and stayed in Denmark?

With a year and a half at Theresienstadt behind them and a further three weeks in Sweden, the Danish Jews in the first week of May were sent back home to Denmark. By then the International Red Cross had taken Theresienstadt under its wing. In the commandant's building a document was discovered announcing that 10 May was the date fixed for razing the entire ghetto to the ground. The Soviet army passed Theresienstadt on 8 May, however, on its march towards Prague, and on the 13th a Russian major took command of 'model ghetto' Theresienstadt.

11

The White Buses: Ravensbrück

One of the drivers of the Swedish buses described the transportation from Ravensbrück:

> Early in the morning we drove the buses up to where embarkation would take place. Our passengers-to-be were already lined up in long rows while mainly female SS officers strutted around in their impeccable uniforms. The first transport – the Scandinavians – were sent on board with true German attention to detail. Lists of names and accuracy in checking them off. The second and third time round, though, we just loaded in as many as there was room for without too much control. Many people were dressed in the prisoners' striped clothing, while others wore a mix of civilian clothing, such as an overcoat with the compulsory big white cross on the back. Most had short hair, some of them with crew cuts which they tried to hide with a head scarf or a rag . Their clothes and shoes were worn out, filthy and shoddy. People's ages were anything between young teenagers and middle-aged folk. They were grey, thin and tired in appearance, but most of them could walk without assistance. They naturally brightened up when they realised we were going to take care of them. They did, however, tell us that the SS women had tried to dampen their spirits by saying that they were now going to leave to be gassed and cremated.
>
> The second transport was mostly made up of French, Belgian and Dutch women. I remember how, when we stopped for them to

relieve themselves – which the Germans required be done in open fields so no one would try to escape – the women ran around looking for green herbs, which they picked and ate. Particular favourites were dandelion plants, the leaves of which had just begun to sprout in the spring weather. Using twigs and their fingers, they dug up the plants by the roots, cleaned off the soil and ate them.[1]

Germany-based Swedish Citizens Are Brought Home

Back in February 1945, prior to Bernadotte's trip to Berlin, a small Red Cross convoy had been sent to Berlin to bring back those Swedes who wished to return home to Sweden. The people concerned were chiefly women married to German citizens. Captain Hultgren was in charge of that transport, and he was among those who had returned to Sweden on 5 April together with the producer-gas-powered buses, now in a battered condition. Bernadotte decided then that the detachment that had remained in Germany would bring these Swedish people home too.

My primary sources say very little about these transport operations. The only name among those women quoted in the memoirs is that of a well-known film actress, Kristina Söderbaum. She had married the film director Veit Harlan in Germany, a man notorious for his blatantly anti-Semitic propaganda film *Jud Süss*. One of those responsible for these transports, the Countess Majlis von Eickstedt (née Lüning), wrote some fascinating memoirs about her work in Germany in 1939–45. She described how the Gestapo at the last moment denied Söderbaum a permit to leave Germany, and so Söderbaum landed up in a British internment camp.[2]

Records of police interviews with scores of these women are available for study at Malmö city archives. Most of them had had Swedish parents but had married in Germany and thereby lost their Swedish citizenship. The tales they told were a motley collection of highly dramatic moments experienced in the course of their lives. The compulsory question of 'political stance' more often than not gave the response 'had no political affiliation and no interest in politics' or, more briefly, 'not politically interested' or even more appropriate 'neutral standing'. Several women declared themselves anti-Nazi and had in a number of cases been directly affected by Gestapo methods. One of these (no. 6795 in the register) was of Jewish origin and her son had refused to report for military service. Another (no. 6858), a man of German nationality but half-Jewish, had been threatened with his life but managed to reach Sweden with a provisional Swedish passport and under a false name. A woman known as IB (no. 6742) had been evacuated to Dachau, where she had 'caught a glimpse of what conditions were like at a concentration camp'. On the occasion of the second White Bus expedition to Dachau she had managed to get a lift in the convoy's petrol-driven car as far as Aumühle. Several women maintained that they had been ardent National Socialists from the beginning but had changed their opinions as time went on. There were two, nevertheless, who held on to their Nazi ideas. IW (no. 6678) had been working as recently as January 1945 with the German radio station broadcasting from Königsberg to the Nordic countries.

There were quite probably more Swedish women with a Nazi background among those who now seized an opportunity to leave the country with the Third Reich in its death throes. Folke Schimanski, for instance, told the story in 1999 of how he, his mother and his sister Vera were rescued in 1945 by the White Buses and brought to Sweden. His mother had worked as a censor of letters at the German Defence Staff while his sister Vera, before marrying Assar Oredsson, had been married to the Swedish Nazi leader Sven-Olof Lindholm. After the war, in her capacity of Vera Oredsson, she came to be known as one of the leading lights in the Swedish Nazi movement.

In Frykman's book, Lieutenant Agartz described his many trips accompanying these German Swedes. Starting in February, they had been assembled at Lübeck where the Swedish Church served as a meeting point. (Bernadotte and Frykman also mention Aumühle, near Hamburg, as a meeting point.) Most of them had luggage to take with them. Responsibility for the work at Lübeck lay with legation secretary Count Lewenhaupt, the Reverend Hellqvist and Countess von Eickstedt. Board and lodging would be guaranteed and all the necessary documents and passports put in order. In the final stages of the war the number of applicants grew rapidly. Many people then suddenly remembered distant relatives in Sweden, or as in an example quoted by Agartz 'my husband's aunt had a servant girl who was married to a man whose cousin had been engaged to a Swedish girl!'

As soon as transport facilities had been granted a so-called *Schnellvisa* would be issued for the hundred or so fortunate ones. Those selected were then informed and requested to be ready to be fetched at different points in and around Lübeck. The business of boarding the buses turned out to present one of the biggest difficulties: everybody wanted to sit at the front! Sometimes the Swedish drivers only went as far as Padborg, and sometimes they drove straight to Copenhagen. It was a long journey and there were slim chances of being able to sleep for any length of time. Things were not made any better by some passengers complaining it was too cold in the bus and others that it was too hot – some thought the bus drove too fast and others too slowly.

At times someone would try the Swedish drivers' patience to the limits – a Swedish lady complained there was no brandy on board the bus. Another lady angrily wondered whether she was really expected to spend the night at a Danish youth hostel sleeping on straw on the floor. Neither was Red Cross official Eric Karlsson over-pleased with the transportation of these women. They didn't seem to care two hoots about the help they were receiving. The mood changed for the better, however, in Denmark when the passengers were fed Danish food and milk in limitless quantities. According to Agartz, a total of 1,400 'German Swedes' were moved from Lübeck to Denmark.

Nonetheless, this is a surprisingly high figure. Both Bernadotte and Frykman reported after the war that only about 400 'German Swedes' had been gathered together and brought to Sweden by the detachment. The National Swedish Office for Aliens, on the other hand, on 19 April reported to Möller, minister of social affairs, that between 26 March and 18 April 794 'German Swedes' had reached Malmö via Red Cross transportation. By the same date 741 Danes (including the 421 Jews), 444 Norwegians and the two French women had come to Sweden. This would mean that in this first batch the White Buses would have brought more 'German Swedes' home than Danes or Norwegians! Sergeant Lööw much later on related how between 15 and 20 April his Danish bus fetched the last Swedes out of a Berlin almost completely encircled. Lööw managed to extract twenty-two Swedes from a Berlin in flames via a narrow corridor north of the city wedged in between the Soviet Eastern Front and the British–American forces flanking the south-west. The vicar at the Swedish Church in Berlin, Myrgren, chose to remain at his post – he was later to be taken prisoner by the Russians, who burnt down the church. Myrgren, however, was able to make his way home to Sweden via Moscow and Leningrad.

In the light of these events the Foreign Office's and Bernadotte's actions concerning the Swedish Jews within the German sphere of authority has a special interest. Engzell at the Foreign Office sent a message on 19 April to Brandel – who was also present at Friedrichsruh – stating 'the particular desirability of doing everything possible to find the Swedish Jews from Theresienstadt', and especially the Hess and Hartogson families and Mrs Behrendt. The Foreign Office also added a reminder about the Bondy children. This message from Engzell included a special petition to Bernadotte dated 14 April concerning the Hess family: husband, wife and five-year-old daughter. They had been living in the Netherlands in 1943 and had acquired Swedish citizenship, which the German authorities had not recognised, and in 1944 the family was deported to Theresienstadt. In his hurried reply Bernadotte was unable to ascertain whether the family formed part of the transport leaving Theresienstadt, although he suspected that they had not been passed as Scandinavians this time either.

There was no cause for too much concern, however: Bernadotte had found out that the Germans were not going to evacuate the camp but would hand it over to the Allies. He had pencilled in details concerning the Hartogson family. There were two children, and the wife was Swedish-born and had her Swedish citizenship restored, while the husband was a Danish national. We have seen earlier that both Bernadotte and Kersten had made great efforts to secure the release of the Bondy children but without success. On 8 April Bernadotte instructed Sturmbannführer Danziger, a Gestapo liaison officer, to fetch the Bondy children from Bergen-Belsen, but Danziger was evidently hindered from doing so by the course of events. Bergen-Belsen was liberated by the British on 15 April and the children's whereabouts were not discovered by the Swedes until July.

The French Prisoners

During his 1944 visit to Paris Bernadotte had been inspired to come to the aid of French prisoners in the German concentration camps. Nordling, the consul general, had originally proposed assistance for the perhaps 20,000 French women imprisoned at Ravensbrück.[3] Foreign Office instructions of 27 March had extended Bernadotte's mandate to include transportation to Neuengamme of 'approximately 25,000 French women'. It is of course easy to speculate on whether Bernadotte's own French origins were influential in selecting the French after the Scandinavians. Nevertheless, during his third round of talks in Germany Bernadotte had not succeeded in obtaining more than just a permit for the Swedish detachment to provide the French women at Ravensbrück with 15,000 food parcels. These were to be delivered directly to the camp by the Red Cross buses at the same time as the Scandinavian women were picked up. Bernadotte's petition to Himmler for the 25,000 French women as well to be taken to Neuengamme had been rejected, even though a dozen or so did eventually travel straight to Sweden.

In the final stages of the war there was the semblance of an unofficial race between the Swedes and the Swiss to rescue prisoners from the concentration camps in Germany. In both cases it was the respective Red Cross organisations that were active. As far as Ravensbrück was concerned, at the start of April it seemed that the Swiss were the more successful. The Swedish Foreign Office received news from Berne that Burckhardt, president of the ICRC, had had a meeting with high-ranking Nazi officials at Konstanz. Burckhardt had secured German consent in principle for the Red Cross to repatriate Belgian and French female prisoners. About one hundred vehicles stood in preparation on the Swiss side of the border. No permit had yet been received by the Swiss, however, by 17 April, and unlike Bernadotte Burckhardt had not had the opportunity to meet Himmler. That same day Sverker Åström composed a memo dealing with queries from Burckhardt, sent partly to the Swedish legation in Berne and partly directly to the Salén shipping company in Stockholm, as to the possibility of a Swedish ship fetching the Belgian and French women prisoners by sea and then accommodating them in Sweden. The Swedes were in agreement in principle, but pointed to the huge risks involved with such a transport operation over the seas, and added a reminder that all repatriation procedures up to that time had had to be carried out overland through Denmark.

Bernadotte took the train to Malmö on 18 April, and via Copenhagen reached Friedrichsruh on the evening of the 19th. He conveyed a formal request from Prince Carl, the Red Cross chairman, to obtain permission from the German authorities for the Swedish Red Cross detachment to move the French civilian prisoners from Ravensbrück to Neuengamme. These prisoners would subsequently be placed on the same footing as the Norwegian and Danish civilian prisoners, in the event of a transfer from Neuengamme as well.

The White Buses Hit by the War

On their way to Theresienstadt the Swedes had noticed more and more German army vehicles, as well as passenger cars carrying German officers, painted white and decorated with a red cross. Apart from the fact that this contravened international law it produced in the Swedes dismal premonitions. The moment this German abuse became known to the Allies' intelligence services the White Bus symbol would lose its protective character and the transport operations would face greater danger. Previously British and American aircraft had swooped threateningly at a low height over the buses, but had tipped their wings at the last moment as a sign of recognition and then flown on.

In Stockholm on 11 April the military attaché at the British legation had sent the Swedish Foreign Office the alarming warning that the British Air Force's 'tactical battle zone' was now approaching the area in which Bernadotte's expedition was operating. Danger grew of Allied aircraft attacks on all road traffic. The Foreign Office forwarded the message to minister of defence Sköld and to Bernadotte.

The Allies' low-flying fighter planes (dubbed *Tiefflieger* by the Germans) pursuing the retreating German military convoys now became more and more troublesome for the White Buses. On 18 April the Danish base camp at Friedrichsruh was subjected to an unabashed fighter plane attack, probably American in the judgement of the Danes but British according to the Swedish report. Four Danish bus drivers and a Danish nurse were slightly injured by the machine-gun fire, while a dozen Danish vehicles were blown up. Most of the Swedish personnel and vehicles had not yet returned from the Theresienstadt expedition at the time. The Swedish minister in anger ascertained as a fact that according to all the eye-witnesses the attack had been carried out after due reconnaisance flight. A day later another Danish bus driver was injured by *Tiefflieger* while plying the route from Friedrichsruh to Hamburg.

The following night plans were drawn up for a big evacuation operation from Neuengamme and the detachment's decampment from Friedrichsruh. The British army had now crossed the Elbe at several points and flanked Neuengamme on both sides. It was a matter of days and hours, therefore, if the Scandinavians were to be rescued from Neuengamme before the war was upon them. While planning was going on under cover of dark the Friedrichsruh castle gardens were lit up by 'the magical, sinister glare of the flares'. Shortly after, Friedrichsruh was attacked by a wave of bombers and the palace was laid in ruins. The Swiss consul general, his wife and some of the staff were killed, but all the Scandinavians survived. Later on Field Marshal Montgomery's adjutant Keating would claim that the British Air Force intentionally bombed Friedrichsruh castle on the conviction that the SS (and Himmler too?) had established its headquarters there.

One of the Danish buses suffered a *Tiefflieger* attack while Neuengamme was being evacuated on 22 April and two people – a Dane and a Norwegian – were killed while eight were injured.

Neuengamme Is Evacuated and the Scandinavians Are Taken To Denmark

The process by which it was decided to evacuate Neuengamme is not easy to reconstruct. One leading factor was the hectic, chaotic state of affairs prevailing during the final days of the Third Reich and the little time left over for documentation. Large chunks of Germany's infrastructure were now falling to pieces, and it became all the more difficult to keep communications functioning. More and more decisions were being made locally. For a week or so the Swedish legation in Berlin had been moving house to Friedrichsruh and when the evacuation took place Richert, the minister, joined it and returned to Sweden – for good. His colleagues went too, and the reporting material stemming from the legation, previously so abundant when it was in Berlin, petered out completely around 18–20 April. Bernadotte, leader of the entire Red Cross expedition, had been back in Sweden, and when he then returned to Germany issues concerning the rescue operations would occupy less space in his reports – talks dealing with the politics of the great powers were to take precedence. Carlgren's draft to the *White Book 1956* summarised the situation: 'Foreign Office documents concerning the talks covering the progress of the rescue action which Bernadotte in any case must have conducted with Himmler and his assistants contain very scanty information, and in particular no reports from Bernadotte himself.' Unfortunately the same has to be said of his own documents which Bernadotte left behind.

Once back home in Sweden, Bernadotte did not seem to have been particularly worried about Neuengamme's future. On his previous visit to Germany he had of course received undertakings from Himmler and Schellenberg that the concentration camps would be surrendered intact to the Allies and that a special such order would be issued to the commandant at Neuengamme.[4] Bernadotte's report to the National Board of Information of 16 April mentioned an agreement reached with camp commandant Pauly to move the Scandinavians to Denmark at such time as the Allies approached Neuengamme. The Swedish detachment would then be capable of transporting 800–900 people at a time. Bernadotte now revealed that the Jyllandskorps, the secret Danish organisation, which had a transport capacity of 5,000–6,000 people at a time, was fully prepared for the relief of Neuengamme. Bernadotte concluded that Himmler's refusal to allow all the Norwegians and Danes to be ferried over to Sweden had not caused too much harm. 'We could reckon with the remaining Scandinavians falling into Allied hands and the Swedish delegates staying on at the camp.' Swedish food aid had been geared on a long-term basis to satisfy the requirements of Scandinavian prisoners who might remain in Germany. Richert in Berlin had at the same time suggested to Schellenberg that the internees be evacuated to Denmark.

At Friedrichsruh the initiative now appeared to have transferred to Danish hands. Frykman said that it was Hvass who towards the middle of April considered the time was ripe to try to press the German authorities into arranging transport home for the Scandinavians. According to both Bernadotte and Holm it was minister Yde, Denmark's consul general in Hamburg, who on 18 April obtained permission from the Hamburg gauleiter Karl Kaufmann for the immediate transportation of all Scandinavians from Neuengamme to Denmark. Kaufmann's decision was his own since connections with Berlin had been cut off.[5] The same evening, however, a counter-order arrived from Dr Rennau. The Hamburg Gestapo staff had established contact with Berlin and the Reichssicherheitshauptamt had given a flat refusal.

Bernadotte (and Yde too in his report) stated that it was Himmler himself who stopped the transport from Neuengamme, and who also prohibited further movement of sick people to Sweden. Rennau was forced to intervene in Professor Rundberg's last transport (which had already been cleared) of 336 'chronically ill prisoners' to Sweden. The mood at Friedrichsruh, which had had its ups and downs of late, took a turn for the worse. The days were employed in frantic preparations for the journey home, while two Swedish bus platoons were expected back soon from Denmark. In the woods around Friedrichsruh an entire fleet of Danish cars and buses and large ten-ton fish-market vans was being assembled.

It was at this stage, according to Frykman and Trier Mørch, that Bernadotte, notified of the critical situation, flew to the south of the Danish mainland and was driven from there by a Swedish car to Friedrichsruh. In Hvass's, Koch's and Mørch's versions it was, again, Bernadotte who personally received final confirmation from Himmler in Berlin that all Danish and Norwegian prisoners could now be moved to Denmark. Nevertheless, there was no support for this information in Bernadotte's own account. On the contrary, Bernadotte reported that it was the German liaison officer, Rennau, who announced that the entire Neuengamme camp was to be evacuated and the Scandinavians immediately to be moved to Denmark. Yde's report to the Danish Foreign Ministry was unclear as to when or how Himmler's consent was obtained.

Whatever the case, on the evening of 19 April a council of war was held concerning the evacuation of Neuengamme. Bernadotte, Frykman, Richert and Obersturmbannführer Rennau were present, while Denmark was represented by Mohr, Hvass and the secretary Paulson. In Rennau's opinion it was impossible to transport almost five thousand prisoners in the vehicles available and suggested half of them marching northwards on foot. Frykman expressed his regret that the Swedish detachment was equipped with so few vehicles: could the Danes lend a hand, preferably with a hundred or so vehicles? Paulson gave it a moment's thought and briefly responded . . . Yes, indeed!

Koch has estimated that that night ninety-four Danish buses, as well as a stream of passenger cars, ambulances, motor cycles and trucks, were sent off from Padborg to Neuengamme. Frykman gave notice now that everybody would be able to leave in the vehicles by the fixed time: 7 p.m. the following evening. Rennau protested, still insisting on the foot march. Bernadotte brought the discussion to an end: 'If the head of the detachment has said he can cope with the task, then I am confident he will carry it through and transportation will proceed according to the plan he draws up!' At four o'clock in the morning the first transport departed, and at 6.30 p.m. on 20 April the last prisoner was heaved on board. By then the Swedish buses had had time to return from Denmark and swiftly load on board more internees.

All the other non-Scandinavian prisoners were evacuated from Neuengamme at the same time. This took place in the Germans' customary brutal manner. The prisoners, many of whom could hardly stand upright, were packed into goods wagons. When the Swedes asked where these prisoners would be going the commandant's listless reply was: '*Keine Ahnung!* (No idea!)'

All in all there were 4,255 Danish and Norwegian prisoners transferred to Denmark between 20 and 21 April. The Danish effort drew unqualified praise from the Swedes. Rundberg estimated that of the 120 buses involved in the operation about a hundred were Danish and twenty Swedish, although a later Danish special survey raised the Danish figure to 120.[6] Bernadotte, too, praised the Danes:

> I had arranged with the Danish authorities that if the signal was given (evacuation, that is) we could get Danish transport facilities to go and fetch everyone at once. This Danish organisation worked

exceptionally well. Twenty-four hours after the order had gone out we had 150–200 buses from Denmark in the north of Germany. A huge organisational problem had been resolved in a remarkably efficient way. The buses were painted white with Danish flags and red crosses, and everything went smoothly.[7]

The Danish Red Cross catering centre at Kruså also performed marvellous work, providing up to five thousand starving Scandinavians with food and drink within the space of twenty-four hours. Most of the prisoners were accommodated in Denmark in the notorious concentration camp at Frøslev. As there was not enough room here, the Danes saw themselves compelled in all haste to set up a provisional camp at Møgelkjaer outside Horsens. This consisted of a large farming complex which had been expanded to house unemployed young people. It was not protected by barbed wire but patrolled instead by German guards and Danish Nazis – so-called *stikkere* – and escape was not impossible. On 25 April some forty Danish prisoners were reported missing. The Germans then demanded that all the Danes be moved and put behind barbed wire fencing at Frøslev, and in future all transport was to be carried out using sealed Swedish buses.

The Swedish Red Cross delegates were now operating inside the Frøslev and Møgelkjaer camps. One of them, Eric Karlsson, was threatened with a pistol by one of the Danish Nazis but was rescued by two burly Stockholm drivers who promised to smash the Danish *stikkere*'s head in with an engine crank if Karlsson was shot at. Professor Rundberg, now in charge of transportation from Frøslev and Møgelkjaer over to Sweden, was obliged to demand from the Danes their word of honour that no more escape attempts would take place. The following day Rundberg managed to persuade Schellenberg to allow all the Danes and Norwegians at Møgelkjaer to be moved straight to Sweden. As a result, on 27 April a convoy of 600 Norwegians left Frøslev and another convoy of 600 Danes left Møgelkjaer, bound for Sweden. Nevertheless, during the journey through Denmark between the 28th and the 29th no less than about 345 Danes took the opportunity to escape. In return, however, it seems that these escapees were 'replaced' by other Danes who grabbed the opportunity to take advantage of a comfortable exit out of Denmark!

The staff of the Swedish detachment was moved to Lübeck during the period 23–28 April. Here Major Frykman was able to initiate fruitful collaboration with the chief delegate of the ICRC, the diplomat de Blonay, who placed some twenty vehicles at the disposal of the Swedish expedition. The military situation in Germany was then making all operations impossible, and the Swedish staff were therefore transferred on 28 April to Padborg over on the Danish side. Captain Melin was placed in charge and made responsible for the transport of Scandinavians from Denmark to Sweden while Frykman remained in Lübeck. It was then that Hjalmarsson, the motor-cycle dispatch rider who had got himself lost from the convoy leaving Theresienstadt, suddenly appeared. In spite of not knowing a word of German, he had 'begged for, exchanged, threatened and stolen his way to petrol from German soldiers, led his motor-cycle past road blocks, crept down in ditches out of the way of *Tiefflieger*', and thus managed to find his way through the bottleneck between the two war fronts as far as the Swedish legation in Berlin and from there back to Friedrichsruh.

Kersten and Masur in Talks with Himmler

After a potentially perilous but in the end incident-free journey by air from Sweden, Felix Kersten, accompanied by Norbert Masur, arrived at Kersten's country estate in Germany, Hartzwalde, on the evening of 19 April. Kersten brought with him lists from the Swedish Foreign Office for Himmler with specific Swedish requests. On the night of the 21st, from 2.30 a.m. for a period of two-and-a-half hours, these two gentlemen from Sweden had a meeting with Heinrich Himmler, his adjutant Dr Brandt and Walter Schellenberg. For the first time Himmler met a representative of the Jewish people he had spent years systematically wiping out. Masur emphasised the fact, however, that he had come in the capacity of a private person and not as a representative of the WJC. A number of records exist of the talks that took place at Hartzwalde during these early morning hours, but unfortunately they are not entirely in accord with each other.

The previous day – 20 April, Hitler's birthday – Kersten and Schellenberg had conversed alone. In Kersten's version the conversation centred around getting Himmler to heed the Swedish requests and Masur's desire to set as many Jews free as possible. Schellenberg raised the objection that

Himmler would not be prepared to make such sweeping concessions. Top party policy required Himmler to act in line with Hitler's orders, which stipulated that in the event of his regime collapsing the largest number possible of his enemies were to be destroyed. Gradually Kersten managed to persuade Schellenberg to approach Himmler and put forward his own opinion that the attitude adopted by the party leadership was untenable, and to support Masur's wishes. Masur, too, was given an opportunity that same day to join Schellenberg for breakfast and share a walk in the forest with him.

Masur confirmed Schellenberg's promises to back all of Masur's requests to Himmler. The so-called 'Trosa memo' (composed by Schellenberg in Sweden during a brief stay after the war) included no mention, however, of the promises made that day, while it did instead air Schellenberg's own difficulties *vis-à-vis* Kaltenbrunner in particular. On the other hand Schellenberg referred to Kersten's discussion of the Germans' talks with Musy where he said that a happy solution to the Jewish problem would be to remove it from *der geldlichen Atmosphäre* (the money sphere), leaving the money deposited with the International Red Cross.[8]

On Himmler's arrival Kersten managed – still in his own version – alone with Himmler to get him to pledge to 'bury the hatchet with the Jews'. Himmler is supposed to have said: 'If I had had my way things would have turned out differently, but the Führer has ordered the very strictest measures from me regarding the Jews.' As far as the lists from von Post and Engzell were concerned, Kersten succeeded in securing the release of all the people appearing on the lists he presented to Himmler. Engzell's own more specific records, however, classified Himmler's pledges as follows:

- release of fifty Jews (and their transfer to Sweden) interned at Berg in Norway: *granted by Himmler* (a Swedish order to this effect on 23 April was sent to the consulate-general in Oslo);
- release of Swedish citizens under arrest in Norway: *Himmler promised benevolent inquiry*;
- request for the Swedish Norway Aid action to send extra rations to political prisoners at Grini: *granted, and Himmler will issue orders to Oslo*;

• gift parcels and medication for Jews in German camps: *consent given, should go via International Red Cross and Swedish Red Cross*;
• release of Swedish hard labour prisoners in Germany: *the majority already freed, including those under sentence of death*!;
• release of people of various nationalities specified by name: *granted, if possible in practice*;
• release of approximately one thousand women from Ravensbrück, including about three hundred French women: *granted, although the action had already to a large extent been carried out*;
• release of Norwegian prisoners in Norway following requests expressed by minister Ditleff: *Himmler pledged benevolent inquiry*.

It is not difficult to see that Himmler's pledges, all of them verbal, do not in many cases add up to much more than 'benevolent inquiries'.[9]

In respect of the Jews, a tougher posture was encountered. Kersten stated that the talks between Himmler and Masur ended in deadlock – Kersten had to confer with Himmler in private. Himmler's comment was that Hitler had forbidden any further release of the Jews. Himmler had experienced some ugly scenes with the Führer on account of the release of the Jews to Switzerland. Gradually, however, Kersten succeeded in getting Himmler to agree to the release of one thousand Jewish women from Ravensbrück. In order to evade Hitler's ban, however, they would be called 'Polish prisoners'. Thus everything would be settled – by Kersten! – in collaboration with the Swedish Red Cross and the WJC. Masur was then summoned into the room and informed – by Kersten! – that Himmler was prepared to release one thousand Jewish women from Ravensbrück, and that this would be arranged from 'our' side using Swedish Red Cross buses. While confirming this Himmler assigned Brandt the task of confirming all the other agreements in writing. In written form, however – as far as I have been able to find – Kersten only received a letter from Brandt in which Himmler had authorised the International Red Cross to send 'affectionate gift parcels' and medicine to Jews in the German camps. In talks among themselves, however, Schellenberg and Brandt – still according to Kersten – had also given the assurance that the number of Jews released might be considerably higher if technically possible.

196

In Norbert Masur's little book, *En jude talar med Himmler* (A Jew Talks to Himmler), published as early as 1945, it is Masur himself who was the active negotiator with Himmler. It is Masur who stressed the need to rescue the Jews, backed up by Kersten. The two men insisted time and time again that the prisoners at Ravensbrück must be allowed to be evacuated to Sweden. In his summary of events set out in his report to the Foreign Office Masur stated that Himmler, in addition to the assurances to Kersten already mentioned, also gave:

- a definite pledge that no Jews would be shot;
- a pledge that no forced marches would take place even if the war fronts came close to the camps;
- a pledge to seek out people whose names had been supplied on further lists, even when this was sure to be practically impossible;
- all these pledges on condition that the visit to Himmler and the conversation with him remained absolutely secret, and that nothing was published regarding the arrival at a neutral country of Jews and non-Jews who had been released.

This implied that Himmler to a large extent had met two of Masur's more general requests but not the third – vaguely formulated – whereby 'should evacuation to a neutral country by means of the assistance of the Red Cross or other neutral aid body still be possible, such voluntary evacuation shall be permitted'. The exception here were the one thousand women at Ravensbrück. Note may be taken of the fact that Masur, according to his report to the Foreign Office, apart from Ravensbrück did not seem to have raised any further demands regarding the release of Jews from any specific concentration camps.[10]

Masur was convinced, however, that in the event of the Red Cross transport convoy succeeding in bringing out the thousand women from Ravensbrück, more women would be released. Furthermore, the Swiss had to be notified via the Swedish legation in Berne so that they as well as the Swedes might try to collect as many Jews as possible from camps in the south of Greater Germany. In contrast to Kersten, however, Masur discovered that Himmler's words were definitely not to be trusted. In his talks with Masur he had been guilty of manifest untruths. Himmler described press reports of conditions at Bergen-Belsen and Buchenwald, after they had been handed over to the Allies, as tales of *Greuelmärchen* (horror). Such descriptions, Masur feared, could actually drive Himmler to destroy all traces of the camps:

> If Nazism is to end in ruins, then at least as many people as possible in Europe and the rest of the world are to share its fate. That is why it is not inconceivable that Himmler or any other of the Nazi leaders – should power slip out of Himmler's hands at the last moment – will issue an order for the assassination of the Jews. For this reason it is so *absolutely essential* to evacuate as many Jews as possible to neutral countries or behind Allied lines, even if admittedly liberation by these armies appears to be just around the corner.

Masur emphasised the value of his talks with Schellenberg, Brandt and Franz Göring. 'They are young men who wish to live on.' In Masur's opinion they would sabotage every order proceeding from Himmler for violent action against the Jews. Such acts of sabotage would not be difficult to carry out in a Germany that was then heavily disorganised.

For more than two hours Norbert Masur, a free Jew, had spoken to the dreaded head of the Gestapo face to face:

> No doubt Himmler was both intelligent and educated, but he was no master in the art of dissimulation. His cynicism particularly came into expression when he painted a picture of the catastrophes that were expected. The words were typical which he uttered in bidding Kersten goodbye: 'The worthwhile portion of the German people will accompany us into ruin – what happens to the rest is of no significance.' As opposed to Hitler he was a rational being in his relationship with the Jews. Hitler, of course, had a pronounced aversion to them. Himmler's actions were not emotionally tinged. He had people cold-bloodedly murdered as long as it suited his purposes, and was capable of choosing another path when it was more convenient for his policies and for himself.
>
> What motives can Himmler have had for the minor concessions he made during the final months of the war, and to us as well? He

never demanded anything in return. Neither did he believe, surely, that with these concessions he would manage to save his own skin. He was too intelligent for that; he knew quite well that his list of sins was too long. Possibly he wished to stand in the annals of history in a more favourable light than those who bore the main responsibility for Germany's crimes.[11]

The very same day, Kersten and Masur flew out a Berlin that was being pounded by Soviet artillery fire. This time they could no longer fly direct to Stockholm but only as far as Copenhagen, whence via ferry and train they reached their home destination. Straightaway, on 23 April, they delivered their reports to the foreign minister in Stockholm. In these Masur expressed his sincere gratitude to Kersten for his 'active and whole-hearted collaboration', while Kersten praised Masur for having 'very capably carried through the negotiations'. Once home in Stockholm, Kersten wrote a letter to Storch on 27 April about the result of the talks, adding that the number of women for release from Ravensbrück – one thousand – could certainly be increased, and explaining why the Jewish prisoners released had to be classified as 'Polish prisoners'.

Soon, however, Kersten, Masur and Storch were at odds with each other on the question of credit for the result of the talks.

Folke Bernadotte and His Talks in Germany: Fourth and Last Round

Bernadotte had solicited fresh talks with Himmler. These could not take place in Berlin as Bernadotte had planned, but instead he was once more forced to drive to Hohenlychen, now converted into a military hospital. On the morning of 21 April, at 6 a.m., a very tired Himmler appeared at the breakfast table, complaining that for the last few nights he had had no sleep at all. Bernadotte's notes indicated that Himmler had come straight from the Eastern Front while the draft copy of his book *Last Days* . . . gives a more correct version – that Himmler had come 'straight from treatment by his masseur, medical counsellor Kersten, who possessed a country estate not far from Hohenlychen'. This rough draft also showed that the evening before Himmler had had a discussion with finance minister

Schwerin von Krosigk about what could be done to minimise the disaster that was overshadowing Germany. Both of these interesting pieces of information have been excised from the published version of *Last Days* . . . and with them the only passage that showed that Bernadotte was aware of Kersten's involvement. All of this pointed to the probability that Himmler now communicated to Bernadotte something of the talks he had just had with Kersten and Masur only a few hours earlier.

Over breakfast Bernadotte repeated his request to Himmler for the Scandinavian prisoners, now under transportation to Denmark, to be moved straight on to Sweden. Himmler's response once again was that this was impossible since Hitler had forbidden it. Bernadotte's next proposal, however, was that in the event of hostilities breaking out in Denmark the Scandinavian prisoners should be ferried over to Sweden by the Red Cross, and to this Himmler gave his immediate approval.[12]

Bernadotte then suggested that the Swedish Red Cross should fetch all the French women from the Ravensbrück concentration camp. Himmler not only gave his consent but also expressed the wish that the Swedes transport women of every nationality from Ravensbrück to Sweden. This camp was going to fall into the Russians' hands in a very short time anyway, Himmler declared. Bernadotte travelled back to Friedrichsruh immediately breakfast was over and issued orders for the Red Cross detachment to collect the women from Ravensbrück.

According to the report sent home to Stockholm, the order implied that the detachment in its first stage would collect all the French women (now estimated to be down to only three hundred) plus Polish, Belgian and Dutch women (a total of 750). This was also the substance of the letter Bernadotte sent the same day to the camp commandant at Ravensbrück, and in which he gave notice of Himmler's permission for the Swedish Red Cross to take back to Sweden every woman at present at the camp: first 'sämtliche französische Frauen', whereupon equally 'die Polinnen, Holländerinnen und Belgierinnen' should be made ready in preparation for the transport. Bernadotte had thus induced Himmler to raise the offer to Kersten and Masur of the release of one thousand women to a level at which all the women at the camp in principle would be collected. At this stage Himmler was prepared to surrender all the concentration camps on the Western

Front to the British and Americans undamaged. According to Storch's later accounts, however, Himmler's pledge did not include camps on the Eastern Front liberated by the Soviet troops.[13]

Bit by bit Bernadotte came to be criticised for having given priority to the rescue from Ravensbrück of *'west European'* women. This is true inasmuch as it was the French women who on 21 April Bernadotte first mentioned – this was, of course, the priority to be given as expressed by the Foreign Office in the instructions Bernadotte had received on 27 March. But Bernadotte then ordered the rescue of Polish women (by no means capable of being construed as 'west European') as well as all women at the camp. Similarly Eric Karlsson wrote that the information the Swedes received was that all the Swedish vehicles were now to proceed to Ravensbrück in order to collect women *'of every nationality, mostly Polish women'*.

This version was reinforced by Schellenberg's portrayal of the meeting between Bernadotte and Himmler when Bernadotte was given the promise for all *Polish* women to be brought from Ravensbrück to Sweden. Seen from Hitler's angle this would be not only a humanitarian deed but also a cornerstone of his policy towards Russia. Radziwill, the Polish prince, had already in January handed over a list to Schellenberg from Geneva detailing Polish women at Ravensbrück who should be released. For the same political reasons, in the dying stages of the war (24 April), Schellenberg had been able to have Bor, the Polish general, rescued over the border to Switzerland. There were moreover, Schellenberg hinted, racial qualities in the Polish people to be considered: he could have brought up the case of his own wife, whose mother was Polish. In a similar fashion Trevor-Roper too would later remark that Himmler's pledge concerning Polish women was a way of procuring Hitler's recommendation by presenting the concession to Bernadotte as an anti-Russian gesture.[14]

It is therefore odd that Åke Svenson would later maintain that his orders in respect of Ravensbrück were to rescue 'in the first place . . . all *west European* women', earlier stated more precisely as 'in the first place . . . French, Dutch and Belgian women' as well as – but only if 'space allowed' – 'to take along with us Polish women'. Sigurd Melin, too, in his notes wrote about 'orders from Bernadotte to fetch about six thousand *west European* women'. This statement, seconded by a Dane, Kjerulf-Jensen, has lain at the root of later accusations directed at Bernadotte. As indicated above, this criticism appears to be totally mistaken – rather was it the case that the Polish women occupied a position of priority with Bernadotte (and Schellenberg). The only primary source with a tendency to corroborate Svenson's, Melin's and Kjerulf-Jensen's versions was an interesting note from 22 April at the Danish Foreign Ministry in which Sweden's minister in Copenhagen, von Dardel, informed the Danes that Sweden was willing to admit 'one thousand mainly French and Belgian women plus a further five thousand women of the same nationality'. Was it this Swedish–Danish communication that reached Svenson and Melin, and was the Foreign Office back in Stockholm in that case advocating a line of policy concerning the Polish women other than Bernadotte's?

Bernadotte spent the following days in Denmark where he inspected the 'exceptional measures' being taken by the Danish Red Cross and other Danish authorities to take care of all the prisoners coming from Neuengamme. Especially touching was the moment on his visit to the Frøslev camp where the prisoners in slow time whistled the Swedish national anthem as a tribute to Bernadotte – contravening every rule in the book for the Gestapo guards.

He met Schellenberg again on 23 April, this time at the Swedish consulate in Flensburg near the border with Denmark. Schellenberg then let a bomb drop: Hitler was dying in Berlin and did not have many more days to live. Himmler had therefore decided to try to see General Eisenhower to let him know he was prepared to surrender on the Western Front. Was Bernadotte prepared to forward such a message to Eisenhower? Bernadotte's response was that he was only ready to pass on the message to foreign minister Günther and only on condition that Denmark and Norway also formed part of the entreaty of surrender. Bernadotte also stressed how improbable it was that the Allies would agree to such terms of surrender. If Himmler wanted to surrender, no meeting with Eisenhower was necessary – all Himmler had to do was to issue orders for the German military commanders to lay down their arms. On the other hand there were no western Allied troops in Denmark or Norway, and a meeting between Eisenhower and Himmler could be justified by the need to discuss the technical details behind surrender operations. Bernadotte was ready to meet Heinrich Himmler once more.

This meeting – the fourth and the last one – took place on the night of 23–24 April at the Swedish legation's temporary offices in Lübeck.

> I'll not very easily forget that night with its uncanny atmosphere of approaching doom. Himmler arrived at the Swedish legation's Dienstställe in Lübeck around half past eleven. Straightaway the air-raid sirens began to wail. I asked Himmler if he wanted to go down into the air-raid shelter, pointing out that I couldn't guarantee that we would be alone – we couldn't, could we, prevent other people or passers-by seeking shelter in the cellar. There was a moment's hesitation, and then Himmler decided to go down there. A tiny group of Swedes and Germans had already gathered there – Himmler chatted with the Germans and asked how they were getting on: he was clearly trying to get an idea of the mood of the people. It was also quite plain that he hadn't been recognised. I gave him the occasional glance during the hour we were down in the air-raid shelter. He seemed enormously tired and nervous, and by all accounts was struggling hard to keep up a calm appearance.[15]

After the 'all-clear' had sounded talks proceeded between Bernadotte and Himmler in Schellenberg's presence. The electric lighting had failed and everything took place around a table 'while a couple of wax candles gave off their feeble flames'. Himmler explained that he had understood that Bernadotte on the three occasions they had met had tried to per-suade him to put an end to the war since Germany was in a hopeless posi-tion. Himmler personally was of the same conviction – it was just that he couldn't break his word with Hitler. Now the situation had changed. Hit-ler had made up his mind to remain in a hedged-in Berlin in order to meet his death there. Berlin's fall was a matter of days, and Hitler might already be dead. Himmler considered he now had a free hand to act as he wished, and announced to Bernadotte his recognition of Germany's defeat.

> With the purpose of sparing as large a part as possible of Germany from occupation by the Russian troops, he would therefore wish

to surrender on the Western Front and allow the western Allies to forge eastwards, whereupon the German troops on the Western Front would lay down their arms and let themselves be made prisoner. Nevertheless, he was not prepared to surrender on the Eastern Front since he had always been, and always would be, a sworn enemy of Bolshevism. Thus it was that he had most decidedly opposed the German–Russian alliance at the start of the world conflict. He asked me if I was prepared to forward such a message to the Swedish foreign minister so that he could brief the western Allies about his proposal.[16]

This proposal sounded even more interesting in Schellenberg's version, which had Himmler saying that the Germans would continue fighting against the Russians on the Eastern Front until the western Powers' front, so to speak, had replaced the fighting German front.[17]

Bernadotte emphasised the practically impossible nature of Himmler's proposal – the western Allied troops would not interrupt their advance when they reached the Germans' halting places on the Eastern Front. Bernadotte repeated what he had said to Schellenberg, that he was not prepared to hand Himmler's message to Günther unless Norway and Denmark were included in the surrender terms. Himmler then declared that he agreed to such a surrender, and that he was willing to have American, British or Swedish troops occupy Denmark and Norway – but the occupation should not be performed using Russian troops.

Himmler said that this was the bitterest day of his life: he had had to admit to a foreigner that Germany had definitely lost the war. He was, however, now prepared to tell General Eisenhower the following: 'I recognise the defeat of the German armed forces by the western Allies. I am prepared to surrender on the Western Front unconditionally, and I am likewise prepared to discuss technical procedures for the surrender of the German military forces in Norway and Denmark.'[18]

Bernadotte then put forward proposals – evidently at the end of the conversation – to the effect that German sentences of capital punishment in Denmark should now be revoked, and that King Leopold of Belgium, imprisoned in Germany, be released. Himmler's responses in both cases were in principle positive. It is however noteworthy that in line with his own notes Bernadotte did not raise the question of transporting the Scandinavian prisoners in Denmark to Sweden. It was not until his press conference on 5 May that Bernadotte mentioned that during that fateful night Himmler had promised: 'I could bring back home everything it was possible to bring back home, including Danish and Norwegian prisoners.' Schellenberg testified to the truth of this promise given to Bernadotte on 24 April. Bernadotte was at this stage so embroiled in Great Power politics that in recording events in his notes the rescue of prisoners from concentration camps to Sweden seemed completely to have slipped his mind, an operation that was his original and only mandate for the talks in Germany.

In reply to Bernadotte's proposals Himmler, by the light of the two candles, then wrote a letter in a sprawling hand:

> Your Excellency,
>
> I have asked Count Bernadotte together with you to deal with a number of problems that I have had occasion to discuss with him today. Please accept my gratitude in advance for devoting your time and interest to these matters.
>
> In expressing my most deeply felt respect I remain
> Very respectfully yours,
> H. Himmler.[19]

The two men parted at 2.30 a.m. on 24 April. The agreement was that Schellenberg would accompany Bernadotte as far as Flensburg after which Bernadotte would return to Sweden as fast as possible and then forward the reply to Himmler's petition via Schellenberg. Leaving the Swedish diplomatic quarters Himmler insisted on doing the driving himself and ended up careering straight into the legations's barbed wire fence. It was only with great effort the Swedish staff were able to free the car from barbed wire and grating. Bernadotte, the legation secretary Brandel and the attaché Lewenhaupt joined in concluding that Himmler's exit could very well be interpreted symbolically. The same day Bernadotte flew home from Copenhagen airport to Stockholm.

Thus – as observed by the *Swedish Foreign Office White Book 1956* – came to an end the Swedish–German talks relating to the release of Danish and

Norwegian prisoners at camps in Germany. It 'only' remained now in the final stages of the war to carry into effect all that Himmler's pledges would be making possible. The big Ravensbrück operation went into high gear.

Ravensbrück

In November 1938 camp prisoners began building a special concentration camp for women at Ravensbrück – Frauen-Konzentrationslager Ravensbrück – in a marshy zone some eighty kilometres north of Berlin.[20] Subsequently Ravensbrück became the largest female concentration camp built in history. Originally the camp was designed for six to seven thousand inhabitants. On 31 December 1944 there were 45,637 prisoners registered at the camp. When the camp was liberated between 30 April and 1 May 1945 by the Soviet and Polish armies there remained only some three thousand sick women. All the rest had been killed or evacuated – either by the White Buses or by forced death marches.

The camp's own internal records showed that between 1938 and 1945 a total of 132,000 women from twenty nations were imprisoned at Ravensbrück. Most of the women came from Poland (24.9 per cent), Germany (19.9 per cent), the Soviet Union (19.1 per cent) or were Jews (15.1 per cent). A number of these were sent on to Auschwitz, Mauthausen or other camps. Some 92,000 prisoners died, however, at the main camp and its *Aussenkommandon*, producing a mortality rate of 70 per cent.

With the exception of the extermination camps, no other concentration camp recorded such a high mortality rate. The women died of undernourishment, strenuous work, torture and plain execution. Ravensbrück also became notorious for the medical experiments performed on female internees in atrociously unscrupulous forms, with sterilisation experiments given priority. A large number of *Aussenkommandon* came under the supervision of Ravensbrück, and in these women were used as a free work force. The giant German company Siemenswerke built a factory directly connected to the Ravensbrück camp.

The commandant at Ravensbrück in 1945 was Sturmbannführer Fritz Suhren. In October 1944 he received orders from the SS to raise the death toll at Ravensbrück: twelve thousand women were to be executed over a six-month period. A new double-unit gas chamber was constructed. In the month of March 1945 alone, hundreds of women were killed every night. Suhren had the gas chambers destroyed on 23 April, before the arrival of the liberating forces. Fritz Suhren was tried and put to death in 1954.

The first three Norwegian women entered Ravensbrück in 1941. They were Miriam Kristiansen and Helene Strand Johansen, both married to prominent members of the Norwegian Communist Party, both born in Russia and both of Jewish descent. They were to die at Auschwitz in May 1942. The third lady was Olga Marie Eltwig, arrested twice by the Germans at her home in Oslo before arriving at the camp. She was rescued in 1945. The last transportation of women, six of them, from Norway took place on 6 July 1944. In all 102 Norwegian women were deported to Ravensbrück. Seven of them died there or at Auschwitz and one from spotted fever in Sweden in April 1945 following her release. The Norwegian women made up a small, favoured minority at Ravensbrück, where they received support in various shapes and forms from the Norwegian government-in-exile in London and the Norwegian legation in Stockholm, from Red Cross units in Sweden, Norway and Denmark and from the International Red Cross, as well as in Germany from Norwegians at Gross Kreutz and the Norwegian seamen's chaplains in Hamburg. The parcels reaching the Norwegian women plus their own inward harmony were factors in their ability to survive. The camp also held a score of Danish women in 1945 whose situation very probably resembled that of the Norwegians.

One of the Norwegian female internees at Ravensbrück was Sylvia Salvesen, married to Professor Harald Salvesen at the Oslo State Hospital. She managed to obtain work at the camp cottage hospital where she made the acquaintance of Gerda Schröder, a German nurse who unlike the rest of the German staff did a professional job and took good care of the patients. Wanda Hjort who belonged to the Norwegian colony at Gross Kreutz had come into contact with Salvesen, who in all secrecy made up lists of the Norwegian women imprisoned at Ravensbrück. Via Wanda Hjort, and with nurse Gerda running as courier, the lists travelled to Gross Kreutz and on to the Swedish legation in Berlin and finally Stockholm, reaching Bernadotte's Red Cross expedition literally in the nick of time. After the war Bernadotte would thank Sylvia Salvesen for the 'extraordinary help' her lists of names had meant for the Swedish relief operation to Ravensbrück.

The Scandinavian women at Ravensbrück were collected by the Swedish White Buses on 8 April. Axel Molin's diary mentioned that a convoy of eight buses and three trucks left Friedrichsruh on the 7th, loaded with five thousand gift parcels for the French women at the camp plus 'other important necessities for women'. At 1.30 a.m. on the 8th embarkation began at Ravensbrück, after which the convoy drove straight to Padborg in Denmark. It was a twenty-four-hour journey, very taxing for the passengers who, according to Molin, were in rather poor condition. How many rescued women there actually were is difficult to say. The transport plan spoke of 125 women to be collected, while statistics from 17 April quoted 124 as having been brought from Ravensbrück to Sweden, although 'the lists are not fully reliable'. As we shall soon see there can hardly have been as many as 124. The Danish report – that ninety-eight Scandinavian women plus two French women had been rescued and taken to Padborg on 8 April – is very probably nearer the truth. The two French women must have been the countesses, de Fleurieu and de Rambuteau.

This is how the liberation was witnessed from inside the camp:

Information reached us from '*nach vorne*' on Saturday afternoon 7 April that the Scandinavian prisoners were to make themselves ready for transport. It wasn't clear-cut information, though. What happened first was that through the camp's bush telegraph news had reached the clothing department that civilian clothes were to be made ready for 120 Danish prisoners. So much was clear. It came straight from the commandant's office, so we just had to follow orders. The only thing was that there weren't 120 Danish prisoners at the camp and never had been. At that point there were no more than twenty Danish women there. They'd come down over the course of the last year and were, just like the Norwegians, spread over a number of different places. The total number of Danish and Norwegian prisoners normally would have amounted to only 120. Nor were there that many, because of the hundred or so Norwegian prisoners registered at the camp from 1941 to 1944, six were already dead, eighteen had been sent by NN transportation to Mauthausen as recently as just over a month earlier, and three were at some place or other in southern Germany. The information reaching the clothing department evidently must concern both Norwegian and Danish prisoners.[21]

A white-painted bus bearing a Swedish flag then drove into the camp. The order came from the camp commandant himself: *'Achtung! Achtung! Alle skandinavische Fangen vortreten.'* This was the signal for the first stoppage of work in the history of the camp. All the Scandinavian prisoners went straight to their barracks and packed their few possessions. They were then summoned (the NN prisoners included) to the bath house where they spent the rest of the night. Commandant Suhren there announced that the Reichsführer-SS had decided everyone was to be driven to an assembly camp in Germany by the Swedish Red Cross – *'Gute Heimfahrt!* (Have a good trip home!)'.

> In front of the building stood a number of shining white Swedish buses, all of them decorated with the Red Cross sign and with a Swedish flag. And in front of the buses stood a flock of smiling, friendly Swedes, men and women. What they had in common were their field-grey Red Cross uniforms with the Red Cross armband. 'Come along now, ladies,' could be heard from the first bus. Ladies! You had to pinch yourself to believe it – were they really ladies again? Was that the way the Red Cross saw them? They took their seats, stealing a swift glance to left and to right. The Swedes politely drew their attention to the need for all conversation for the time being to be in German, and that representatives of the German authorities would be on board the buses, two on each of them. Then, as soon as everyone was seated, a motor-cycle dispatch rider rode up. He exchanged a word or two with the driver of the leading Swedish bus. The Swedish Red Cross officer bade the SS officer, who was standing strictly to attention, goodbye. And then off went the convoy.[22]

To Sweden from Ravensbrück: At Least Seven Thousand Women Rescued

A convoy of fifteen Danish ambulances left Friedrichsruh on 22 April led by Swedish Captain Arnoldsson in order to collect all the sick internees at Ravensbrück.[23] Captain Ankarcrona, who had joined the Swedish Red Cross delegation at Neuengamme, travelled with the convoy. Ankarcrona was later to remain at Ravensbrück and he played an important rôle in organising affairs during the final state of chaos. When they reached Ravensbrück police-inspector Göring and Musy jr (son of the former president of the Swiss Confederation) were already at the camp. The commandant, Sturmbannführer Suhren, notified Arnoldsson that the entire camp was about to be evacuated and that he, Arnoldsson, was welcome to take charge of all the French, Polish, Dutch and Belgian women – a total of fifteen thousand women. Arnoldsson immediately gave his consent despite the fact that he knew this to be three times the number the detachment until then had managed to liberate in the course of almost two months.

As the ambulances rolled into the camp desperate women literally stormed the vehicles. Up to fifteen fortunate internees were packed into each ambulance, and in this way 112 sick people (Ankarcrona's figures) could be transported to Lübeck. Transportation through Denmark en route to Sweden was, as before, the responsibility of the Danes. In Lübeck Bernadotte was reached by telephone, and he promised Arnoldsson he would expend every ounce of effort, both Danish and Swedish, to ensure the operation was successful. Arnoldsson also secured permission from de Blonay, the Swiss head of International Red Cross operations, to employ twelve of their trucks. These had until then been used for transporting gift parcels, but in future would be plying the Ravensbrück route to collect as many women as possible.

On 24 April Arnoldsson and Göring were back in Ravensbrück, where the news from Suhren was that he had been issued with fresh orders from Gruppenführer Glücks, chief inspector of the German concentration camp network: a Führerbefehl required all prisoners to be retained at the camps. The order, then, had come straight from Hitler! What had happened?

According to Franz Göring's account of events, at Schellenberg's bidding Göring had made his way to Ravensbrück on 22 April, but there he had come up against an uncooperative Sturmbannführer Suhren, who claimed that all the camp's files and case records had been destroyed. The following day Suhren told Göring in private that via Kaltenbrunner he had been given Hitler's express order to keep the prisoners at the camp and liquidate them as enemy troops approached. He also let Göring into his confidence revealing that at the camp he had a number of women (fifty-four Polish and seventeen French) for whom strict orders had been issued that they were not to be handed over: they had been subjected to medical experiments. They were the so-called *Kaninchen* (guinea pigs). Germs were inoculated, the prisoners fell ill, and afterwards the women were 'cured' by means of muscle and bone surgery.

Göring succeeded in telephoning to obtain Himmler's permission, via Brandt, for all the prisoners, including the *Kaninchen*, to be released. Dr Arnoldsson was notified and was to see personally that these instructions were carried out. Arnoldsson later confessed, however, that in the hurly-burly he had had no time to check this thoroughly (Ankarcrona reported that Suhren had managed to retain fourteen of the women, although they did leave with the next transport). In this context it may be added that Swedish archives contained details of women who had suffered these medical experiments at Ravensbrück and who had been brought to Sweden and received Swedish medical attention.[24]

In parallel with this the severely overworked Swedish detachment had left Padborg at 6 a.m. on the morning of 22 April after almost uninterrupted missions, first to Theresienstadt and Copenhagen followed by the evacuation of Neuengamme. The detachment was split into two convoys when Captain Folke joined them in Lübeck. In the evening one of the convoys reached Ravensbrück, where Suhren told the Swedes that the Russians, having cut off the route to Berlin, were now capable of getting to Ravensbrück in a matter of hours, but that probably instead they would detour in a south-westerly direction and complete the encirclement of Berlin. Suhren therefore demanded an immediate departure, that very evening. Ankarcrona shared his view. Captain Folke knew, however, that the bus drivers, totally exhausted, needed a few hours' rest. In Suhren's presence Folke threatened Ankarcrona that he would personally shoot him if he, Ankarcrona, refused to act on Folke's decision. The drivers were given their period of rest. Reveille was sounded at 3 a.m. and 786 women, most of them French, were loaded on board and travelled straight to Padborg. The second convoy would fetch 360 more French women.

The prisoners were deeply suspicious of the Swedes at the start. Folke had made the mistake of supervising the boarding of the buses side by side with the camp commandant. The women's icy gaze was an expression of their conviction that they were going to be moved to another concentration camp. Once on the buses, they told how the SS female officers had said that they were being transported away to be gassed and cremated. Their outbursts of joy as soon as they realised they were heading for freedom were enormous. Of all the transportations undertaken by the expedition this one, with the French women, was received the most gratefully. They seized every opportunity to show their gratitude, and in Padborg were welcomed heartily by the Danes in French. It was a deeply moving moment when the 'Marseillaise' echoed out from the buses in homage to liberty. In Denmark they were given the usual sumptuous Danish reception with food and drink, and could enjoy a little sleep before being put on Danish trains for transport to Sweden.

The Swedish officers invited a number of the English-speaking French women to dinner at Padborg on 23 April. These women told how only a fraction of the five thousand so-called 'Swedish parcels' delivered on 8 April had actually reached the internees. They also described the gruesome brutality perpetrated at Ravensbrück, not least by the female SS officers, and the medical experiments carried out. Furthermore, they recounted the way the camp had been 'tidied up' before the arrival of the Swedes. All those irremediably sick had been exterminated, a number of women sent to the gas chambers, which then had been destroyed, while the male prisoners who helped to carry out the destruction had been shot.

The following morning, on 24 April, the Swedish detachment began its final trip to Ravensbrück. Conditions inside Germany became more and more difficult. The *Tiefflieger* – the Allied planes – were causing havoc everywhere, and they could not be warded off. German traffic had been reduced almost to a standstill. But Ravensbrück might fall at any moment, and transport chief Svenson ordered the rescue operation to go ahead. For long distances the Swedes were now completely alone on the highway while German vehicles stood abandoned or burnt out by the roadside. As they approached Berlin the stream of refugees increased. Berlin was now surrounded, and all those civilians and military personnel who were able to hastily made their way westwards. Every conceivable vehicle came into use – fire engine, horse and cart, bicycle and handcart. Svenson urged the drivers to keep almost bumper to bumper so that no German vehicles could slip in between the Swedish ones. The convoy slowly advanced and by nightfall still had a number of kilometres left to reach Ravensbrück. Svenson was forced to bivouac for the night, and the convoy finally got to its destination at the break of day on 25 April.

By then, eight hundred women had been waiting in line all prepared for transport since the day before, with no sign of the buses. In the meantime Arnoldsson had driven to the Harzwalde country estate, where he picked up a couple of unidentified people of 'Swedish descent' (they must have been the brother of Kersten's wife and Elisabeth Lüben, both German citizens). The French women, waiting patiently although there were as yet still no buses in sight at nightfall, were in excellent spirits all the same – they were of course free! Arnoldsson's suggestion that the sickest among them, at least, should spend the night with a roof over their heads inside the camp was met by a storm of protests. Finally the convoy of Danish ambulances turned up followed by the International Red Cross trucks shortly after. Sixty-five people were packed into the cargo space of each truck – a grand total of 706 French, Belgian, Dutch and Polish women. Ninety-odd women had to be left behind – the following morning they were scooped up by the next (Swedish) convoy.

On the way back the war really caught up with the Danish/international expedition. German resistance had almost entirely collapsed. The roads were chock-a-block with retreating soldiers, prisoners of war on the march in every direction, and civilians fleeing in panic from a Berlin in flames – all going west, away from the Russians. Tank formations could break through at any moment from the west. The Allied *Tiefflieger* were unchallenged in the air and patrolled the motorways uninterruptedly. At night they launched attacks when they saw the tiniest glimmer of light, and the expedition no longer dared drive through the hours of darkness. The Allied pilots' former respect for the symbolic markings of the White

Buses had now practically vanished. The convoy of International Red Cross trucks driven by Canadians who were former camp prisoners was headed by a Swedish vehicle with Eric Ringman at the wheel and convoy leader Gösta Hallqvist at his side. The following day, 25 April, Hallqvist's convoy was attacked west of Schwerin.

The convoy was brought to a halt and took shelter while the aircraft circled above them without firing. Believing all danger over, Hallqvist gave the order to make preparations to continue the journey. Then the aircraft went on the attack, killing Ringman, a Canadian driver and five women – thirteen women according to another source. Sixteen people were badly injured, among them Hallqvist who miraculously survived. Hallqvist, with bits of bullets and splinters still lodged in his head, suffered from recurrent headaches from that time and was alive until 2006. The other convoy made up of Danish ambulances was attacked near Wismar and saw four people die and ten receive serious injuries.

Frykman's report home to the Foreign Office stated that both attacks followed reconnaisance flights by the aircraft, both were entirely intentional, and the planes were probably British. The remains of the convoy, led by Lieutenant Löthman, continued its way but suffered a new attack from the air at Plön, where twenty passengers were killed according to Frykman's account. The injured were picked up by Danish ambulances and brought to Denmark where several of those in a critical condition died. In Arnoldsson's estimation this transport operation all in all between Ravensbrück and Padborg in Denmark cost twenty-five lives, a figure that presumably took into account those who died later.

Meanwhile Svenson's convoy had filled its twenty buses with 934 internees. First of all the Swedes, working from their lists, had some seventy or so sick French and Belgian women summoned on board. Captain Folke had also got a list of eight English names smuggled in. Initially the commandant would not acknowledge their existence but gradually Danziger, the Gestapo liaison official, got the Germans to produce twenty-two British and American women. The majority of the women travelling with the transport were Polish, however, some fifty of them accompanied by the children they had given birth to at the camp. As the day went on more and more confusion arose at the camp, and soon enough the Swedes stopped negotiating about this and that contingent and took with them everybody they could without asking.

It was a motley collection of people that left Ravensbrück. On board the buses there were now South American women, a Chinese, breast-feeding mothers and others in an advanced stage of pregnancy, a few Belgian and Dutch men who had managed to sneak their way in as well as a Swede with his German wife and mother-in-law. Up to sixty women were squeezed into buses whose regulation capacity was twenty-five passengers. Including German and Swedish personnel the transport operation involved more than one thousand people. The journey home was one long nightmare in the midst of a chaotic stream of Germans fleeing in panic. Horror stories involving the Russians were rife – Goebbels had done his propaganda work very effectively. Once again Svenson was forced to bivouac for the night, during which one of the Poles gave birth. The baby was nicknamed 'Per Albin' after the bus that had provisionally been converted into a maternity ward and after the Swedish prime minister. A less felicitous circumstance was the night attack from fighter planes, which happily resulted in no injuries. On 26 April Lieutenant Svenson succeeded in reaching Denmark without further mishap, along with almost one thousand women.

By 25 April, according to Ankarcrona's account, 1,300 women had been transferred to safety, the majority of them Polish Jewish women – presumably the 360 plus 934 accounted for above. Still languishing in the misery of Ravensbrück on 26 April were about two hundred sick women, two thousand Polish women, and between eighteen and twenty-two Dutch women working on a farm in the vicinity. On 30 April the Soviet army marched into Ravensbrück.

This was to be the Swedish detachment's last transport operation in Germany. The Allies' war fronts were now fast approaching one another, Germany was in a state of collapse, and further transport along the motorways was deemed far too hazardous. Ravensbrück and the other women's camps were considered no longer feasible to reach. Frykman notified the Foreign Office on 26 April that further transportation by the Red Cross detachment had been discontinued until such time as adequate guarantees could be offered by the Allies that the air attacks would not be repeated.

Two days later Bernadotte arrived at Padborg. Frykman's assessment of the situation was that the Swedish detachment was now needed in Denmark, where thousands of Scandinavians were awaiting transportation to Sweden. The International Red Cross vehicles could only be used in Germany, and they could continue to be employed there. Bernadotte expressed his full comprehension of Frykman's evaluation – operations in Germany could no longer continue.

Frykman requested that Sweden send 'the most energetic protests' to the British, American and French legations over the air attacks on the Swedish Red Cross detachment. Whether they were sent or not I do not know. On 1 May, however, the British minister in Stockholm did express the British government's duty-bound regret at the attacks 'claimed' to be British, at the same time reminding the Swedish Foreign Office of the warnings issued previously.[25]

The Swedes had understood at an early stage at Ravensbrück that other means of transport would be needed in order to release as many women as possible and as fast as possible. It was greatly to their surprise that, after Arnoldsson, Frykman, Folke and Göring had called on railway chief Reichsbahnspräsident Bauer in Lübeck, they found they had at their disposal an entire train of goods wagons. This train left Ravensbrück on 25 April, eighty women crammed into each of fifty wagons. On departure, each woman was given an American Red Cross parcel. The train later disappeared, but was gradually traced to a spot some kilometres from Lübeck, its locomotive broken down. When four days later, on 29 April, the train reached Lübeck railway station Arnoldsson and his colleagues opened the wagon doors dreading the worst. Things were better than they had feared, however: only two women had died and a dozen had to be rushed to hospital. After due nourishment the women travelled on the same train to Denmark, where Danish trains with real passenger carriages were waiting. This 'ghost train', as it came to be known, rescued a further 3,989 women from Ravensbrück.

Adding together all the figures quoted above, the combined Swedish–Danish–international rescue operation by road between 22 and 26 April would have brought a total of 2,904 women from Ravensbrück to Denmark for further transportation to Sweden. The figures are not entirely conclusive, however, and vary from source to source. Bernadotte has compiled a pencilled list (not dated, unfortunately) on the back of an Air Training corps stencil. It specified 2,873 women (from) 'Ravensbrück and *Aussenkommandon* from Neuengamme', a figure broken down into 946 Polish women, 254 French, 51 Belgian, 15 Dutch and 1,607 Jewish of different nationalities.

The same sheet of paper gave another specification: 'arrived Sweden Friday–Saturday' (4–5 May?), adding up to 3,175 people – in other words, more or less the same figures as those quoted above. If we add the four thousand who came by 'ghost train', the expedition would have rescued at least seven thousand women from Ravensbrück in the course of less than a week. Norbert Masur similarly reported in 1945 that seven thousand women, approximately half of them Jewish, were rescued from Ravensbrück by the Swedish Red Cross. German documentation concerning Ravensbrück stated that 7,500 were evacuated 'within the framework of the Bernadotte operation'. The same figure was quoted by Captain Melin, while Arnoldsson, head of the whole operation, claimed that 'we' rescued about eight thousand women from Ravensbrück.[26]

Dr Hans Arnoldsson from Gothenburg in Sweden would never forget his last day at Ravensbrück, when commandant Suhren was preparing the evacuation march out of the camp of ten thousand Russian women. (It is noteworthy that Ankarcrona's report made no mention at all of these Russian women. The German collection of source material estmated that on evacuation of the camp on 27 April there were still 18,000–30,000 prisoners remaining there.) Suhren assured Arnoldsson that the Germans were still in possession of a secret, as yet untested, weapon which would grant Germany final victory. He would be back at the camp in a few weeks with his Russian women, of this Suhren had no doubts whatsoever. While evacuation was proceeding and Russian guns could be heard thundering in the near distance, a detachment of SS women in rigid step paraded around the camp chanting improvidently:

'*Wir werden weiter marschieren, wenn alles in Scherben fällt, denn heute gehört uns Deutschland und morgen die ganze Welt.*' (We shall go marching on, though all around us fall to bits, for today Germany belongs to us, and tomorrow the entire world.)[27]

The Rescue Expedition's Work Is Concluded

After being moved to a base at Padborg the White Buses were used from 28 April onwards for transporting prisoners from their temporary quarters at Frøslev and Møgelkjaer. Both drivers and material were absolutely worn-out. The drivers had kept themselves awake for the night trips by taking amphetamine in both tablet form and dissolved in chocolate. The amphetamine tablets were provided, one at a time, by the expedition nursing staff. Many of the journeys were by now being undertaken by Danish vehicles. The final journey back to Sweden set off on 30 April, which traditionally ushers in the Scandinavian spring. The triumphal journey through Denmark in Axel Molin's description was met with incredible ovations on the part of the Danish population. After being treated in princely fashion at a reception at the Blegdam hospital that night the detachment's remaining personnel were ferried across to Malmö on 1 May. The Swedish national anthem was sung on the ferry, after which the vehicles, carrying the coffin of the dead driver Ringman, landed on Swedish soil. The detachment's tasks had been completed.

Rescue work in Germany, however, was not entirely over. Remnants of the Red Cross detachment, staff belonging to the Swedish Church and individual Swedes resident in Germany had admittedly left Lübeck on 28 April when the British were reported to be approaching from the west and the Russians from the east. Captain Ankarcrona, Dr Arnoldsson, a further doctor and three drivers remained, however. Their job was to take care of those wounded when the convoy was attacked, including Lieutenant Hallqvist, and to supervise the final stages of the transport operations from Ravensbrück. What this last task involved is not too clear. It might have to do with women on the so-called 'ghost train', and it might have to do with the injured people from the air attack who had been hospitalised in Lübeck. Arnoldsson also knew that about three hundred Norwegian citizens were still confined in German prisons but he did not know where. Very shortly more transports would be taking place, but this time without the Swedish buses.

218

Ankarcrona had pluckily begun an adventurous journey on 28 April to the Neu Brandenburg camp as part of a reconnaissance patrol for an International Red Cross convoy. At that time, the camp lay within shooting range of the war front, and all the prisoners bar those who were ill had been sent off on a march. When the main convoy reached the camp the war front had already passed the camp and the vehicles suddenly found themselves inside a Soviet military zone. It took the convoy eight days to return to Lübeck, but on their way back they were able to pick up two hundred of the women who otherwise were marching to their deaths along the roads.

Franz Göring ascertained that in Hamburg and its surroundings there were still about 2,000 women (960 Jewish, 790 Polish and 250 French women), transferred from various *Aussenkommandon* to Neuengamme. They were transported by a new goods train, personally requisitioned by Göring, into Denmark where the Danish Red Cross assumed responsibility before they were shipped to Sweden. On arrival in Denmark on 2 May the starving women, without food for several days, scrambled out of the wagons, half naked and howling with distress, in search of food. Potato peelings, grass and bits of bread which the local population threw to them led to clashes and scuffles. The Danish quarantine camp at Padborg was then in the process of being wound up, and the Danes, taken by surprise, required some time to arrange for proper food to be brought from the hospital at Sønderborg.[28] There is an element of uncertainty, however, about this last large transport operation by train. Two other Danish sources report up to 2,800 women arriving on this train, and they are supposed to have come from Ravensbrück.

Dr Arnoldsson on 29 April received an anonymous letter informing him of what had happened to the rest of the prisoners at Neuengamme when the camp was emptied on 20 April. The prisoners had been taken by goods train to Lübeck where the following day they were locked up in four cramped vessels in the harbour. By chance the Swedish ships the *Magdalena* and the *Lillie Matthiessen* were anchored in the same harbour after having delivered their cargo of prisoner of war parcels. Arnoldsson suggested to the German authorities that he take charge of 250 prisoners from the German ship *Athen* and send them with the Swedish ships on to

Sweden. At the same time a German officer asked Arnoldsson if he would take care of some seriously ill prisoners from the German vessel *Cap Arcona* who were currently housed in a barn at Süssel, a few kilometres north of Lübeck. They were fetched by Bjørn Heger and driven to the quayside in cars provided by the International Red Cross. The Norwegian Heger had been kitted out by Arnoldsson in Swedish uniform and incorporated into the Swedish force.

The two Swedish boats on 30 April were reported to be standing by for departure for Malmö, the *Magdalena* accommodating 223 ex-prisoners and the *Lillie Matthiessen* 225 women. They were French, Belgian, Dutch and Polish women, all in a precarious state of health. Arnoldsson, in despair, was forced to leave thousands of other prisoners living under the most wretched conditions. He tried to console them with the fact that it was only a matter of days before the British would arrive. And so it turned out. On 3 May the port was raided by British aircraft and three of the German ships with concentration camp prisoners on board sank, with very few survivors. Arnoldsson estimated that at least ten thousand of the prisoners from Neuengamme drowned that day, while German documentation reported that at dawn the following day the sea, as smooth as glass, revealed the corpses of almost eight thousand people. A day after the liberators – the British – had entered and occupied Lübeck, those same British forces took the lives of thousands of prisoners who had endured years of suffering in German concentration camps. The sinking of the *Cap Arcona* alone cost the lives of nearly five thousand prisoners – far more than the death toll of the *Titanic* and *Estonia* disasters. Ten or eight thousand drowned ex-prisoners was hardly worthy of a headline in any newspaper on 3 May 1945.[29]

The last batch of women was ferried over to Sweden on 4 May 1945. The same day a last group of five hundred Danish policemen and ninety-five political prisoners would be transferred to Sweden. A huge crowd had congregated at Copenhagen's free port zone to give the Danish prisoners a hearty send-off. Their departure was delayed hour after hour in an atmosphere of tense expectation. Prince George, who had collaborated with the Swedish Red Cross detachment, tried to persuade the German police inspector on board the ferry to release the policemen. In the end the

Gestapo headquarters yielded after pressure from the Danish Ministry of Foreign Affairs.

Resounding shouts of joy greeted the Danish police as they went ashore – free men. The ferry slowly started to ease away from the quayside. The Swedish head of detachment, Major Frykman, was now approached by a Danish political prisoner who wondered whether they too, the political prisoners, couldn't obtain their liberty. When the German police inspector commented that he was not in a position to assume responsibility for such a move, Frykman replied that Germany's surrender was expected at any moment. Frykman informed the representative of the Danish Ministry of Social Affairs that he personally at his own risk was releasing all of the ninety-five prisoners. This was announced on the ferry's loudspeaker system, the captain ordered the vessel to move astern, and the overjoyed Danes swarmed over the rails to join their countrymen. The transportation of prisoners over the Öresund Straits was thus at an end. The same evening the Germans surrendered in Denmark. Enormous peace celebrations broke out in Copenhagen – and the Swedes were more popular than ever.

12

Operation Rescue Norway!

The Swedish foreign minister, Christian Günther, wrote on the day peace was declared in 1945:

8 May 1945: Peace! Peace? Tonight armistice with Germany comes into effect.

Days full of unbearable strain have preceded the announcement; the radio's been on all the time, newspapers have been snapped up. Latest developments have gone tremendously fast. A constant worry has been: would the Germans in Denmark and Norway, especially Norway, surrender without putting up a fight, or would we be forced to intervene in a conflict that might have been anything but simple, and in which we might even have had to risk becoming acquainted with V1 and V2 rockets?

When the news came yesterday of an unconditional surrender we felt an immense relief. Denmark and Norway free, Sweden spared the war, and war in Europe over. Stockholm can't ever have enjoyed such scenes of jubilation.

Today. Well, today the shadows are there to see and they're dark. Europe, continental Europe, destroyed, in ruins. An overriding hatred. A hatred between nations and within nations. Impoverished, without food, without roof, without tools. The liberated countries at least have a hope. But Germany? There's no hope there. Not even here have I heard a word of sympathy. It's quite natural that in the liberated countries there's not much room for sympathy, but even

222

here people forget too easily that in Germany too there are millions of innocent people suffering horribly, both mentally and physically, without a glimmer of hope. Decidedly, compassion is not *comme il faut* at this moment.

And the dark shadow of Russia. Powerful as never before, and more powerful still now that the United States and Britain apply all their strength to defeating Japan. Powerful and opaque. As far as Sweden is concerned there are two issues of current interest. Would the Russians accept the German surrender on Bornholm and at Narvik and 'temporarily' occupy them, subsequently never to leave? A nightmare!

What's hidden behind the Russian lines? Nobody knows, not even the Allies. What's going on there? Kalmuk and Kirghiz people in Berlin. How many Germans are being dragged to Russia? Where are our Berlin friends? Don't even know anything about the remaining members of our legation even though it's been so many days now since Berlin collapsed. Best not to think about it.

And yet . . . The first steps have been taken, they must be taken before any improvement can take place. Arms are silent in Europe, for the time being at least. And by a miracle and by wise decisions Sweden has avoided being drawn in.[1]

Sweden and Scandinavia: From Submissiveness to Military Intervention?

The Swedish policy of complying with Germany's course of action during the first years of the war had led to tough reactions surfacing in the occupied neighbouring countries of Norway and Denmark. After Germany had attacked Denmark and Norway on 9 April 1940 the Swedish government declared that it would observe a strictly neutral policy. There were particularly bitter feelings in Norway, where a certain touchiness still remained from the Swedish–Norwegian union of 1814–1905. The Norwegians considered that Sweden ought to have been able to act more forcefully during and after the German invasion. The Swedish decision of 18 April to permit 'humanitarian' German rail transport through Swedish territory of beleaguered German troops in the Narvik area was seen by the Norwegians as an unnecessary Swedish stab in the back to the combined British–French–Norwegian military operations in the north of Norway, up till then successful. The uninterrupted export of Swedish iron ore to Germany was viewed as a Swedish contribution to the German war effort.

Following the surrender of the Norwegian fighting forces in the north of Norway and the retreat of the Allied troops, the Swedish government on 18 June had abided by Germany's request also to use Swedish territory for the transit of German soldiers, so-called 'soldiers on leave', and munitions to Norway. This concession led to protests from the Norwegian and the British governments, which both saw the action as a departure from a strict policy of neutrality.

Norwegian criticism was also directed at the Swedish government's refusal to allow Norwegian ships to leave Swedish ports. Instead the vessels were requisitioned and later, via a series of legal procedures, embargoed (the so-called embargoed ships, referred to earlier in the book). The Norwegian government-in-exile in London, which had placed the entire Norwegian merchant fleet at the Allies' disposal, requested that Sweden permit the Norwegian ships to leave for Britain.

Relations between the Norwegian London government and Stockholm were frosty in general for a long time.[2] During the first years of the war the London government felt it was treated in an unfriendly and condescending way by the Swedish government, which had refused to recognise the Norwegian government-in-exile as the only lawful Norwegian government. Stockholm regarded the Norwegian London government rather as a British puppet government and chose instead to establish contacts with the leaders of the Norwegian resistance movement, the Hjemmefronten. The Swedish government probably counted on the Norwegian government-in-exile expending itself politically by the end of the war, and that the Hjemmefronten people would then seize power. Thus, when the Norwegian minister in Stockholm died in 1940 the Swedish government refused to accept the appointment of a new fully authorised proxy. Norway would have to be content with a chargé d'affaires until December 1943. The remaining Norwegian legation in Stockholm, however, was to become quite important not only for the London government's contact with Sweden but also for its indirect links to the Norwegian resistance movement. The Swedish government had, moreover, as we have already seen, close and informal contacts in Stockholm with Norway's former minister in Warsaw, Niels Christian Ditleff, who rejoiced in the title of Envoyé Extraordinaire et Ministre Plénipotentiaire faisant fonctions de Conseiller à la Légation de Norvège, Stockholm.

The Swedish policy of appeasement towards Germany had also come up against a small but opinion-wise considerable opposition. In Stockholm Ture Nerman's *Trots Allt!* magazine was an important mouthpiece for Swedish support for Norway. Most crucial, perhaps, was the Gothenburg *Göteborgs Handels- och Sjöfarts-Tidning* daily newspaper with its aggressive chief editor, Torgny Segerstedt. Segerstedt consistently and forcefully criticised Nazi Germany right from the moment Hitler seized power in 1933. His criticism of the coalition government's compliance with Nazi Germany took into consideration, not least, its handling of connections with the Norwegian sister nation. Gothenburg in 1940–5 lay, as indeed it does today, much closer to Oslo in every respect than it did to Stockholm.

In line with the German military setbacks from autumn 1942 onwards, Stockholm's attitudes towards the Germans became more brazen. Swedish forceful rearmament then reached such a strength that German threats could be met with a greater degree of confidence. The pro-Norwegian opinion in Sweden, which in general also expressed itself in favour of the Allies, gained more and more attention for its demands, while German proposals were treated all the more curtly by Stockholm. Transit of German troops, the 'soldiers on leave', and equipment was soft-pedalled and revoked in July 1943. The Swedish policy of neutrality, which had previously shown clear German bias, was now largely back to a balanced position. From 1943 onwards it gradually moved in a pro-Allied direction. During autumn 1944 Swedish ports were closed to German shipping and Swedish iron ore exports to Germany stopped. By the turn of the year (1944–5) Swedish–German commerce had been almost suspended from the Swedish side.

Growing pressure of opinion from mainly liberal and Social Democratic quarters saw to it that prime minister Hansson's and foreign secretary Günther's problems at the end of the war focused all the more on impeding 100 per cent support for the western Allies. Too drastic concessions to London and Washington from the Swedish side would lead, in the first place, to doubts arising on the Soviet side as to Sweden's sincerity in declaring its neutrality and remaining outside the two major power blocs. It was clear by the turn of the year (1944–5) that after the war the Soviet Union would be replacing Germany as Sweden's big influential neighbour on the Baltic. In the second place the coalition government's most important task was still to keep Sweden out of the conflict. This would really be put to the test at the tail end of the war.

The Nordic dimension began to assume more and more importance for Swedish foreign policy from 1943: partly it was a question of helping the Nordic neighbouring countries in their quest for a happy ending to war and occupation, and partly an endeavour to prepare the way for harmonious Nordic cooperation after the war was over.

Some fifty thousand Norwegian refugees fled to Sweden during the war. A petition from the Norwegian government-in-exile was granted by the Swedish government in 1943 allowing so-called Norwegian 'police battalions' to be trained in Sweden, with twelve thousand men and women recruited by 1945. They were equipped from Swedish military stores, not merely with light small arms but also with mortars, cannons and light anti-aircraft artillery. They were permitted to hold regular manoeuvres on Swedish soil. Even though officially, and particularly in respect of the Germans, they were called 'police troops', there is no doubt that in 1945 they had risen to become fairly well-armed and well-trained military units. The aim was for these battalions, on leaving Swedish territory, to be placed under General Eisenhower's Supreme Headquarters Allied Expeditionary Forces – to be incorporated, that is, in the western Allies' warfare organisation.

Only a handful of these Norwegian battalions were to take part in the liberation of Norway. Most of them entered Norway following the German surrender of 7–8 May. Some companies, however, had already at the beginning of 1945 been transferred to the Norwegian Lapp territory known as Finnmarken, which had just been liberated by Soviet troops. These Norwegian companies were transported and provided for by nine American aircraft which had been stationed from December 1944 at the

Kallax airport near Luleå in Sweden. Plainly the training of Norwegian military personnel on Swedish soil, as well as the location of American military aircraft at a Swedish air base in order to lend support to Norwegian military units in Norway, implied a departure from the principles of neutrality.

In the final phases of the war the German *Festung Europa* swiftly collapsed on the continent. In the Nordic countries, on the other hand, German troop contingents remained intact, both in Denmark and in Norway. Günther estimated the German war machine in Norway on 27 April 1945 at 160,000 men and women, 225 aircraft at the most, 150–200 U-boats plus a number of heavy surface vessels. The head of the German Supreme Command, Oberkommando der Wehrmacht Field Marshal Keitel, on 6 March 1945 had given the German troops in Norway the order to continue the military struggle whatever the outcome of the battle scene on the central European front. A German map manoeuvre in late winter 1945 had demonstrated to the German command that they would no longer be able to halt a large-scale *Swedish* military invasion of Norway. The Swedish/German military balance of power had now swung over in Sweden's favour.[3]

Trygve Lie, foreign minister in the Norwegian government-in-exile, had visited Stockholm in October 1944 to celebrate the first Swedish–Norwegian summit meeting during the war. Lie's talks with prime minister Hansson and foreign minister Günther had ironed out all misconceptions and resulted in a Swedish–Norwegian reconciliation. Lie had announced in London that 'the Swedes will do what we ask them, if required also march into Norway with armed forces'. The Norwegian government-in-exile now – 12 April 1945 – forwarded a formal request to Sweden for an armed Swedish invasion of Norway should the Germans choose to continue their defence of *Festung Norwegen*.

> The Norwegian government ventures to express its conviction that Sweden will be prepared to undertake such an intervention should it prove necessary in order to spare the Norwegian people further suffering which would cast dark and enduring shadows over all the Nordic countries.[4]

Lie also proposed full military preparedness in Sweden, although this was coolly rejected by the Swedish government. In Stockholm the notion was that everything pointed to the conclusion that the Germans were ready to give up their struggle in Norway. This assessment was backed up by reports the government was receiving of Bernadotte's talks in Germany with Heinrich Himmler.

The West was toying with similar notions about Swedish entry into the war. The western Allies lacked sufficient resources to invade *Festung Norwegen* from the sea and were directing their energies towards smashing the Germans' defence on the continental central front. At Eisenhower's SHAEF headquarters his operations section in April 1945 found the only realistic plan was to carry out an invasion from Swedish territory. 'Up to 250,000 strong Allied troop units would be sent via Gothenburg to the Swedish provinces of Dalsland/Värmland and Jämtland in order to attack Oslo and Trondheim. The units would receive support from the Swedish armed forces, who would thus be placed under Eisenhower's command.'[5]

Military involvement on the part of Sweden in the liberation of Norway had already been a topic of discussion in British war planning in the early part of 1945. Following Norwegian overtures to Sweden in February the British Foreign Office advised the Norwegian foreign minister against Swedish entry into the war: 'The disadvantages of so doing outweigh the advantages.' In such a case Sweden itself would be in need of military assistance, which could be supplied only by the Russians. The latter would probably be disinclined to divert huge resources from their main front line in Germany – in addition, there existed strong political objections to allowing the Russians more muscle in Sweden. Sweden's best contribution, if needed, would be to assist in maintaining order in Norway after Germany's collapse.

The British approach soon changed tack, however. It is not easy to pinpoint the reasons for this. It can be assumed, nevertheless, that in the final stages of the war it was becoming increasingly evident – not least for prime minister Churchill – that the British and Soviet troops were involved in a race to see who would first liberate Norway, and thus become the dominant Great Power in Scandinavia. On 9 March the British military attaché in Stockholm issued a warning to the effect that German forces would carry on the war from Norwegian territory even after Germany itself had collapsed, and that the Germans in Norway were preparing continued U-boat warfare. Couldn't Sweden in this case provide its neighbours with valuable assistance 'by entering Norway to maintain order, to check excesses by both (sic!) sides, to protect communications and to prevent massacres?' While reports were coming in suggesting that the Norwegian Hjemmefronten did not believe the Germans would put up any resistance in Norway following Germany's collapse, the war leader himself, Winston Churchill, took command in a 15 April memo to the Foreign Office:

> Few questions are more important than bringing the Swedes into the war to liberate their Norwegian brother State. In this way Sweden would assume an honourable position among the Allies, her previous neutrality having a strong foundation in the great danger she ran until quite recently from the German power . . . The war might be delayed for a long, vexatious and wasteful month by the resistance of this group of German divisions, albeit of low morale, and the very large U-boat force whose operations they will shelter. A protracted resistance here by the Germans would force the British navy to remain at full stretch, delaying necessary movements both to the Far East and to Mountbatten . . .
>
> This is a matter to finish up as quickly as possible. Will you please endeavour to persuade President Truman to prepare a joint note or parallel notes from us to the Swedish government perhaps pointing out that this is the last opportunity they are likely to have of being of service to the Allies as well as to their own neighbours. I regard this matter as of the greatest importance and urgency.[6]

Four days later Churchill returned to the question of 'Swedish Aid to Liberate Norway' in an even more sharply worded memo, this time to General Ismay, Chiefs of Staff Committee:

> It is easy for the Swedes to talk of this matter as if it were not urgent. A vast expense and burden are placed upon us by the continuance of the U-boat menace, and I see in this morning's report that 25,000

tons of shipping have been sunk in one single previous day. Indeed I think that the Swedes should be forced by Britain and America, under severe pressure, to begin their mobilisation at once and to concert with General Eisenhower the necessary measures . . . Even if the Swedish mobilisation would not be complete, the fact that we could move some of our troops in through Sweden after Denmark has been liberated would be a very great advantage.

I regard this as the last opportunity for the Swedes to save their name before the world. Up till a few months ago, they could plead they were frightened. Now they have no excuse except a calculating selfishness, which has distinguished them in both the wars against Germany.[7]

The Swedes, however, maintained their sang-froid. Boheman on 17 April let the British minister Mallet know that Denmark, too, had requested Swedish mobilisation. Yet Swedish mobilisation, Boheman pointed out, immediately coming as it would to the knowledge of the Germans, might well provoke them into the same desperate type of resistance they had shown in the Netherlands. The Swedish army could be mobilised in a matter of a fortnight and then push into Norway. Should both the Norwegian and the Allied governments make the request, the Swedish government was prepared for military action in Norway. The Soviet minister in Stockholm, however, had not been informed of this, as the Russians had previously made it clear that the Soviet government would not approve of Swedish intervention in Norway.

After Churchill's plain language the matter of 'Entry of Sweden into the war' was passed on to the military people and the combined chiefs of staff. On 21 April they notified foreign ministers Stettinius and Eden that General Eisenhower was of the opinion that the Germans would put up organised resistance in Norway, that Norway could be reached effectively only through Sweden, and that 'Swedish cooperation will be forthcoming'. The Allies, however, must proceed with caution – otherwise 'an injudicious approach might result in frightening the Swedes into a flat refusal'. The next step would therefore be to request staff talks with Sweden in order to coordinate 'Swedish action with that of the other (sic!) Allies'. Russian cooperation in liberating Norway was not a military necessity.[8]

On 30 April 1945 the heads of the British and American legations in Stockholm were issued with instructions to persuade the Swedish government to agree to talks between Eisenhower's staff and the Swedish defence staff. The aim of the staff discussions would be to work out a plan for a joint western Allies–Swedish attack on Norway. Within the space of three hours the ministers were able to cable home that foreign minister Günther had accepted the Allies' proposition. Günther's sole Swedish proviso appears to have been that the western Allies' military representatives use civilian dress ('conceal their ranks').[9]

Germany Collapses: Norway and Denmark Are Spared the Final Battle

It was on 25 April 1945 that advance detachments of American and Soviet troops for the first time joined forces in the heart of Germany, at Torgau south of Berlin on the River Elbe. Berlin was now completely encircled and the Soviet troops had penetrated the central districts. On 30 April they proceeded to hoist the Red flag over the German parliament building. On the same day British forces crossed the Elbe in northern Germany. From here they fanned out over north Germany in the direction of Denmark. By 2 May they had reached Lübeck, while on the 3rd Hamburg, Kiel and Flensburg surrendered and were declared open cities, with the entire German front collapsing before the British forces. On 1 May German radio announced Hitler's death the previous day, and that he had been succeeded by the head of the navy, Admiral Dönitz.

Bernadotte had returned to Stockholm on 24 April.[10] In the evening he reported to foreign minister Günther, cabinet secretary Boheman and Foreign Office political department head Eric von Post the sensational news of Himmler's offer to surrender on the Western Front. It was agreed that the prime minister should be informed and that Sweden could not neglect to pass on such an important message. It would have to be done, however, in such a way as not to give the impression that the Swedish government was party to a wedge being driven in between the western Allies and the Soviet Union. Herschel Johnson, the American minister, and his British colleague, Sir Victor Mallet, were summoned. The two ministers together with Boheman and Bernadotte later that night drafted identical telegrams to London and Washington. Marked 'Top Secret', they contained Himmler's offer to surrender 'on the whole Western Front and in Norway and Denmark', while the two ministers at the same time pointed out that this appeared to them to be a final attempt to sow discord between the western Allies and Russia.

How the British reacted can be read in Churchill's book *Triumph and Tragedy*, which devoted a full four pages to the Himmler–Bernadotte talks. Churchill immediately summoned his war cabinet (25 April) and then phoned the new United States president Harry Truman – Roosevelt having died on 12 April. The two leaders came to an agreement and Truman gave his support to Churchill's communication to Stalin. Earlier the same day Churchill had already informed Stalin by telegram of Himmler's offer, but had stressed that the British government regarded only unconditional surrender simultaneously to all three Great Powers acceptable. German fighting forces, on the other hand, either as individuals or as units, could surrender locally to the Allied forces or their representatives. Stalin's reply of thanks was 'the sweetest communication I (Churchill) had ever received from him!'[11]

On the evening of 26 April Boheman and Bernadotte received Truman's response at the American legation: 'A German surrender will only be accepted on condition that full surrender take place on all fronts to Great Britain, the Soviet Union and the United States of America alike. When these conditions are satisfied German fighting forces on all fronts and at every battle scene shall immediately surrender to respective local Allied commanders. Wherever resistance is shown, the Allied offensive will continue mercilessly until total victory is proclaimed.'[12]

Although he expected a completely negative response, Günther reasoned that Bernadotte should immediately deliver the message to Schellenberg. Bernadotte would advise Schellenberg to try, in spite of everything, to get Himmler to go ahead with his plan to surrender, in Norway and Denmark at least. Great care must be taken, however: on no account must Himmler be led to believe that the Swedish government was working towards a split between the western Allies and the Soviet Union.

The advice was to be proffered by Bernadotte as a purely personal gesture (he stated parenthetically his disappointment over the Allies' rejection). Bernadotte immediately flew to Denmark, and on 27 April, this time in Odense, he met Schellenberg once again.

To Schellenberg's mind the matter now was without solution. Nevertheless, the same day Bernadotte had been sent instructions from the Swedish foreign minister to suggest to Himmler – as his own private proposal – the idea of the German troops in Norway, on surrender, being able to enter Sweden where they would be interned. This could be arranged through direct talks between German and Swedish representatives, without Allied intervention, that is. Not until after this would the 'Danish issue' be resolved. This new variation captured Schellenberg's interest and a fresh meeting with Himmler in Lübeck was planned for the following day. The same day, however, the dramatic news of Himmler's offer of surrender with a detailed report of the secret talks between Himmler and Bernadotte came through on the British pirate radio, Radio Atlantic, an occurrence that made Bernadotte furious. This sort of publicity could ruin – or in any event considerably complicate – subsequent talks with Himmler. Schellenberg encountered an equally furious Himmler, who held Schellenberg personally responsible for the fact that the world's press had now been able to publish his offer to Eisenhower and the Allies' humiliating rebuff.[13]

In the end, however, Himmler declared himself prepared to appoint Schellenberg Sonderbevollmächtig, assigned together with the Swedish government to achieve a peaceful solution in the Nordic countries. To begin with, this would involve the Germans formally revoking their occupation of Norway, followed by the internment in Sweden of the German troops for as long as the war lasted. Himmler was also prepared to accept a similar situation for Denmark, but in this case Schellenberg would first have to groom the Reichsbevollmächtigen Dr Best. Himmler refused to see Bernadotte again; the official reason given was that Himmler on that day would be in the Bremen area, now a war zone.

Schellenberg met Bernadotte on 30 April in Copenhagen where Best took Himmler's line. Subsequently at the Swedish legation Schellenberg saw Bernadotte together with a Swedish delegation sent down in all secrecy from the Foreign Office in Stockholm: foreign counsellor von Post, first secretary Sverker Åström and Major Carl von Horn, head of the military bureau at Swedish Rail. Attendance at the talks with Schellenberg, however, was confined to Bernadotte and von Post. Schellenberg notified the Swedes that Himmler on no account would surrender until such time as Hitler was dead, for then he (Himmler) would then automatically have supreme power in the land. Nor would Himmler accept any arrangement in which German troops were handed over to the Russians, which would be the case in the event of their internment in Sweden.

Von Post's response was that such an internment operation should in point of fact be seen as a great act of courtesy on the part of Sweden and a clear advantage for the Germans. As a neutral state Sweden was in no way duty bound to absorb foreign military forces, but rather had the obligation to repel them. What Sweden could guarantee was that the German internees would be handed over to an inter-Allied control commission – not, that is, solely to the Soviet Union – when internment in Sweden was over. Sweden could not make any declaration concerning what would happen to the prisoners of war following their return home to Germany. Nor did von Post believe that the issue of their return home would be very urgent: the Allies would be concerned with a great deal of other issues in the months to come. The Swedish offer of internment would apply only if a series of conditions were agreed to by the Germans:

- the Norwegians spared acts of violence or arrests;
- no Norwegian property damaged;
- immediate release of all Norwegian political prisoners and internees;
- no Norwegian prisoners of war, internees, deportees or those in labour camps be subjected to poor treatment;
- all German military and other plants in Norway, including weapons and stores, to be left in undamaged state.

Von Post repeatedly warned of the urgency of the matter: the general course of the war et cetera might otherwise 'put a spoke in the wheel' for the Swedish plans. Schellenberg, for his part, countered by stressing the importance of maintaining full secrecy so that not even the Norwegians, and other Allies, should be informed by the Swedes. Both parties observed furthermore that neither had the authority to conclude a binding agreement, with Schellenberg having to report back to Himmler and von Post and his retinue to Stockholm.[14]

There existed, therefore, for a number of hours in the course of 30 April the draft of a German–Swedish plan for German surrender in Norway, manifestly without the knowledge of the Allied forces. That very same day, however, the Foreign Office in Stockholm received a request straight from General Eisenhower for Swedish staff negotiations with SHAEF in order to plan operations to be performed jointly by the western Allies and Sweden against the Germans in Norway. According to the foreign minister's presentation to the Swedish Advisory Council on Foreign Affairs, the western Allies now expressly requested the talks being kept secret from the Russians, as 'in Anglo-Saxon circles Norway was considered a western Allied question'. The Russians already had troops in the northern tip of Norway, and it was now essential the western Powers get to the rest of Norway before the Russians. The West's proposal was immediately accepted by the Swedes, who must have realised that a Swedish go-it-alone policy involving German surrender would be a tricky enterprise – or at any event would have to be undertaken at exceptional speed.

The following day the world heard of Hitler's death, and that Admiral Dönitz had succeeded him in the rôle of German 'State President'. Hitler's last will and testament had expelled Himmler from the National Socialist party and stripped him of all his posts. The reason was Himmler's secret talks with the enemy (via Bernadotte), which had come to Hitler's notice in his bunker in the bowels of Berlin. In Trevor-Roper's reconstruction of the event Hitler was blind with rage: the faithful Heinrich's betrayal was the final stab in the back. Hitler gave up, wrote his will and committed suicide. First, however, he went through a marriage ceremony – finally – with Eva Braun, and before that had Hermann Fegelein, married to Eva's sister, shot. It is unclear why this execution took place. According to Trevor-Roper Fegelein had been charged not only with desertion but also with having been acquainted with Himmler's secret meetings with Bernadotte. Padfield's speculations centred around Hitler's belief that it was Fegelein via a lover who had leaked information from the bunker to the well-informed British Radio Atlantic.[15]

Himmler's fall from grace came as a shock to all of those who, in Stockholm at least, had assumed that he was the one who would be succeeding Hitler. Relations with Himmler and his closest colleague Schellenberg which the Swedes had laboriously built up would now supposedly be of no use.

On returning to Germany Schellenberg discovered that he too had been deprived of all his posts, in his case by Kaltenbrunner. Dönitz, however, in his first government reshuffle, replaced Ribbentrop as foreign minister with Count Schwerin von Krosigk, who was more inclined to negotiate. Schellenberg met Himmler and handed over his report on the talks with von Post, Bernadotte and Best. Himmler and Schellenberg agreed that von Krosigk was also bent on a peaceful outcome to the Nordic situation while the military men Dönitz, Keitel and Jodl, on the other hand, were not prepared to surrender *Festung Norwegen* without a fight.

Schellenberg was back in Copenhagen on 2 May. His travels around Denmark were made all the easier because he was able to use Bernadotte's own Red Cross car, ironically enough one that Bernadotte had been provided with by the Norwegian legation. The only unpleasant aspect of all this, wrote Schellenberg in his diary, was all the warm greetings that were showered on him in his supposed capacity of Swedish citizen, and all the autographs he had to sign for school children and Danish adults, in his rôle as Swedish Red Cross worker. Schellenberg once again saw von Post and Åström, notifying them that his plan still had Himmler's support and the new foreign minister's too. Von Post's report back home, however, spoke of the failure of Schellenberg to discuss with Himmler those issues, highly relevant for Sweden, that concerned the scope of the internment clause and the details pertaining to a possible settlement. Himmler's sole worry appeared to have been that the coastal fortifications not fall into the hands of the Russians. Von Post countered by saying that an eventual Allied occupation of Norway would probably be undertaken by the British while any equipment left behind by the Germans could be requisitioned by the Norwegian police force which had received its training in Sweden. The closer a German surrender seemed likely, however, the less interest the Swedes showed in separate arrangements for Norway. Von Post concluded that there was no longer any concrete Swedish proposal to hand.

The negotiators agreed that time was running out and binding proposals had to be made and exchanged, the sooner the better.[16]

Schellenberg hadn't given up. On 3 May, after a nightmarish journey through the chaos of a Germany in a state of collapse in which he survived twelve raids from Allied *Tiefflieger*, he managed to gain an audience with both foreign minister von Krosigk and Admiral Dönitz. Germany's new foreign minister was very understanding, but Dönitz initially would not have anything to do with the Swedish offer. Schellenberg pointed out that Sweden in the near future would be the only neutral country of any importance to a totally demolished Germany. A long series of sessions joined by generals Keitel and Jodl resulted in Schellenberg on 4 May obtaining letters of authority from Dönitz. The German state government gave him full powers: 'to conduct talks with His Swedish Majesty's government concerning matters which may arise in respect of Swedish–German relations as a result of the German armed forces' occupation of Norway being revoked'.

That evening saw Schellenberg back in Copenhagen. His car – Bernadotte's Red Cross car, that is – got stuck in the cavalcade of tens of thousands of Danes anticipating German surrender in the central square, Rådhuspladsen. Bernadotte's car was soon recognised, and Schellenberg swiftly had to fasten doors and windows while dozens of enthusiastic Danes climbed up all over the bonnet, mudguards and roof. It took a perspiring hour and a half for the Germans, nodding and doffing their hats and muttering rudimentary Swedish, to force their way through the crowds and seek refuge in the Swedish legation. Then it was off to Malmö by Danish Red Cross plane and finally to Stockholm on board a Swedish bomber. It was now 5 May and Åström took Schellenberg, now converted into a Gesandter (German emissary) to Bernadotte's living quarters, where Boheman and von Post were waiting. Bernadotte had suggested to the Foreign Office that he accommodate Schellenberg at his home if that was deemed convenient for reasons of secrecy.[17]

According to notes taken by Åström, Schellenberg now informed his Swedish hosts that German headquarters had already issued orders to General Böhme, commander of the German troops in Norway, not to fire a single shot. He claimed to have the authority, in his capacity as

Gesandter, to be able to arrange for Swedish troops to cross into Norway and on Norwegian soil take command of surrendering German forces. He also considered he was in a position to hold direct talks with the western Powers. Schellenberg further maintained that it was he who had seen to it that the Germans' offer of surrender to Montgomery on 3 May covered Denmark as well. Von Post then insisted that 'the Allies' must of course be informed, and a meeting between Schellenberg and Eisenhower might also possibly be arranged. Bernadotte's report stated that it was only the 'western Allies' representatives' in Stockholm who were first given the opportunity to acquaint their governments with the matter, and they also 'contemplated' informing the Soviet Union's chargé d'affaires, but not until advised to do so by London and Washington. Should the United States and Britain consider it convenient, Sweden wished to have the opportunity to inform the Russians first.

The Swedes wanted the fullest secrecy – only the Norwegian minister was given immediate information. Eisenhower's staff nevertheless asked Sweden to inform the Russians. In the course of the evening of 5 May the Soviet Union's representative in Stockholm, Chernyshev, was told of Schellenberg's authorisation to declare 'the surrender of the German troops in Norway, possibly in collaboration with Sweden'. Boheman's handwritten report showed that the Swedish Foreign Office via the British minister in Stockholm made an urgent request by telegram for a SHAEF mission to be sent to Stockholm as fast as possible for direct talks in which Sweden was expected to 'make itself benevolently available every proposal SHAEF provisional internment German troops'. President Truman, however, interpreted the Swedish offer as even more far-reaching: that the Swedish government had now approved an Allied suggestion for an 'attack launched from Swedish territory . . . on the German troops in Norway'. He considered it extremely doubtful, however, that Sweden would declare war on Germany.[18]

Things were happening fast now and every hour was precious. That same evening the German minister in Stockholm, Hans Thomsen, flew to the Norwegian border in a Swedish military aircraft, and there instead of General Böhme he met his subordinate Colonel Uberhack. He was coolly informed that Böhme had no intention whatsoever of surrendering without direct instructions from Admiral Dönitz. Böhme's forces in Norway were fully intact and capable of holding their ground for several months. A series of feverish telephone calls were made from the German legation in Stockholm, Schellenberg talking to Oslo and Schellenberg talking to Dönitz and to von Krosigk, all of them duly recorded by the Radio Institute of the Swedish Armed Forces. Schellenberg was told that the German government had established direct contact with Eisenhower, and the issue of Norway was included. If the matter of a total German surrender could be settled between them, it was not certain that the Swedish government need be involved at all.[19]

In conjunction with all this, troublesome reports were coming in from Denmark. The Russians had started bombing the Danish island of Bornholm in the Baltic and would soon be going ashore there. Rumours were circulating that Soviet troops had been parachuted on to the main Danish island of Själland and that a Russian offensive into Denmark was coming from Warnemünde on the north German coast. The Swedish minister in Copenhagen on 7 May notified the Swedish government of an imminent request from Best and Schellenberg for Swedish cooperation in an effort to bring a swift end to German occupation. It would require the Germans laying down their arms in the presence of some 150 Swedish officers in order for Denmark thus to avoid a possible Russian occupation.

The western Allies, however, and the British in particular, were now not in the least interested in allotting the stubbornly neutral Sweden an important rôle in the dying moments of the Second World War. During the war Sweden had been regarded as a British 'sphere of interest'. Churchill, long distrustful of Swedish 'outsidership' during the war, sent a curt reply on 5 May to the Swedish proposal: 'From the prime minister. General Eisenhower has the matter in hand. It would only cross the wires if the Swedish Gov. started negotiations with Schellenberg. I attach importance to this.'[20]

And so the war ended, without the collaboration of Sweden. On the evening of 4 May the German fighting forces in north-west Germany, the Netherlands, Schleswig-Holstein and Denmark surrendered to the British supreme commander, Field Marshal Montgomery. The following day Churchill informed his foreign minister that Denmark had been rapidly occupied by British armoured troops, and a small force was being dispatched to Copenhagen by air. In light of this, and 'the Danes' joyful emotions', the British 'would quite certainly be able to impede our Soviet friends' further incursion'.

Nonetheless, full surrender was delayed a few days more, enabling as many Germans as could somehow to escape the Russian sphere. In the space of three days two and a half million Germans, including a million soldiers at least, handed themselves over to British command. On 7 May, at General Eisenhower's headquarters at Reims, the general terms of an unconditional German surrender were signed by the German general Jodl, with French and Soviet officers in attendance as witnesses. The following day the Germans surrendered in Norway and the first British military advance unit reached Oslo. SHAEF's military mission never left for Stockholm but went to Oslo instead. At midnight on 8 May 1945 a ceasefire was declared – the Second World War in Europe was over.[21] Denmark and Norway would in future be part of the British sphere of interest.

Hitler's thousand-year German empire lay in ruins. The victorious powers had already, however, begun choosing sides in order to share the booty. The Cold War was about to break out, and fresh chilly winds would soon be sweeping over neutral Sweden. As soon as 2 May the American and British ministers called on Boheman at the Swedish Foreign Office and requested that Sweden take charge of the German legation's and the German consulate's archives and place them at the Allies' disposal. Boheman's guarded response was that Sweden would definitely take charge of the archives, but would then itself decide what the Allies might have access to. Concerning the German legation staff and personnel at other German institutions, these people would be divided into two categories (as Günther was later to report to the Foreign Affairs Committee): Germans found to be 'compromised' would be interned in Sweden while the remainder would be offered 'living accommodation outside Stockholm'.

The American legation counsellor, Ravndal, called on Grafström on 4 May bringing the news that the Russians had now banned all American flights between Luleå in the north of Sweden and Kirkenes in the very north of Norway. The Americans feared the Russians intended penetrating further into Norway, even occupying the area around Narvik.

Something had to be done to try to stop the Russians, Ravndal urged, which was why the staff talks planned for Stockholm between Sweden and SHAEF were of the 'utmost importance'.

The announcement of the Germans' unconditional surrender reached Bernadotte on 7 May straight from von Krosigk, making him probably the first Swede to hear that the war in Europe was over. Bernadotte expressed his boundless relief at an end to the merciless war, as well as his gratitude for perhaps having had a hand in hastening an end to the conflict. The first secretary – twenty-nine-year-old Sverker Åström – celebrated VE day by driving Schellenberg to the NK department store in order to buy under-wear for the newly recruited Gesandter, and a blue and yellow tie, the colours of the Swedish flag, for himself. As he passed the jubilant crowds milling on the streets of Stockholm, Åström reflected on the chances of a small nation such as Sweden playing a rôle on the scene of world history.

For the Swedish government, in April 1945, to accept staff talks with one of the warring parties in order to prepare an armed assault on the other party, implied a clear departure from the tenets of Swedish neutral-ity. The deviation, however, involved the tiniest of risks: the judgement made – that the Germans would surrender in Norway without Swedish intervention – proved correct. Sweden in fact never had to decide whether to carry out an armed attack on the Germans in Norway, in order to lib-erate the sister nation. Swedish defence staff had, nevertheless, planned in all secrecy a Swedish military intervention on a large scale in order to rescue Norway (Operation Rescue Norway) as they had with Denmark (Operation Rescue Denmark) in the event of the Germans refusing to sur-render. Swedish defence staff had calculated that this would require the employment of at least half a million men or a large portion of the entire field army plus air force and navy. In the words of both Leifland and Sver-drup: after 1943 Sweden had passed from being a non-belligerent state with German sympathies to being in 1945 a non-belligerent state on the side of the Allies.

In fact the Swedish government had extended itself even further. Defence minister Sköld on 6 April 1945 signed a General Order to the effect that personnel attached to the Swedish–Norwegian Voluntary Corps be summoned to emergency service duty. The aim was for Swedish volunteers to help liberate Norway with armed force. The decision was trumpeted abroad not only by Stockholm's evening newspapers but also by the *New York Times*. In just a few weeks the Voluntary Corps had mobilised 6,400 members, of whom more than six hundred joined up for military training. On 25 April the first fifty volunteers had been given a send-off at Gothenburg central railway station. They were led by Bengt Segerson, a communist member of the local city council and veteran of the Spanish Civil War.

The Swedish Norway battalion was not, however, allowed to take part in the liberation of Norway, although the Swedish government was prepared to let it march into Norway. The Norwegian government did, however, on 12 May express its warm gratitude to those Swedes who had been prepared to risk their lives for Norway. As things turned out, though, the Norwegian government found that the Swedish volunteers' assistance was not necessary. Trygve Lie, the Norwegian foreign minister, had in fact as early as 12 April informed the British in London that the Norwegian government-in-exile was anxious for the Swedish troops not to participate in Norway's liberation. The Norwegians would rather their country be liberated without Swedish help.

On the day peace was proclaimed (8 May) the Swedish foreign minister, Christian Günther, a man of exceptional sang-froid, jotted down his innermost thoughts in a highly unusual gesture. His thoughts included how relieved he was that Denmark and Norway had been liberated without military intervention from Sweden. The perspicacious minister had no illusions about the future, as we saw from the lines quoted at the beginning of this chapter. He had already sensed the imminence of the 'cold war' with the Soviet Union. With Germany now defeated, Russia was to cast its 'dark shadow' in future years over democratic Sweden.

13

Final Days

We were transported by train and all of us thought we were heading for the crematorium, but we got to Hamburg instead [said one of those 'rescued by Bernadotte'].

The train continued and then came to a stop. For four hours. We just waited and waited. Suddenly we saw how the German soldiers who were guarding us disappeared. Somebody opened the doors of the goods wagons. Hundreds of people came up to the train and gave us food to eat, and shouted: 'You're free!' We didn't believe our ears! We were in Denmark and just couldn't believe it.

Somebody said that Bernadotte had taken our train full of Jews and Gentiles and exchanged it for a train with German soldiers. After five or six years of inhuman suffering we'd reached freedom. We'd never dared that this could ever happen.

We were very, very well received in Sweden. I still remember nurse Inga. The war went on another couple of days and then it was the ninth of May. Groups of Swedish people came to us and sang and told us the war was over, and that we really were free. The first few days we thought we were living in a dream. We were not so old then, just fourteen or fifteen.

The doctors gave us a thorough examination, I think we weighed about twenty-one kilos. Everything was so finely laid out, tents, bedding and clothing. It was the first time in five or six years that we'd had a real bed. They shoved a thermometer in our mouths.

We stayed in quarantine in Helsingborg for six weeks. The Swedes came and asked us questions and to hear more from us. They weren't allowed to give us any food parcels, though. They'd done that with another transport and those people had eaten from the parcels and got sick. Some of them had even died. I must admit that during these weeks I really thought we were dreaming.[1]

Over the Straits and Back to Life

The Swedish Red Cross on 27 April wished to issue an official communiqué concerning the Swedish relief expedition to Germany. With one single exception – that of *Dagens Nyheter* at the beginning of March – the Swedish press had observed a total silence with regard to the White Buses. This had been a prerequisite for the successful outcome of the operation. If its activities had come to Hitler's knowledge the operation would undoubtedly have been stopped at once. The Nazi German leadership was amazingly well informed about what the Swedish newspapers were writing. Now, the leading journalists in the Swedish press rushed to the south of their country to report on the avalanche of prisoners released from German concentration camps who were arriving. Four thousand internees had arrived in the southern province of Skåne on 1 May, and Bernadotte held a press conference. Subsequently, three thousand more refugees arrived daily. This is what Attis Ljungström, writing in the *Svenska Dagbladet*, had to say on 3 May under the heading 'Over the Straits and back to life':

> In pouring rain and with a fierce wind blowing the huge contingent stepped ashore off the midday ferry: five hundred Norwegians, all men, and a large body of women, mostly Polish. In thin rags which once had been summer clothes, shoes made of paper and wood and odds and ends, with pieces of cloth wrapped around their heads and their few belongings in bags, bundles, cardboard boxes and their bare hands, they arrived – some of them quite normal in appearance but most with legs as thin as match sticks. Their young, hollowed faces bore deep furrows, twenty years too early. They were greyhaired, but their eyes were still the blue eyes of a baby.

'I'm so afraid of waking up. I'm convinced I'm dreaming that I'm free and that I'm seeing friendly faces all around me and that I'll soon be coming home.' This is how a young, fair-haired Polish girl spontaneously expressed what she felt. If there are a lot of us here at these camps, do we get a bed each? was a question often put. Getting a bed of your own they cherished as one of life's most precious gifts.

The way the Polish women looked was matched by others who had come from the concentration camps. At present in Sweden there are more than twenty-four nations represented; among the women, apart from the Norwegians and Danes, mostly French, Polish, Dutch and Belgian women. We met a number of representatives of various nations in a couple of the camps, and the friendly faces we had seen down on the quayside we saw to an even greater extent up here. There's been a radical change in Malmö: in the new Malmö Museum, which has been requisitioned as camp headquarters, a group of well-dressed, spotlessly clean and well-groomed women, many of them still skinny but their faces now with smoother skin and less haggard, were walking around or sitting or lying down, in a spirit of greater ease and security. On arrival all of them were able to choose their new clothes, obtain the necessary toilet accessories and a handful of pocket money. What sort of psychological impact this must have had – to put on good-looking, smart clothes after years of filth and rags– you probably have to be a woman to be able to appreciate. It's quite a lesson to watch them as they go about choosing their new garments, said one of the Swedish officials. They fondle their frocks, give them a kiss and dance around with them like little children.

The Salén shipping line's *Lillie Matthiessen* and *Magdalena*, hired by the International Red Cross to convey eight hundred former camp prisoners to Trelleborg on the south coast of Sweden, turned up on 2 May. While awaiting escort by a German mine-sweeping vessel their voyage had been delayed, and two passengers had died in the course of a rough passage. During the trip one of the passengers had been recognised as a German tormentor from one of the camps and was on the point of being lynched. He had robbed his last fatal victim of his prison clothes and dressed in these tried to smuggle himself into Sweden. The *Trelleborgs Tidning* reported on 3 May on 'singular adventures, and frightening and touching scenes':

> Another episode – one of the sweeter and more touching kind – could be witnessed yesterday morning down at the Customs House where a large number of prisoners of war were awaiting further treatment involving disinfection and settlement. In one section in the southern part of the building all the female refugees were gathered while the big customs-clearance hall was filled with male refugees.
>
> Suddenly there was heard a loud shriek, coming from a rather young woman, who dashed into the male section straight up to a man she had discovered among a group of men walking through the hall. She seized the man by both of his arms and stared at his face. Then she could be heard weeping, laughing out loud, and finally she threw her arms around his neck. It was! It really was! It was her husband!
>
> It was an emotional scene, watching the married couple reunited and their joy. For almost three years they had been completely unaware of each other's fate and had both been on board the *Lillie Matthiessen* on the trip over from Lübeck to Trelleborg. It was not until they were on Swedish soil that they found each other again.

Approximately nine thousand foreigners were estimated to have been brought to Sweden by the Red Cross detachment by 30 April and the following day a further four thousand were expected to arrive, a thousand of them by ferry from Lübeck. The week after two thousand Danish and Norwegian former Neuengamme internees would be arriving. At his press conference on 5 May Bernadotte announced that when that day the last contingent had arrived, in total some nineteen thousand people representing twenty-seven nationalities would have been 'affected' by the Red Cross expedition. He stressed that these were approximate figures and by no means reliable.

For many, however, the Swedish relief and compassion came too late: 110 of the former prisoners died at the Swedish camps during April and

May 1945, more than half of them of tuberculosis. Most of the casualties – forty-four – were Polish, and it was the Poles, many of them Jews, who had been treated worst of all in the German concentration camps.

How Many Were Rescued?

At the start of the Swedish rescue expedition's work German officialdom was still working perfectly and the number of prisoners the Swedes were allowed to transport was checked assiduously. During the final weeks, however, the red tape and due order broke down, and the Swedes, just like the Danes, were able to squeeze into their vehicles as many prisoners as they could. There was evidently no longer time for accurate records of the exact number of prisoners rescued. Figures differ considerably for many of the final transports, and it is therefore not unexpected that the total number of men and women rescued should vary from source to source, even though the differences at times appear suspiciously disparate.

There does exist an accurately specified account, however. In 1988 Koblik referred to a 'Red Cross document' that stated that exactly 20,937 'internees' had been transported to Sweden 'before the end of the war.' The breakdown was:

- Danes and Norwegians: 8,000
- Poles: 5,911
- French: 2,629
- stateless Jews: 1,615
- Germans: 1,124
- Belgians: 632
- Dutch: 387
- Hungarians: 290
- Balts: 191
- Luxemburgers: 79
- Slovakians: 28
- British: 14
- Americans: 9
- Rumanians: 6
- Finns: 5

- Italians: 4
- Spaniards: 3
- others : 9^2

I have checked the box in the Red Cross archives where Koblik found these figures. This list does indeed exist with these precise figures, but there is no description of what the figures refer to. This sheet of paper is filed close to a situation report from Dr Arnoldsson from Lübeck dated 11 May. Arnoldsson then reported that relief work was continuing there and that a further thousand people from concentration camps were being cared for. It might of course be the same Arnoldsson who had carefully compiled a list of all of the internees who until then had been sent home to Sweden. Nobody better than he could have been in a position to do this. Why, then, had he not repeated this account in his book *Natt och dimma* (Night and Fog)? The book includes accurate statistics concerning the 9,273 'patients' for whom he himself organised the transport, between Lübeck and Sweden, in collaboration with UNRRA, from 23 June to 25 July 1945. This transportation of sick prisoners from the concentration camps, mainly Bergen-Belsen, was the result of an express request made to Sweden by the Allies.[3]

The most accurate statistics I have discovered are Danish. Finn Nielsen's private archives contain a handwritten 'transport list' from the first Danish transport home of two hundred policemen during 5 and 10 December 1944 up until the fortieth transport on 4 May (over to Sweden) bringing 1,627 women. Judging by the handwriting, it was Finn Nielsen himself who continuously compiled the material, in the same way as he later summed up the forty transports. The summation revealed that the Danes themselves were able to bring back 598 people from Germany, who were then released or interned at Frøslev (499 of these were policemen or gendarmes). 'Very soon' 10,689 people were transferred to Sweden: 1,141 Danes and Norwegians, 423 (Danish) Jews and 9,125 women (mainly French and Polish). To Denmark, first of all, and afterwards to Sweden, a further 5,536 people (approximately 2,700 Norwegians and 2,836 Danes) were transported. Another 530 people (in all certainty Danish policemen) were sent straight from Frøslev to Sweden as well.

The total number of people transferred to Sweden in accordance with Nielsen's calculations, then, was 16,755, 7,630 of whom were Danes and Norwegians.[4] We shall have to add at least eight hundred to account for those who went by ship directly from Lübeck to Sweden. My grand total of at least 17,555 ex-prisoners rescued and brought to Sweden by 5 May is therefore a lower figure than that traditionally used. One explanation for the discrepancy may perhaps be found in the transport home of 'German Swedes' whose number oscillated between 400 (Bernadotte and Frykman) and up to 1,400 (Agartz). If we include these 1,400 the number roughly corresponds to the 19,000 Bernadotte judged were 'affected' by his Red Cross expedition.

Even more difficult to assess is the controversial question of how many *Jews* were rescued by the Bernadotte expedition. We know that all of the 423 Danish Jews were brought back from Theresienstadt, that only three Norwegian Jews were rescued and that 1,615 stateless Jews were conveyed from Ravensbrück. In all other cases the Swedish authorities as well as the Danish refused to use the classification 'Jew' but included them under their respective nationality. Masur, however, estimated that half of those who were rescued from Ravensbrück were Jewish women, some 3,500 in all. Among these it is *possible* that all of those defined above as 'stateless' may be included. The Bernadotte operation of April–May 1945 would then have rescued and brought to Sweden at least four thousand Jews. Inga Gottfarb searching in the Jewish Community's archives found hand-written statistics from August 1945 showing 3,112 Jewish refugees having been rescued and brought to Sweden by the Bernadotte operation and a further 5,112 by the UNRRA operation. This would mean a total of 8,224 Jews rescued, the vast majority women: only 1,340 were men.

There were probably far more. Whenever the Swedish authorities raised questions regarding the newcomers' religion, the Jews had learnt their bitter lessons from Germany not to make a show of their Jewish identity. The definition of 'Jew' is another debatable point: whether to use a narrow interpretation (both parents Jews or practising the Jewish religion) or going by a broader definition such as the Nazi German one, that is including the so-called *Mischlinge* and others.

Storch, who we should consider competent enough to make a reasonable assessment, between 1956 and 1979 claimed that between six and seven thousand Jews had been rescued and brought to Sweden by the Red Cross before the end of the war – and *that it was chiefly to Folke Bernadotte's credit that this had happened.*[5]

Many of those who had been rescued from the German inferno in 1945, however, were not transported by the White Buses but by train and ship. The trains were German and Danish, and the ships were Swedish but chartered by the International Red Cross. Many of the famous White Buses were not Swedish either, but Danish, as were the ambulances and the fish vans. It is even possible that the majority of the transports were carried out using Danish vehicles, in any case during the month of April. This is not to downgrade the Swedish achievement: during March all the transportation took place with Swedish vehicles and in April it was the Swedish White Buses that accomplished the long and dangerous trips to the south of Germany, to Theresienstadt and to Ravensbrück. The Swedish buses, equipped with petrol–gas combustion, were much better suited to the prevailing conditions than the Danish buses, which were responsible for the shorter trips from Neuengamme to Denmark and along the Danish roads.

Folke Bernadotte and *'Last Days . . .'*
Bernadotte acted fast: within six weeks of the end of the war he had published his book *Last Days. My Humanitarian Work in Germany in the Spring of 1945 and Its Political Consequences.* The book was the first published anywhere in the world to give an insight into what lay behind the scenes during the final days of the German Third Reich, and was an enormous success. It was serialised in the *Daily Telegraph* and translated into eighteen languages. Bernadotte became known throughout the world and tokens of respect and decorations were showered on him. He was made chairman of the Swedish Red Cross in January 1946, with responsibility for the large Swedish Red Cross relief work in occupied Germany during the years to come. He was one of the leading figures within the international Red Cross movement and unchallenged as chairman for the seventeenth International Red Cross Conference in Stockholm in 1948. It was here

that the principles were established for the 1949 Geneva Convention. In 1948 he was made the United Nations' first – and last – mediator in the Palestine question. His life was brutally brought to an end on 17 September 1948 when his body was riddled with bullets fired by Jewish terrorists in an ambush laid in the Jewish quarter of Jerusalem.

Bernadotte has subsequently been charged by many with taking too naïve an attitude. His negotiation strategies in 1945 with the Nazi leaders, it must be said, however, do not point as much to naivety as to a cold-blooded approach and what is sometimes referred to as a salami-slice strategy. In February he had requested only an insignificant number of German concessions concerning the return of Swedish women to Sweden (easing the burden of maintenance for the Germans) and the concentration of Norwegian and Danish prisoners in one camp, still inside Germany. At the same time, however, he also arranged for Swedish military vehicles, even if camouflaged as Red Cross transport, to enter German territory and ply German highway routes. These tiny concessions were later used as wedges to dig into the German resistance. Gradually this resistance was broken down completely and led to wholesale German concessions in the final stages of the war. Undoubtedly Bernadotte had negotiated with the Germans after consulting the Stockholm Foreign Office on tactics, as well as Richert in Berlin. The Danes engaged in their talks in parallel, of course, and Kersten was always there in the background preparing the way for Bernadotte.

It was nonetheless Bernadotte who in person engaged Kaltenbrunner, Ribbentrop, Schellenberg and, four times round, Germany's second most powerful man, Himmler, in talks. Initially Bernadotte was without detailed instructions from the Foreign Office in Stockholm. On 3 March a manifestly irritated Sven Grafström wrote in his diary that the Foreign Office political department 'had turned into a Red Cross branch office and nothing less'. Bernadotte's own notes jotted down from the talks showed a tougher – and much more cynical – negotiator than what the censored version of *Last Days* . . . could reveal. Bernadotte's surreptitious threat to Kaltenbrunner – of Sweden participating in the final stages of the war, feasibly on Norway's side – was probably Boheman's idea and approved by Günther. Bernadotte's suggestion on 23–24 April concerning the German

251

troops' surrender in Norway and Denmark, however, was Bernadotte's initiative as told by Günther in 1956. Bernadotte could well be characterised, as Koblik has done, as a 'skilful negotiator who endeavoured to provide the groundwork for further agreements'.[6]

What Koblik and other researchers have been unaware of is Bernadotte's recurrent hint in talks with the Germans of the risk of Europe being 'Bolshevised', and the direct proposals put to the German leaders to open up the Western Front for the Allies and instead concentrate German military resources on the Eastern Front against the Soviet Union. This was meticulously censored out of *Last Days . . .* and out of the *Foreign Office White Book 1956*. Nor are these proposals, which demonstrate Bernadotte's powers of prediction as early as February–April 1945 of an approaching Cold War, reflected in any of the instructions and documents emerging from the Foreign Office in Stockholm. They certainly coincided, however, with foreign minister Günther's apprehension about future Soviet dominance in eastern and central Europe and with cabinet secretary Boheman's feelings of sympathy for the West. It was surely a conscious strategy on Bernadotte's part to use his anti-Bolshevik sentiments in order to build a common platform with the Nazi German leaders. It was evidently also a successful strategy in light of the concrete results that gradually surfaced.

We supposedly will never know whether Bernadotte's anti-Soviet negotiation stance was sanctioned from home. It probably enjoyed support in leading circles at the Foreign Office but hardly within the Swedish coalition government. It was treated as a taboo when the wholly Social Democratic government took power in July 1945, with Östen Undén as the relatively Russia-friendly foreign minister bridging ideologies. Günther was subsequently pushed aside and placed in Rome, Boheman in Paris and von Post was moved to Ankara. Richert was demoted to the Chamber of Commerce and later landed up in provincial Vänersborg. Bernadotte was no longer appointed to any commissions by the Swedish government. His mediation in Palestine in 1948 was a United Nations job and it was given very casual interest by the Swedish government.[7]

Following Bernadotte's brutal assassination in 1948 accusations against him and his work were not long in coming. The Jewish right-wing extremists who were responsible for his murder had a clear-cut reason for justifying their cowardly deed by belittling his efforts on behalf of the Jews in 1945 and directly or indirectly portraying him as an anti-Semite. At the beginning of the 1950s Felix Kersten started to spread his forged letter in which Bernadotte in March 1945 not only was to have declared to Himmler that Jews were unwelcome in Sweden but even have delivered a sketch of British military targets! The path now lay open for the first general assault on Bernadotte.[8]

It was delivered by the British historian H.R. Trevor-Roper who in 1947 gained fame for his book *The Last Days of Hitler*. In this, Bernadotte had been allotted a modest rôle for the events marking the final stages of the war, and this led to a grumpy exchange of letters between the two men. In February 1953, however, Trevor-Roper used hammer and tongs against Bernadotte's version of events, doing so in the pages of the *Atlantic Monthly*. He gave Felix Kersten the entire credit for the rescue expedition's success in 1945 while labelling Bernadotte as 'a transport officer, no more'. This was a quotation from one of Himmler's closest but unnamed men. Trevor-Roper uncritically reproduced Kersten's version, including the latter's claim that Bernadotte had both refused to bring back Jews to Sweden and to supply letters to the WJO in Stockholm.[9]

Trevor-Roper's assault, entirely based on Kersten's testimony, on anonymous former Nazi German sources and on the Dutch professor Posthumus's inquiries, created a storm of protests in Sweden. The Foreign Office in a press release described Trevor-Roper's information as 'improbable': it was Bernadotte and no other who was the leader of the 1945 operation and the Swedish officials who had been present at talks with the Germans had testified to Bernadotte's 'unfailing interest in the rescue of as many Jews as possible from Germany to Sweden'. The two officials employed at the legation in Berlin who most closely served Bernadotte in the 1945 talks both supported him in this matter.

In a confidential letter written in 1953 legation consultant Lennart Nylander explained that Bernadotte's alleged negative attitude towards the Jewish prisoners 'in no way corresponded with reality'. On the contrary, Bernadotte often expressed the hope that the relief expedition would be 'expanded to include people other than Scandinavians, irrespective of race'. Legation secretary Torsten Brandel, who attended talks with Himmler, in 1984 (after the publication of Holm's book) affirmed that 'no distinction was made between Jews and non-Jews'. He also portrayed Bernadotte as 'an exceptionally skilful and discerning' negotiator who, even if acting on instructions from the Foreign Office, had a fairly wide margin of discretion.

Trevor-Roper, however, was not to be deterred. Kersten's memoirs were published in a new version in 1956, this time in English. The introduction to the book was written by Trevor-Roper, who maintained all his previous accusations concerning Bernadotte, albeit in a somewhat milder shape. Trevor-Roper then admitted that there was no reason to believe that Bernadotte had been an anti-Semite but that he had still made use of an 'anti-Semitic language' in his refusal to take Jews along with him to Sweden. As proof of Bernadotte's 'anti-Semitic language' Trevor-Roper displayed the forged Bernadotte–Himmler letter from 10 March 1945 in a modest footnote, adding that 'its authenticity had not been able to be proved', together with a 1952 certificate from Himmler's chief of staff, Gottlob Berger. Trevor-Roper guessed that Bernadotte had misunderstood his instructions in 1945.

In 1955 Trevor-Roper obtained access to the Foreign Office memo from 27 March 1945, which he now merely mentioned in passing – either Trevor-Roper had not understood, or he did not want to understand, the meaning of the Foreign Office instructions to Bernadotte. Or was Professor Trevor-Roper insinuating that Bernadotte was unable to read correctly what was written? Trevor-Roper maintained that Bernadotte had been no more than an ambassador with authority to discuss details with Himmler – the real political decisions had already been made by Günther and negotiated by Kersten. Trevor-Roper saw Bernadotte as a mere 'instrument, selected in order to stand for the technical execution'. Finally Trevor-Roper claimed that it had not been sufficient for Bernadotte just to be an ambassador but that Bernadotte had seen fit to inflate his own actions in order to 'monopolise credit for the success'. The real negotiator with Himmler had been Felix Kersten was Trevor-Roper's conclusion.[10]

Trevor-Roper's fresh assault brought on a new round of stormy debate in Sweden, and led to the Foreign Office publishing the *White Book 1956*. Preparatory work on the book had already been done in 1953 by Wilhelm

Carlgren, keeper of public records, following Trevor-Roper's first series of accusations. The *White Book* did full justice to Ditleff's, Günther's and Kersten's efforts in 1945 and reduced Bernadotte's rôle correspondingly. Trevor-Roper's presentation of Bernadotte's rôle, however, was totally dismissed by Carlgren, who concluded that Trevor-Roper was 'unilaterally pro-Kersten and anti-Bernadotte, that he in a number of instances launches inadequate criticism at his sources and not infrequently offers purely incorrect information'.[11]

It is important to see Bernadotte's achievements in Germany in spring 1945 from the perspective of the negotiating table. What did Bernadotte, representing the Swedish government, have to offer the German leadership at this point? He was able to threaten with Sweden's entry into the war scene on the side of the Allies, and chiefly a military intervention in order to liberate a neighbouring country, Norway – which is what Bernadotte did on more than one occasion. This must have been of some significance in the Germans' peaceful surrender in Norway and in Denmark. He was able to play on the common fear of future Soviet dominance in central and eastern Europe – and this became a frequent theme in Bernadotte's talks with Himmler. Bernadotte was also in a position to offer Swedish mediation when the Germans put feelers out for separate peace terms with the western Powers, something both Schellenberg and Himmler were eager for. Moreover, he could discreetly offer a safe haven in Sweden to those who had made contributions to the rescue work, which is what he did in the case of Schellenberg, Rennau and Göring, who were all helped over to Sweden before the end of the war.[12]

Nowadays after the event, with the cold war over, we should also be willing to admit that it was Bernadotte in 1945 who was sufficiently perspicacious and uncompromising to anticipate the Russians' aims and purposes, while Undén and the new Swedish foreign policy-makers from July 1945 onwards were naïve enough to adopt a meek attitude towards the Soviet superpower.

The fact that Bernadotte did not bring up the subject of the *Jews* in his talks with the Germans, and above all with Himmler, should also be seen from the angle of negotiation strategy. The Swedes could expect that the Nazi German leaders would be more inclined to agree to concessions in respect of 'Aryan' Scandinavians. Making an express request for the release of Jews, the Nazis' chief opponents, would very likely lead to the immediate collapse of talks. Himmler's pledges to release thousands of Jewish women were camouflaged up to the very last moment by calling them 'Polish women' to Hitler.

Bernadotte also knew of course that there existed in Sweden a certain resistance to the mass influx of Jews, not least among the very leaders of the Jewish community in Stockholm. In Germany he had met with lukewarm interest from the Danish legation in regard to the Danish Jews' situation at Theresienstadt. It would be a bit presumptuous to require Bernadotte in spring 1945 to apply more energy to the fate of the Jews in Germany than that shown by leading Jews in Stockholm – something that nobody had demonstrated better than Gilel Storch.

Criticism aimed at Bernadotte after 1945, and particularly after his assassination in 1948, has been unjustified and in part directly mendacious. It was Bernadotte in person who was the undisputed leader of the entire expedition. It was Bernadotte who carried through the decisive negotiations with the German leaders, and he was the one who conveyed Himmler's offer of a separate surrender on the Western Front. On the other hand, it is quite evident that Bernadotte's involvement during the month of April 1945 shifted towards the Great Power talks and he gave less priority to the real task assigned by the Swedish government: rescuing prisoners in German concentration camps and jails and bringing them over to Sweden. The final rescue of these unfortunate prisoners instead was the result of energetic field operations performed by men such as Hans Arnoldsson, Sven Frykman, Harald Folke, Åke Svenson, Gerhard Rundberg and other Swedes, but to an equally large extent through the enormous efforts of the Danes.

Endnotes

INTRODUCTION

1   At this time I was commanding a sort of British intelligence commando called 'T' Force. Our job
     was to secure valuable intelligence targets as the army advanced. We found, for example, one of Nazi
     Germany's few remaining nuclear laboratories. We were the first Allied unit to reach the Bergen–
     Belsen concentration camp. We finished up in Denmark.
2   Sune Persson wrote a groundbreaking book, *Mediation & Assassination: Count Bernadotte's Mission to
     Palestine in 1948* (London 1979), on Bernadotte's assassination.

CHAPTER 1

1   This short biography is based on pp.225–7 of my dissertation *Mediation & Assassination: Count Bernadotte's
     Mission to Palestine in 1948* (London 1979). This includes a comprehensive list of books on Bernadotte,
     which were all published between 1945 and 1950 and were in the nature of tributes. Among them may
     be mentioned the British journalist Ralph Hewins' *Count Folke Bernadotte. His Life and Work* (London
     1950). Since then have appeared: the Israeli Amitzur Ilan's malicious *Bernadotte in Palestine, 1948. A
     Study in Contemporary Humanitarian Knight-Errantry* (London 1989); the American journalist Kati Marton's
     appreciative book *A Death in Jerusalem* (New York 1996); and a superficial biography in Swedish by Stig
     Hadenius, *Vem var Folke Bernadotte? (Who was Folke Bernadotte?)* (Lund 2007). The quote on p.7 is from
     'Answers to Questions from Dr Amitzur Ilan', dictated by Estelle Ekstrand, December 1983; copy in
     Barbro Jerring's private archives. The 1943 visit to Geneva: Kristian Ottosen, *Redningen. Veien ut av
     fangenskapet våren 1945 (The Rescue: Emerging from Imprisonment Spring 1945)* (Oslo 1998), p.92; the 1944
     visits to London and Versailles are described in handwritten notes in the Count Folke Bernadotte
     archives, vol. 3 and 2, SRA. For relations between the International Committee of the Red Cross
     (ICRC) and the Swedish Red Cross (SRK), see Jean-Claude Favez, *The Red Cross and the Holocaust*
     (Cambridge 1999), pp.261, 278.

CHAPTER 2

1   *Norway's Relations With Sweden During the War Years 1940–45*, Official documents published by the
     Norwegian Foreign Office, III, p.474 (reported in the Swedish evening newspaper *Aftonbladet* on
     8 March 1945).
2   This short background sketch is based on the classic works by Alan Bullock, *Hitler. A Study in Tyranny*
     (rev. edn Harmondsworth 1962, 1st edn 1952) and by Joachim Fest, *Hitler. Eine Biographie (Hitler. A
     Biography)* (Berlin 1973). Still unsurpassed as an analysis of Hitler during the final stages of the war
     is H.R. Trevor-Roper, *The Last Days of Hitler* (rev. edn London 1973, 1st edn 1947); Hitler's will and
     testament here in facsimile, p.252.

ENDNOTES

3   The main sources here are Eugen Kogon, *The SS State. The German Concentration Camp System* (1st
     German edn 1947), Bullock's biography of Hitler as well as those of Himmler and Kaltenbrunner, i.e.
     Peter Padfield, *Himmler. Reichsführer-SS* (London 1990) and Peter R. Black, *Ernst Kaltenbrunner. Ideological
     Soldier of the Third Reich* (Princeton NJ 1984). Also relevant is Walter Schellenberg, *The Labyrinth.
     The Memoirs of Hitler's Secret Service Chief* (New York 1956). I have not however made use of these
     later notes but instead used Walter Schellenberg, *Tagebuchskizze*, his so-called Trosa Memorandum,
     completed at Trosa in Sweden prior to 9 June 1945. Trevor-Roper, in *The Last Days of Hitler*, is very
     critical of Schellenberg as a source yet makes abundant use of him. Undoubtedly Schellenberg *after
     the war* carefully minimised his own responsibility for the Nazis' violent deeds while inflating his own
     excellence. Odder is the fact that Trevor-Roper in 1947 did not show the same scepticism towards
     Albert Speer as a source or, later during his feud with Bernadotte, concerning information from Felix
     Kersten (Himmler's masseur) or from Gottlob Berger (Himmler's chief of staff).
4   Five million Jews dead: Raul Hilberg, *The Destruction of the European Jews* (Chicago 1961), p.11; more
     than six million Jews dead: Stephane Bruchfeld & Paul A. Levine, *Tell Ye Your Children . . . A Book About
     the Holocaust in Europe 1933–1945* (Stockholm 1998), p.2.

CHAPTER 3

1   Communiqué issued by the chairman of the Jewish Community in Stockholm, Gunnar Josephson,
     and published by the Swedish Central News Agency on 25 and 26 January 1945. From the Jewish
     Community archives, IG 39:15, SRA.
2   Literature dealing with the Second World War and the Holocaust is now immense. The most important
     works on the Holocaust must still be the standard work by Hilberg, *The Destruction of the European Jews*
     and that of Yehuda Bauer, *Jews for Sale? Nazi-Jewish Negotiations, 1933–1945* (New Haven 1994).
3   The main source of the subsequent short summary is Monty Noam Penkower, *The Jews Were Expendable.
     Free World Diplomacy and the Holocaust* (Urbana & Chicago 1983), particularly ch. 8 'The World Jewish
     Congress Confronts the International Red Cross', pp.223–88, and ch. 9 'The Sternbuchs, Storch, and
     the Reichsführer SS', pp.359–76.
4   The ICRC published a White Book after the war on its sharply criticised policies: *Documents Relating to
     the Work of the International Committee of the Red Cross for the Benefit of Civilian Detainees in German Concentration
     Camps between 1939 and 1945* (Geneva 1975). The standard work is now Jean-Claude Favez, *The Red Cross
     and the Holocaust* (Cambridge 1995), see pp.260–72.
5   Regarding the War Refugee Board and Office of Strategic Services (OSS) in Sweden, see Meredith
     Hindley, 'Negotiating the Boundary of Unconditional Surrender: The War Refugee Board in Sweden
     and Nazi Proposals to Ransom Jews, 1944–1945', *Holocaust and Genocide Studies*, 10:1 (spring 1996),
     pp.52–77, and Wilhelm Agrell, *Skuggor runt Wallenberg. Uppdrag i Ungern 1943–1945* (*Shadows Around
     Wallenberg. Assignment in Hungary 1943–1945*) (Lund 2006).
6   The figures for 'those rescued in 1945' taken from Jewish Community minutes 1946, annual report
     2 May 1946, Jewish Community archives (Stockholm), p.5. Inga Gottfarb, *Den livsfarliga glömskan
     (The Perils of Oblivion)* (Höganäs 1986), pp.87–91. David Köpniwsky, *Några ord och siffror om Mosaiska
     församlingens i Stockholm flyktinghjälp 1933–1950 (A Few Words and Figures about the Assistance to Refugees by
     the Mosaic Community in Stockholm, 1933–1950)* (Stockholm 1951), pp.1–64, stencil in Jewish Community
     archives, SRA, IG 36:13.
7   Storch's views on the Jewish Community from my interview with him: Stockholm, 27 July 1979.
8   Inga Gottfarb in letters to me: Stockholm, 29 September 2000, and Paris, 12 April 2001.
9   Miriam Nathanson, telephone conversation with me: Stockholm, 8 November 2000.
10   Jewish Community minutes, no.7, 15 May 1945, Jewish Community archives (Stockholm).
11   For details concerning Storch, see his case history in P 1370 in the Swedish Security Police archives
     and in his own private archives, now housed at Central Zionist Archives (CZA), Jerusalem, under C4,
     World Jewish Congress, The Representative in Stockholm.
12   A young Swedish diplomat named Göran von Otter at the end of August 1942 was given a detailed
     description of the entire gas execution procedure by a German engineer Kurt Gerstein, who worked for
     the SS 'sanitary department'. What subsequently happened with von Otter's information is unclear. It
     was not until 23 July 1945 that von Otter in Helsinki wrote an *aide-mémoire*, which on 18 August 1945

was delivered to the British Foreign Office. The original copy of this memo is now in SRA, HP 1051. P.A. Levine, *From Indifference to Activism* (Uppsala 1996), pp.127ff., believed however that von Otter's information somehow or other reached the Swedish Foreign Office as early as 1942.

13 Hindley, 'Negotiating the Boundary of Unconditional Surrender', pp.52–68; Penkower, *The Jews Were Expendable*, pp.268ff. Klaus, writing from a hospital, was to send increasingly bitter letters to Storch, claiming that it was he (Klaus) who had already taken the initiative in 1943 in liberating Jews from the German concentration camps; Klaus's unanswered letters in CZA, C/591. Klaus had a Swedish deportation order pending when he died the night prior to the day he was to be deported (1 April 1946); official cause of death a heart attack. Kleist was extradited by Sweden on 27 August 1945 to the British zone in Germany. Bernadotte wrote a letter for Kleist's benefit: 'He helped us in a splendid way by releasing thousands of Baltic subjects from the Baltic states to Sweden,' Bernadotte to General Balfour, Stockholm, 14 September 1946, copy in SRA/SRKA/FBA. Fritz Hesse was arrested in Germany after the war and published his memoirs, *Das Spiel um Deutschland* (München 1953) in which he described (pp.403–19) his secret talks in Stockholm between 19 January and 10 March 1945 with Jacob Wallenberg, Allan Vougt, Gilel Storch and Iver Olsen.

14 Penkower, *The Jews Were Expendable*, pp.268–70. Food parcels: my interview with Storch, Stockholm, 27 January 1979, and also Gottfarb, *Den livsfarliga glömskan*, p.123; interview with Laura Margolis Jarblum, performed by Menahem Kaufman for the United Jewish Appeal, Tel Aviv, 26 April 1976 (extract sent to me by Svante Hansson); letter from Gottfarb to me, Paris, 12 April 2001.

15 Telegram G. Storch to S. Wise, N. Goldmann, A. Tartakower, 28 January 1944 (should read 1945, copy); cable S. Wise, N. Goldmann to G. Storch, New York, 5 February 1945 (copy); both in CZA, 4/588, 590. Zelmanovits's report to the WJC, British section, 10 April 1945, 'Preliminary Survey of the Internal Congress Situation in Sweden' (Strictly Confidential): 'Storch who had done a wonderful job which is recognised and praised by all authorities concerned', copy in CZA, C2/758. Also my interview with Storch, Stockholm, 27 July 1979, and Penkower, *The Jews Were Expendable*, pp.270f.

CHAPTER 4

General note: The whole of this chapter, unless otherwise stated, is based on the official account given in *Norges forhold til Sverige under krigen 1940–45 (Norway's Relations with Sweden During the 1940–45 War)*. Official documents published by the Norwegian Foreign Office. III, pp.344–474: 'Hjelp til nordmenn i tysk fangenskap' (Oslo 1950); Jakob Apalset's semi-official *Heimsending av norske fangar frå Tyskland 1945. Planar og forhandlingar 1944–45 (The Return Home of Norwegian Prisoners from Germany 1945. Planning and Negotiation 1944–45)* (Oslo 1970); Niels Christian Ditleff, *Da Tysklands-fangene ble reddet (When the Prisoners in Germany Were Rescued)* (Oslo 1955); and Ottosen, *Redningen*.

1 Wanda Heger in correspondence with the author, Oslo, 24 January 2002.
2 Samuel Abrahamsen, *Norway's Response to the Holocaust. A Historical Perspective* (New York 1991), pp.2, 4, 125, 133.
3 Ottosen, *Redningen*; Bjarte Bruland in emails to the author, Oslo, 2001.
4 Transport by train: Ottosen, *Aftenposten*, 8 May 1998, and letter from Heger to me, Oslo, 24 January 2002.
5 Wanda Hjort-Heger 20 December 1994. Heger's disavowal in letter sent to me, Oslo, 24 January 2002.
6 Sigurd Melin, *Minnen och intryck från tjänstgöringen vid Svenska Rödakorsdetachementet i Tyskland våren 1945 (Memories of My Service at the Swedish Red Cross Detachment in Germany, Spring 1945)*, typewritten, undated, notes.

CHAPTER 5

General note: Events taking place in 1943–5 are dealt with in a thorough manner in Jörgen Haestrup's masterly work, *Til landets bedste. Hovedtraek af departementschefsstyrets virke 1943–1945 (For the Good of the Country: The Main Features of the Departmental Heads' Work 1943–1945)* (bind I–II, Odense 1966, Copenhagen 1971) and in Departmental Head H.H. Koch, *Socialministeriet under Besaettelsen (The Ministry of Social Affairs under Occupation)*, original manuscript at Finn Nielsens's private archive, dossier 1, DRA.

Brief summary provided in Jörgen H. Barfod, *Helvede har mange navne* (*Hell Has Many Names*) (Copenhagen, 2nd edn 1995), pp.29–39. The meticulous scientific work, published at a later date, by Hans Sode-Madsen, *Reddet fra Hitlers Helvede. Danmark og de Hvide Busser 1941–45* (*Rescued from Hitler's Hell on Earth: Denmark and the White Buses 1941–1945*) (Copenhagen 2005) confirmed the findings of earlier works in all respects, but particularly scrutinised operations involving the White Buses.

1   Letter preserved in the Danish State Archives, Ministry of Social Affairs, J.no.880/1943 in an envelope briefly marked 'in return' (my translation from the German – *author's note*). R.S. was later rescued from Theresienstadt by the White Buses.
2   For the rescue work and preparations, see Leni Yahil, 'Scandinavian Countries to the Rescue of Concentration Camp Prisoners', *Yad Vashem Studies*, VI (Jerusalem 1967), pp.181–220.

CHAPTER 6

General note: This chapter is based mainly on the *Swedish Foreign Office White Book*, written mainly in 1953 by Keeper of the Records Wilhelm Carlgren: *1945 års svenksa hjälpexpedition till Tyskland. Förspel och förhandlingar* (*The 1945 Swedish Relief Expedition to Germany. Prelude and Negotiation*). Official documents published by the Swedish Foreign Office. New series II:8. Stockholm 1956 (quoted as *Swedish Foreign Office White Book 1956*). Quotes in this chapter, unless otherwise stated, are taken from the *White Book 1956*. Carlgren's original manuscript is at UDA, A9G, part 12, section 10.

1   The prime minister's handwritten notes in Per Albin Hansson's manual file, SRA.
2   Himmler: information from Schellenberg at Nuremberg trials, Schellenberg's case history P 6199 in Swedish Security Police archives. Also Gert Nylander, 'Carl Goerdelers fredstrevare via bröderna Wallenberg. Några nya dokument från andra världskriget' ('Carl Goerdeler's Peace Soundings via the Wallenberg Brothers. Some New Documents from the Second World War'), *Scandia*, 1998:2, pp.245–77.
3   *Swedish Foreign Office White Book 1956*, p.14, 'Memo re conversation with W. Schellenberg at the Nuremberg Palace of Justice, 7 December 1945, in the presence of Captain Walter Rapp, a member of Judge Jackson's staff', by Hugo Lindberg, written 24 January 1946, in the Swedish Security Police archives, Schellenberg's case history P 6199. This case history is remarkably meagre, as are similar case histories in the General Security Service's archives, now at SRA. This is not so strange, actually, as all case histories containing (a) wire-tapped telephone conversations, (b) telegrams that had been opened and (c) letters that had been opened were destroyed in 1949 in accordance with a royal ordinance.
4   Kersten has left behind a large number of copies of correspondence with Himmler and other Nazi leaders, but few in original. His memoirs have appeared in many languages but show discrepancies at various points. In 1953 Kersten showed the Swedish chamberlain Dickson a letter allegedly from Bernadotte to Himmler in which Bernadotte explained that Jews were non-desirable elements in Sweden, with a sketch enclosed to help the Germans aim their V rockets better at British military targets. This letter, following inspection by Scotland Yard experts, has been declared a forgery, produced on Kersten's own typewriter. See Gerald Fleming, 'Die Herkunft des Bernadotte-Briefs an Himmler vom 10 März 1945', *Vierteljahrshefte für Zeitgeschichte*, Jahrg. 26 (1978):4, pp.571–600. Questioned directly about this, in conjunction with the *Swedish Foreign Office White Book 1956*, Kersten admitted that the letter of 10 March 1945 was 'half a forgery' and that he was not sure that Bernadotte really had written the letter. The degree of credibility in Kersten's own statements, including his memoirs, *Samtal med Himmler* (Stockholm 1947, published in Swedish), must be considered low. The English edition was called *The Kersten Memoirs, 1940–1945*. With an Introduction by H.R. Trevor-Roper (London 1956).
5   'Translation of Statement no. 6 by Schellenberg handed in 16 July 1945. Subject 1. – Dr Kersten' (Secret), US National Archives (USNA), RG 226, location 190/7/19/03, Box 2. 'Never got a single penny from Himmler': Memo, Å. Kromnow and W. Carlgren, Stockholm, 17 March 1956, UDA, A9G. According to Kersten's son Arno, Felix Kersten obtained permission from Himmler to take 50,000 kronor of his *own* money out of the country: A. Kersten in interview with me, Stockholm, 4 September 2000.

6   Levine, *From Indifference to Activism. Swedish Diplomacy and the Holocaust*; Penkower, *The Jews Were Expendable*, ch. 9, 'The Sternbuchs, Storch, and the Reichsführer SS', pp.247–88; S. Koblik, *The Stones Cry Out. Sweden's Response to the Persecution of the Jews 1933–45*, ch. 4, '"No Truck with Himmler": The Politics of Rescue' (New York 1988), pp.117–40. The *Swedish Foreign Office White Book 1956* offered slender material on Swedish action in Jewish issues.

7   Danish Jews: Leni Yahil's dissertation (Copenhagen 1967), pp.278–318; similarly her 'Scandinavian Countries to the Rescue of the Concentration Camp Prisoners', *Yad Vashem Studies on the European Jewish Catastrophe and Resistance* (Jerusalem 1967), vol. VI, pp.181–200. Hungarian Jews: Björn Runberg, *Valdemar Langlet. Räddare i faran* (*Valdemar Langlet. Saviour from Danger*) (Stockholm 2000) and Agrell, *Skuggor runt Wallenberg*; 'Notes Regarding the Memorandum on the Refugees in Sweden'; probably Gösta Engzell, 11 November 1944, CZA, WJC, British Section, C2/758.

8   Memorandum (secret, '27.1 delivered by the American minister', SRA/UDA, HP 1075.

9   Letters J. Hellman, A. Reiss, A. Tartakower to W. Boström, New York, 19 January 1945; letter E. von Post to A. Richert 25 January 1945; both at SRA/UDA, HP 1050. Letter L. Zelmanovits to G. Storch, London, 23 January 1945, copy sent by Storch to the Swedish Foreign Office, 3 February 1945, and to Bernadotte, 23 February 1945; CZA, C4/588. Code telegram Cabinet to Berlin, Stockholm, 3 February 1945; code telegram A. Richert to E. von Post, Alt Döbern, 7 February 1945; SRA/UDA, HP 1050.

10 Memo G. Engzell, 12 February 1945; code telegram Cabinet to Berlin, 12 February 1945; code telegram A. Richert, Alt Döbern 13 February 1945; SRA/UDA, HP 1050.

Chapter 7

1   Footnote in Folke Bernadotte's diary for 1945, SRKA.

2   *Swedish Foreign Office White Book 1956*, p.19.

3   *Swedish Foreign Office White Book 1956*, p.17.

4   'Eidesstattliche Erklärung' by Elisabeth Lüben, 1 September 1948, according to the *Swedish Foreign Office White Book 1956*, p.19. Trevor-Roper claimed that Kersten's phone call on 5 February 1945 had been confirmed by Himmler's chief of staff and secretary; letter H.R. Trevor-Roper to H. Beer, Oxford, 13 February 1953, copy at SRA/SRKA/II/General secretary, fl:23. Kersten's own version in *Samtal med Himmler*, pp.284ff.

5   Sven Grafström, *Anteckningar 1945–1954* (*Notes 1945–1954*) (Stockholm 1989), pp.642ff.

6   Folke Bernadotte, *Last Days of the Reich. The Diary of Count Folke Bernadotte* (London 2009), p.15.

7   Bernadotte, *Last Days . . .*, pp.18–20.

8   Letter G. Storch to L. Zelmanovits, Stockholm, 24 February 1945 (copy), CZA C4/549.

9   My interview with G. Storch, Stockholm, 27 July 1979.

10 Compare Bernadotte, *Last Days . . .*, pp.20ff.

11 Telegram E. von Post to Alt Döbern, Stockholm, 11 February 1945, SRA/UDA, HP 1618.

12 Personal letter C. Günther to A. Richert, Stockholm, 13 February 1945, A. Richert's private archive, provincial record office, Gothenburg.

13 Telegram A. Richert to E. von Post, Alt Döbern, Stockholm, 11 February 1945, SRA/UDA, HP 1618.

14 Bernadotte, *Last Days . . .*, p.41.

15 Prince Carl, memo, Stockholm, 14 February 1945, SRA/SRKA Central Board, vol. 222.

16 The threat of war, which I have given in italics, only appeared in Bernadotte's handwritten notebook but had been erased in his report to the Foreign Office. The description that follows is based on the notes. In Bernadotte, *Last Days . . .* the first round of talks are described on pp.39–75; here, too, the unanimity between Bernadotte and Kaltenbrunner on the subject of the risk of Europe's Bolshevisation has been deleted.

17 According to Hesse, *Das Spiel um Deutschland*, p.385, Ribbentrop too considered using Bernadotte as a mediator to probe for peace with the western Allies but was persuaded by Hesse to refrain since Bernadotte's chances were judged to be very slim.

18 Bernadotte, *Last Days . . .*, p.58.

19 The discussion between Himmler and Bernadotte on the subject of Dresden has been deleted from Bernadotte, *Last Days . . .* and instead a section (p.72) dealing with Himmler and the Jews has been

added, which neither appeared in the original report nor in Bernadotte's draft of the book, and which
was evidently put in as an afterthought and in a mistaken context.

20 Bernadotte, *Last Days . . .*, p.47.
21 Bernadotte, *Last Days...*, p.148. Hitler: 'Mit solchen Mätzchen kann man in diesem Krieg nichts
    nutzen', according to Schellenberg, *Tagebuchskizze*, p.10; copy at CZA, C4/494.

CHAPTER 8

1   Leading article 'Should Berlin Collapse', 19 February 1945, in the Stockholm newspaper *Dagens Nyheter*.
2   Code telegram from Bernadotte to the Swedish Foreign Office, Berlin, 20 February 1945, Swedish
    SRA/UDA, HP 1618.
3   Demand for white-painted vehicles: British Foreign Office to Mallet in Stockholm, 3 March 1945,
    according to Koblik, *The Stones Cry Out*, p.129; Mallet to FO, Stockholm, 5 March 1945, TNA:PRO,
    AIR 20/6241; also in the *Swedish Foreign Office White Book 1956*, p.24. The Danish vehicles too were later
    painted white, with a red cross and the Danish flag, following orders from the Allies.
4   H. Andersson, 'Jag körde en av de vita bussarna' ('I Drove One of the White Buses'), *Wendisten*, 2000:1,
    pp.25, 28.
5   Bernadotte, *Last Days . . .*, pp.78f.
6   Letter E. von Post to A. Richert, Stockholm, 1 March 1945, SRA/UDA, HP 1618.
7   Bernadotte, *Last Days . . .*, pp.75–90.
8   Marc Giron, memo conversations with Göring on 8 March, Berlin, 10 March, SRA/UDA, HP 214.
9   T. Brandel, memo conversations Bernadotte–Minister Mohr–Hvass–Brandel–Giron–Hultgren, Berlin,
    6 March 1945, SRA/UDA, HP 1618.
10 T. Brandel, memo Bernadotte's conversations with Norwegian representatives on 7 March, Berlin,
    7 March 1945, SRA/UDA, HP 1618.
11 Bernadotte's report, Berlin, 15 March 1945.
12 Mohr's picture is clearly based on the notorious report 'Ghetto Theresienstadt. Visité le 23 juin 1944.
    Dr M. Rossel. Délégué du CICR' with the Danes F. Hvass and Dr E. Juel Henningsen as colleagues.
13 The attack launched by Kaltenbrunner on Bernadotte appeared in Otto Carl Mohr's private archives,
    DRA, p.52: he must have been very naïve to believe that he could get all the Norwegian and Danish
    prisoners to Sweden. That would simply mean that they would receive military training in Sweden and
    then be used against Germany! Sent home to Frøslev was quite a different matter: this camp was under
    German control.
14 Kersten's diary note, 21 March 1945: Bernadotte 'käme überhaupt nicht vorwärts'; in the Kersten
    family private archives.
15 Kersten petition to Swedish Foreign Office, 12 June 1945, SRA/UDA, HP 1692.
16 SRA/SRK/FBA contains a copy of the fifteen-year-old Alexander Bondy's adventurous account of his
    trip: '*Tatsächlich hat Graf Bernadotte, der die Sache wie seine eigene behandelte, über uns mit Himmler gesprochen und
    auch von ihm eine besondere Ausreisebewilligung für uns bekommen. Wir hätten sofort der schwedischen Gesandtschaft
    in Berlin ausgeliefert werden sollen, aber wir wurden nicht rechtzeitig geholt. Als Graf B. das nächste Mal nach Berlin
    kam schickte er ein Auto um uns, das aber nicht mer durchkam, weil Belsen inzwischen Kriegsschauplatz geworden war.
    Nach Besetzung des Lager durch die Engländer liess Mutter uns durch schwedische Ärtze dort suchen, aber wir waren
    nicht mehr in Belsen.*'
17 Two copies of a copy of this *Vereinbarung*, both from 1952, are in the Kurt Littorin collection regarding
    medical counsellor Felix Kersten, SRA. Littorin was Kersten's solicitor 1945–53.
18 My interview with Arno Kersten, Stockholm, 7 November 2000.
19 No Swedish Foreign Office minutes from the talks between von Post and Kersten on 23 March 1945
    have been recovered. In CZA, C/4/570, however, there is a copy of 'Besprechungen in Stockholm',
    by Kersten, Stockholm, 17 April 1945, in which Günther is said to have praised Kersten for having
    'performed world history' and in which the worthy diplomat stated that Sweden's doors stood wide
    open for all who were being persecuted by National Socialism – Dutch, Belgians, French and *Jews*; a
    few days later Günther would be talking to Bernadotte about this.
20 Sven Frykman, *Röda Korsexpeditionen till Tyskland* (Stockholm 1945), pp.59–64.
21 Frykman, *Röda Korsexpeditionen till Tyskland*, pp.55–7.

ENDNOTES

22 Daehli's rescue: S. Payne Best, *The Venlo Incident* (London 1950), p.257.

23 Hans Arnoldsson, *Natt och dimma (Night and Fog)* (Stockholm 1945), pp.103f.

24 Frykman, *Röda Korsexpeditionen till Tyskland*, pp.76ff.

25 Based on the report by Professor Gerhard Rundberg in 1945; see also Fritz Bringmann's dossier: *KZ Neuengamme. Berichte, Erinnerungen, Dokumente* (Frankfurt am Main 1981).

26 'Muslims': jargon used at the concentration camps to describe totally exhausted prisoners who, bent forward, were likened with their headlong stance to praying Muslims.

27 This transportation became the centre of controversy in Sweden in 1979, when in a television programme 'Bernadotte's buses' were accused of helping the Germans transfer concentration camp prisoners. According to Gilel Storch, however, the decision concerning these transports had come from 'unidentified heads of detachment' and were unknown to Bernadotte. Storch, who stated he was present on that occasion, reported that Bernadotte was very indignant when he later heard about the transports: *Dagens Nyheter*, 29 September 1979. Ingrid Lomfors, in her book written in Swedish (Stockholm 2005, the English title for which might be *Blind Spot. Memories and Oblivion Surrounding the Swedish Red Cross Relief Expedition to Nazi Germany 1945*) showed that most of the French, Polish and Russian prisoners transferred on 27–28 March by the Swedish buses met certain death in the other German concentration camps. Lomfors has also found a memo dated 27 March 1945 in the Swedish Red Cross archives with Frykman's information on these transports from Neuengamme to Braunschweig. The Swedish Foreign Office had therefore been informed, and possibly Bernadotte too.

28 Åke Svenson, *De vita bussarna* (Stockholm 1945), p.57.

29 The British journalist Ralph Hewins would later (probably in 1956) claim that Björck in fact had been dismissed by Bernadotte 'for not showing the enterprise and initiative expected of every member of the expedition'; undated in SRA/SRKA/II/GS.

CHAPTER 9

General note: This chapter, unless otherwise stated, is entirely based on accounts provided by the NN-prisoner Kristian Ottosen, *Natt og tåke. Historien om Natzweiler-fangene (Night and Fog. The Story of the Natzweiler Prisoners)* (Oslo 1989) and his *Redningen*, pp.34, 148–83, 204–17.

1 Ottosen, *Natt og tåke*, p.328.

2 Axel Molin, *Operation de vita bussarna* (Norrköping 1989), p.7.

3 Ottosen, *Redningen*, p.213.

4 My interview with Molin in Norrköping, Sweden, 20 April 2001. Of the sixteen people rescued from Vaihingen only Kristian Ottosen was still alive in 2001. He had in his possession at that time the registration records for Neuengamme, 'K.L.-Neuengamme, 6 April 1945. Zugänge' with his prisoner number: 'Norw.80.134'. Ottosen died in 2006.

5 Ottosen, *Redningen*, p.216. See also Trygve Bratteli's own account in *Fånge i natt och dimma* (Stockholm 1982), p.169.

6 Arnoldsson, *Natt och dimma*, p.118.

CHAPTER 10

1 Dr Egil Juel Henningsen's report on a visit to Theresienstadt on Friday 22 June 1944. Copy from Finn Nielsen's archives, in the home of Ole Finn Nielsen.

2 Dr Otto Schütz, Report on Theresienstadt, 28 March 1945, SRA (author's translation from the German into Swedish).

3 Memo signed von Post, Stockholm, 27 March 1945, SRA/UDA, HP 1619.

4 Yet . . . 'If any written proof existed, Kersten for his part was not aware of it', from the same 'interrogation' in which Kersten admitted that the supposed Bernadotte–Himmler letter of 10 March 1945 was *'eine halbe Fälschung'*; memo from Å. Kromnow and W. Carlgren, Stockholm, 17 March 1956 UDA, A9G.

5 Thus, for example, in Storch's letter to Kromnow, Stockholm, 4 September 1963, and to Penkower, Stockholm, 27 February 1979, both in Gilel Storch's private archives; letter to Denmark's chief rabbi

Bent Melchior, Stockholm, 14 October 1970, copy in Barbro Jerring's private archive, and similarly in my interview with Storch, Stockholm, 27 July 1979.

6   Letter G. Storch to G. Fleming, Stockholm, 6 September 1976, Gilel Storch's private archives; copy with the author.

7   My interview with Storch, Stockholm, 27 July 1979.

8   Bernadotte, *Last Days* . . ., p.92.

9   F. Bernadotte, draft copy of his book written in Swedish. The published version and the English-language version, *Last Days* . . ., differ slightly.

10   J.B. Holmgård, 'Var Bernadotte antisemit?' ('Was Bernadotte an Anti-Semite?'), *Politiken*, 16 February 1985.

11   F. Bernadotte, draft copy of the Swedish version of *Last Days* . . ., appendix I–II, not preserved in the published version.

12   This account is based on Bernadotte's 'Notes . . .' dated 9 April 1945, in SRA/FBA and in SRA/UDA, HP 1619. In *Last Days* . . ., pp.100–5, Bernadotte's suggestion to Himmler to open up the Western Front and concentrate the Germans' defence on the Russians is omitted.

13   Bernadotte's Notes, dated 9 April 1945; *Last Days* . . ., p.104..

14   Letter G. Storch to F. Kersten, Stockholm, 31 March 1945., copy in CZA, C4/551. In a letter to G. Fleming, Stockholm, 6 September 1976 (copy in the author's private archive), Storch wrote: 'I do not believe it (the Himmler/Kersten agreement) was signed by Himmler . . . This is also a product of many letters and diaries that Kersten was using many years after the war, and most were not even produced by himself. What is important, however, is that the content of the agreement is correct.'

15   My interview with Storch, Stockholm, 27 July 1979; essentially identical, for example, to Storch's letter to G. Fleming, Stockholm, 6 September 1976.

16   A common effort: Storch in my interview with him, Stockholm, 27 July 1979: '*die Verdienste dass die KZ-lager ordnungsgemäss übergeben wurden, Kersten zuzuschrieben und nicht Bernadotte*', letter from Storch to Dr Bienenfeld and Dr Steinberg, Stockholm, 15 May 1957, CZA, C2/197. In memos from the WJC, Swedish Section, signed by Storch and Spivak, Stockholm, 18 June 1947 and 24 March 1956 respectively, Kersten is given the credit but Bernadotte's name is not mentioned; stencils in NUDA, Ad.20.24/3, Bind II, respectively UDA, A9G.

17   Schellenberg, *Tagebuchskizze*, pp.22–6, in CZA, C4/494. Hesse, *Das Spiel um Deutschland*, pp.399f., 418, claimed that Ribbentrop too tried to persuade Himmler to stop the killing of the camp prisoners and that Storch contacted Hesse on this issue.

18   In a telephone conversation with me in the course of 2000 Dov Dinur was unable to confirm these details. Storch's letter to Schellenberg, 16 June 1945, and Schellenberg's reply, Stockholm, 17 June 1945; copies in CZA, C4/551, Schellenberg's in the original in C4/567.

19   Black, *Ernst Kaltenbrunner*, pp.232, 250–2, on Kaltenbrunner; Padfield, *Himmler. Reichsführer-SS*, pp.582, 588, and Trevor-Roper, *The Last Days of Hitler*, pp.147, 151, on Himmler–Hitler. The commandant at Auschwitz, Höss, after the war also claimed that Himmler had issued express orders to the effect that the last remaining concentration camps were to be evacuated, and that Himmler refused to have them placed under Red Cross protection; see *Kommandant in Auschwitz. Autobiographische Aufzeichnungen des Rudolf Höss. Herausgegeben von Martin Broszat* (Munich 1963, 3rd edn 1965), p.186.

20   My interview with Arno Kersten, Stockholm, 7 November 2000. Koblik, *The Stones Cry Out*, p.133, citing Mallet and Churchill. Hindley, 'Negotiating the Boundary of Unconditional Surrender', pp.66ff., similarly reported that it was opposition from the American legation in Stockholm which got the Swedish government to deny Storch a passport. Anja Storch, according to Arno Kersten, 29 March 1996, in L. Einhorn, *Handelsresande i liv. Om vilja och vankelmod i krigets skugga* (*Travelling Salesman in Lives. On Will and Indecision in the Shadow of War*) (Falun 1999) p.395.

21   H. Roesdahl, report from 1946, in Finn Nielsen's private files.

22   Frykman, *Röda Korsexpeditionen till Tyskland*, p.99.

23   F. Göring, *Auszug aus meinem Tagebuch über die Befreiung von Menschen aus der deutschen Konzentrationsläger*, p.11f.; CZA, C4/495.

24   H. Folke, *Officer 37. Memoirs by Colonel Harald Folke*, p.33; unpublished manuscript 1999, sent to me by Folke in October 1999, shortly before his death.

ENDNOTES

25　M. Friediger, *Theresienstadt* (Copenhagen 1946), p.137.

26　H. Andersson, 'Jag körde en av de vita bussarna', *Wendisten* 2000:2, p.11.

CHAPTER 11

1　H. Andersson. 'I Drove One of the White Buses', *Wendisten*, 2000:1, pp.30f.

2　Majlis von Eickstedt-Peterswaldt, *Bro över mörka vatten* (*Bridge over Dark Waters*) (Stockholm 1945), pp.170f. British camp: obituary, *Sydsvenska Dagbladet Snällposten*, 14 February 2001.

3　Bernadotte's handwritten notes in Count Folke Bernadotte's archive, vol.2, SRA.

4　H. Andersson. 'I Drove One of the White Buses', *Wendisten*, 2000:1, pp.153f.

5　Gauleiter Kaufmann collaborated in all secrecy with minister of armaments Speer in circumventing Hitler's instructions to destroy the entire German infrastructure. Kaufmann's object was to spare Hamburg total destruction: this would eventually lead to Hamburg's capitulation on 3 May; Trevor-Roper, *The Last Days of Hitler*, pp.119, 154.

6　One hundred Danish buses: Gerhard Rundberg, *Rapport från Neuengamme* (*Report from Neuengamme*) (Stockholm 1945), p.89. A special Danish article from *Bushistorisk selskab* in 2001 put the number of Danish buses at 'approx. 120': Mikael Hansen, 'Transporterne med de Hvide Busser 1944–1945' ('The White Bus Transports 1944–1945'), *Motstandskampen 1940–1945*, 2001:2, p.7.

7　Bernadotte's speech in a press conference, 5 May 1945, in SRA/UDA, HP 1620; *Last Days...*, p.109: 'exceptional help . . . from the Jyllandskorps.'

8　Kersten's version in a letter to C. Günther, Stockholm, 23 April 1945; Masur's version in memo, Stockholm, 23 April 1945, both in SRA/UDA, HP 1051; see also Norbert Masur, *En jude talar med Himmler* (*A Jew Speaks to Himmler*) (Stockholm 1945), p.13; Schellenberg's version in *Tagebuchskizze*, p.34f., CZA, C4/494.

9　Kersten's address to the Swedish Foreign Office, Stockholm, 12 June 1945, pp.22f. (quotation); memo Gösta Engzell, Stockholm, 25 April 1945, SRA/UDA, HP 1619.

10　N. Masur, report dated Stockholm, 23 April 1945, in SRA/UDA, HP 1051; and Masur, *En jude talar med Himmler*, pp.24–6. Himmler's pledges confirmed by Schellenberg in his *Tagesbuchskizze*, pp.37f., CZA, C4/494.

11　Masur, *En jude talar med Himmler*, pp.29f.

12　'Notes concerning certain talks etc. during Count Folke Bernadotte's stay in Germany 17–24 April 1945', Stockholm, 27 April 1945, SRKA Central Board; ; abbreviated version in Bernadotte, *Last Days...*, pp.110ff.

13　Bernadotte's notes, 27 April 1945, as above; *Last Days...*, p.112, in which the point about the women at Ravensbrück were to be saved from the Russian troops had been censored to read that the camp must 'shortly be evacuated'!); letter Graf Folke Bernadotte an den Herrn Lagerkommandanten des K.L. Ravensbrück, Schloss Friedrichsruh, 21 April 1945, SRKA, dossier 'Folke B Felix K & Trevor-Roper'. Storch on Himmler and the Eastern Front in my interview, Stockholm, 27 July 1979; also in a letter to G. Fleming, Stockholm, 6 September 1976.

14　Schellenberg, *Tagesbuchskizze*, pp.38f., CZA, C4/494; Trevor-Roper, *The Last Days of Hitler*, p.156.

15　Bernadotte, *Last Days...*, pp.115f.

16　Quoted from Bernadotte's notes, 27 April 1945, *Last Days...*, p.119.

17　Schellenberg, *Tagebuchskizze*, p.46, CZA, C4/494.

18　Bernadotte's notes, 27 April 1945, *Last Days...*, p.121.

19　Letter H. Himmler to C. Günther, 24 April 1945, original in Christian Günther's archives in SRA.

20　This whole section is based (if not specified otherwise) on Kristian Ottosen, *Kvinneleiren. Historien om Ravensbrück-fangene* (*The Women's Camp: the Story of the Ravensbrück Prisoners*) (Oslo 1991), quotes from pp.298 and 301 respectively; and Grit Weichelt, 'Das Frauen-Konzentrationslager Ravensbrück vor der Befreiung', *'Ich grüsse Euch als freier Mensch'. Quellenedition zur Befreiung des Frauen-Konzentrationslagers Ravensbrück im April 1945,* Herausgegeben von Sigrid Jacobeit, Stiftung Brandenburgische Gedenkstätten, Schriftenreihe no.6 (Berlin 1995), pp.13–21.

21　Sylvia Salvesen's moving account of her stay at Ravensbrück 1943–5, *Tilgi- men glem ikke* (*Forgive...But Don't Forget*) (Oslo 1947), pp.238–48.

22　Salvesen's account of her stay at Ravensbrück 1943–5: *Tilgi- men glem ikke*, pp.238–48.

23 Basic sources for my description of the Ravensbrück operations are the detailed accounts given by
    Arnoldsson, *Natt och dimma*, pp.121–40; Folke, *Officer 37*, pp.39–43; Frykman, *Röda Korsexpeditionen till
    Tyskland*, pp.135–51, 170–2; Melin, *Minnen och intryck från tjänstgöringen*, pp.21f.; and Svenson, *De vita
    bussarna*, pp.113–142. They do not tally in every detail. I have relied mainly on Arnoldsson and Svenson
    who were in charge of the transports. Frykman appears mostly to have been at staff headquarters in
    Lübeck. Folke's and Melin's memoirs have been written subsequently.
24 Göring, *Auszug aus meinem Tagebuch über die Befreiung von Menschen aus der deutschen Konzentrationslager*,
    pp.13–17, CZA, C4/495; also in Arnoldsson, *Natt och dimma*, pp.128–30.
25 Letter Victor Mallet to C. Günther, Stockholm, 1 May 1945, SRA/UDA, HP 1619.
26 Bernadotte's compilation in SRA/SRKA/FBA; Masur, *En jude talar med Himmler*, p.34. Weichelt, 'Das
    Frauen-Konzentrationslager Ravensbrück vor der Befreiung', p.19: '*ca. 7,500 Frauen aus dem KZ evakuiert
    und in Richtung Schweden in Sicherheit gebracht*'; Melin, *Minnen och intryck från tjänstgöringen*, p.6: 7,500;
    Arnoldsson, *Natt och dimma*, p.138: 'about 8,000'.
27 Arnoldsson, *Natt och dimma*, pp.139f. (quoted on p.133).
28 Göring, *Auszug aus meinem Tagebuch über die Befreiung von Menschen aus der deutschen Konzentrationslager*,
    pp.18f; Arnoldsson, *Natt och dimma*, p.157; Koch, *Socialministeriet under Besaettelsen*, p.27.
29 Description based mainly on Arnoldsson, *Natt och dimma*, pp.157–65, and on Arnoldsson's telephone
    call to Swedish Foreign Office, Lübeck, 29 April 1945, SRA/UDA, HP 1619. There are discrepancies
    in the descriptions, however. In H. Tamm's memo of 30 April 1945, SRA/UDA, HP 1619, it was
    estimated that as many as one thousand people arrived by ship from Lübeck. Regarding the non-
    Scandinavian Neuengamme prisoners' fate from 20 April until the disaster of 3 May 1945, see Fritz
    Bringmann, *KZ Neuengamme. Berichte, Erinnerungen, Dokumente*, pp.108–17. The disturbing report much
    later (1997) in Benjamin Jacob, *The Dentist of Auschwitz*, ch. 17, is quite obviously incorrect: in it,
    though a Polish Jew, on 28 April 1945 he managed to wangle his way on board the 'Swedish trucks'
    but was then refused transport to Sweden on a Swedish ship by Bernadotte since the Swedes only
    accepted 'Westerners'. By 28 April there were no Swedish Red Cross trucks remaining in Germany,
    Bernadotte himself was in Denmark, and among those who were rescued and taken to Sweden in this
    last stage were thousands of Polish Jews. The matter could only have concerned trucks belonging to the
    International Red Cross, the 'count' in Swedish Red Cross uniform may have been Arnoldsson or the
    Norwegian Heger, and the Swedish ship the *Magdalena* or the *Lillie Matthiessen*.

Chapter 12

1   'Extract from notes written in the course of the Second World War', original in Christian Günther's
    archives, vol. 3, SRA.
2   Relations between Sweden and Norway 1940–5 are described mainly on the basis of Alf W. Johansson's
    magnificent *Per Albin och kriget. Samlingsregeringen och utrikespolitiken under andra världskriget* (*Per Albin and the
    War. The Coalition Government and Foreign Policy During the Second World War*) (Falköping 1985), pp.142–76,
    258–70, 285–318, 341–58. See also *Norges forhold til Sverige under krigen 1940–45* (*Norway's Relationship
    with Sweden During the 1940–45 Wars*), Aktstykker utgitt av Det Kgl. Utenrikesdepartement.III (Official
    documents published by the Norwegian Foreign Office) (Oslo 1950); Wilhelm Carlgren's 'Svensk-
    norska regeringsrelationer under andra världskriget' ('Swedish–Norwegian Relations at Government
    Level during the Second World War'), *Broderfolk i ufridstid. Norsk-svenske forbindelser under annen verdenskrig*
    (*Sister Nations in Time of Warfare. Norwegian–Swedish Relations During the Second World War*) (red. S. Ekman
    and O.K. Grimnes; Oslo 1991), pp.18–62; and Jacob Sverdrup, 'Det vanskelige forholdet til Sverige'
    ('The Delicate Relationship with Sweden'), *Inn i storpolitiken 1940–1949, Norsk utenrikspolitikks historie*
    (*Top-level Politics 1940–1949, History of Norwegian Foreign Policy*), Bind 4 (Oslo 1996), pp.149–81.
3   For Swedish–Norwegian relations 1944–5, apart from the works noted above, use has been made of the
    Swedish Foreign Office's official white book *Förhandlingarna 1945 om svensk intervention i Norge och Denmark*
    (*Negotiations in 1945 Concerning Swedish Intervention in Norway and Denmark*). Aktstycken utgivna av Kungl.
    Utrikesdepartementet. Ny serie II:11 (Stockholm 1957); Leif Leifland, *General Böhmes val. Sverige och det
    nazistiska Tyskland våren 1945* (*General Böhme's Options. Sweden and Nazi Germany Spring 1945*) (Södertälje
    1992), pp.65–167. Günther's estimate, confined to a confidential parliamentary meeting on 27 April
    1945, is in Per Albin Hansson's private archives, SRA.

ENDNOTES

4   Beck-Friis to Swedish Foreign Office, London, 12 April 1945, SRA/UDA, HP 192.

5   Leifland, *General Böhmes val*, p.123.

6   British action on the 'Swedish aid to liberate Norway' issue is based on the following documents in TNA:PRO: War Cabinet. Joint Planning Staff, 19 February 1945; Despatch, British Legation, Stockholm, sd. R. Sutton Pratt, 9 March 1945; both at AIR 20/6241; prime minister's personal telegram to Lord Halifax, W.S. Churchill, 15 April 1945, at AIR 20/6242.

7   War Cabinet, Chiefs of Staff Committee Minute (D.117/5) by the prime minister, W.S. Churchill, 19 April 1945, AIR 20/6242/.

8   Telegram Sir V. Mallet to Swedish Foreign Office, Stockholm, 17 April 1945; combined chiefs of staff. Memorandum by the Representatives of the British chiefs of staff, 21 April 1945; all of them in AIR 20/6242. All of these documents in AIR are marked 'Top Secret'.

9   Günther's handwritten comment from 30 April 1945 in draft form, drawn up at the Swedish Foreign Office 29 April and given the prime minister's and foreign minister's approval, SRA/UDA, HP 192.

10   This section is mainly based on Bernadotte's two reports: 'Notes on certain talks etc. during Count Folke Bernadotte's stay in Germany 17–24 April 1945' (which also cover 25–26 April); and 'Notes on Certain Talks etc. during Count Folke Bernadotte's Stay in Denmark 27 April–1 May 1945', Stockholm, unsigned and undated, original running to 7 May; SRKA, in Bernadotte, *Last Days...*, the government's fear of being accused of driving a wedge between the western Allies and the Soviet Union is consistently censored and removed.

11   W.S. Churchill, *The Second World War. Vol. VI: Triumph and Tragedy* (London 1954), pp.465–8.

12   Bernadotte's translation, a trifle modernised, from the report of 27 April 1945.

13   Bernadotte's report as above; in *Last Days...*, pp.126f., Bernadotte has changed his idea: if Himmler's offer of surrender had not been published Himmler would probably have succeeded Hitler and it would have been much more difficult for the Allies to negotiate with a compromised Himmler than with the military man, Dönitz. Conversation Schellenberg–Himmler according to Schellenberg, *Tagebuchskizze*, pp.51–3, in CZA C4/494. According to Padfield, *Himmler. Reichsführer-SS*, pp.595f, it was the British foreign minister Eden, in San Francisco, who leaked the information about Himmler's secret meeting with Bernadotte, thereby torpedoing the fifth meeting planned between the two of them. On 2 May Boheman protested to the British and American ministers in Stockholm about *Eisenhower*'s publication of Bernadotte's talks with Himmler, despite the fact that the telegrams concerning these had been marked 'Top Secret', and he threatened that this reckless lack of scruples 'would not encourage us to give them any further information'; P.M. Boheman, Stockholm, 2 May 1945, SRA/UDA, HP 193.

14   Von Post personal letter to E. Boheman, *en route* to Malmö 30 April 1945, SRA/UDA, HP 192. A draft was approved by the prime minister and foreign minister.

15   Fest, *Hitler. A Biography*, pp.797f.; Padfield, *Himmler. Reichsführer-SS*, p.596; Trevor-Roper, *The Last Days of Hitler*, pp.26, 192, 202–11, 277f. Also in T. Junge, *I Hitlers tjänst. Traudl Junge berättar om sitt liv* (*In the Service of Hitler: The Story of Traudl Junge's Life*), in collaboration with Melissa Müller (Lund 2003), pp.184f. Original German edition: *Bis zur Letzen Stunde* (Munich 2002).

16   Schellenberg, *Tagebuchskizze*, pp.53–7, von Post to E. Boheman, Malmö, 2 May 1945 SRA/UDA, HP 193. Some discrepancies occur in the descriptions.

17   Schellenberg, *Tagebuchskizze*, pp.57–63. Dönitz's authorisation to Schellenberg, 4 May 1945, SRA/ UDA, HP 193.

18   American minister to Boheman, 5 May: 'Eisenhower has been directed to send SHAEF representatives to Stockholm immediately . . . Soviet Gov. should be informed immediately'; SRA/UDA, HP 193. How did Chernyshev react? 'Well, he didn´t react at all, he was drunk, incidentally, so I don't know whether he really grasped what was going on!'; Boheman according to Sven Grafström, *Notes 1940–1945*, p.659. Harry S. Truman's memoirs *Avgörandenas år* (*1945: Year of Decisions*) (Stockholm 1955), p.128.

19   Bernadotte's report 7(?) May 1945, as above. A large quantity of carbon copies of the Radio Institute's phone-tapping of the German legation, 6 May 1945, all marked 'secret', are stored in a special envelope at the SRA/UDA, HP 193; Schellenberg, *Tagebuchskizze*, pp.63–5.

20   Handwritten message 'delivered by Mallet to Boheman 5 May at 4 p.m.', SRA/UDA, HP 193. Sweden a British sphere of interest: Leifland, *General Böhmes val*, p.174. Leifland also quoted (on p.82) Churchill's

comment in this context: 'Why should the Swedish army help clean up Norway after the Germans had left? There would be more point in the Allied armies cleaning up Sweden', TNA:PRO, FO 954/23.

21 Churchill, *Triumph and Tragedy*, pp.469f. The final documents in PRO on the matter are dated 2 and 3 May 1945. On 3 May staff talks with Sweden were to have been initiated 'as soon as possible'; on 2 May Eisenhower announced that his 'information about the capabilities of Swedish Armed Forces is scanty' but that he considered using them mainly 'in operations against the Narvik area': War Cabinet, joint planning staff, 'Staff Conversations with the Swedes', 2 May 1945; chiefs of staff to J.S.M. Washington, 3 May 1945, both 'Top Secret', and at TNA:PRO, AIR 20/6242.

Chapter 13

1 Narrated by 'one of those rescued in 1945', now resident in Israel, to Inga Gottfarb, *Den livsfarliga glömskan*, pp.22f.
2 Koblik, *The Stones Cry Out*, p.138.
3 Arnoldsson's statistics in *Natt och dimma*, p.194.
4 Nielsen's original 'transport list' in Finn Nielsen's private archive, DRA.
5 Storch in my interview with him, Stockholm, 27 July 1979; 6,500 Jews rescued according to Koblik, *The Stones Cry Out*, p.139.
6 Koblik, *The Stones Cry Out*, p.127, note 28.
7 During my work on Bernadotte's involvement in Palestine, *Mediation & Assassination*, I had the privilege of going through all of Bernadotte's documents from 1948. There was not a single letter or communication sent from the Swedish government or from the Swedish Foreign Office. Neither is Bernadotte's mediation mentioned with a single word in *Tage Erlander. Dagböcker 1945–49* (the Swedish prime minister's diaries).
8 The book, for instance, written by one of the men behind the 1948 assassination, Baruch Nadel's *Bernadotte Affaeren* (Copenhagen 1970), in which the forged letter Bernadotte–Himmler from 10 March 1945 is reproduced in full, p.36, with a small footnote indicating that this letter had admittedly been declared false but that 'at the Nuremberg trials it had never been disallowed or repudiated'. This was not surprising as the letter did not turn up until the beginning of the 1950s!
9 H.R. Trevor-Roper, 'Kersten, Himmler, and Count Bernadotte', *The Atlantic Monthly*, 191:2 (February 1953), pp.43–5.
10 H.R. Trevor-Roper, 'Introduction' to Felix Kersten, *The Kersten Memoirs 1940–1945* (London 1956), pp.9–21.
11 Swedish Foreign Office, *The Swedish Relief Expedition to Germany 1945. Prelude and Negotiations* (Stockholm 1956), p.38.
12 This section is the outcome of my discussions with Gilel Storch's son, Marcus, in Stockholm, 21 August and 22 October 2001. Marcus Storch, who had naturally discussed the matter often with his father, claimed that the entire negotiation procedure in 1945 must be seen as a Swedish–German *bartering process* in which the Swedish negotiator, Bernadotte, had to offer the Germans something in exchange for their concessions. This is undoubtedly a correct, albeit cynical, view which it was not politically correct to discuss publicly in 1945.

Index